Watched each other create over so many years — stopping for some serious fun along the way — xxx

I GAVE IT AWAY
DAYS AND NIGHTS AT VINEGAR HILL THEATRE

A Memoir

Ann Porotti

A publication of BookBaby
I Gave It Away: Days and Nights at Vinegar Hill Theatre by Ann Porotti
Copyright ©2022 by Ann Porotti. All rights reserved.

ISBN 978-1-66783-853-3
Library of Congress Cataloging-in-Publication Data
Memoir | Film History | Women in Business | Independent Movie Theatres

Design by Roseberries
Cover photograph by Reid Oeschlin

To Ian who said write your story,
and Dave who gave me everything, the room to excavate.

CONTENTS

Avianca #247 1

1. Italian Girlhood 3
2. Ruined 19
3. Meeting Chief 31
4. Building 45
5. Women in Love 57
6. The Reivers Diaries 81
7. Tumbleweeds 93
8. Four Friends 101
9. Fellini's 117
10. The Rectifier 127
11. Popcorn 139
12. The Long Divorce 149
13. The Summer of '82 161
14. Songs of the Auvergne 179
15. A New Life 195
16. The Year of Living Dangerously 207
17. The Break-Up 223
18. Halapin 237
19. Townwatch 253
20. A Death in Portugal 263
21. A New Lobby 275
22. L'avventura 291
23. I Give It Away 307
24. Fortitude and Fate 323

In the crane shot 329

Avianca #247. We're flying home after two weeks in Colombia, a time spent without music, without a voice from America. Through my ear buds I hear Macy Gray's "Slowly" from her Stripped *release, and I rewind to that moment of our arrival at the* palapas, *or* kogihabs, *as Colombians call them. We are seventy-five hundred feet up in the Sierra Nevada de Santa Marta, a mere twenty-six miles from the Caribbean. No other mountain range in the world rises as abruptly from the sea. I look down at the ocean and the disorganized Ciénega, edging the man-made lagoon that broadens to the coastal vastness of Barranquilla.*

Standing on the side of the world, I am so small. The sky above, not much interference between me and the chill of the cloud forest, its billowing fog. Back and forth, like arms around me. In this extraordinary place.

I am crying.

The bushes move with endemics. I feel like an endemic, one of the hundreds of birds native to the Santa Martas. My window on the world, this sacred vista claims me, even though I know I am only a traveler who happens to fly through.

Santa Marta brushfinches and tanagers, the blue-naped chlorophonia. A flashy hummer, the white-tailed starfrontlet. All seeking warmth from cool clouds. Because I no longer possess a screen of my own, I have gone from watching movies to watching birds.

An olive flycatcher makes a beeline for cover, then stuns himself on impact with our panorama window. Temporarily, we are neighbors. I stay quiet while he dusts himself off and figures the next move.

I am not alone. D. is inside the huge curve of glass, looking out.

But I feel the strength of being alone, in the way that the universe and its parts can convey. All of it. Equally. The birds, the husband, the sicropea *trees, the grey-seeded* grenadilla *fruit I love to crack on car bumpers and suck out the pulp.*

On a mountaintop in Colombia, I acknowledge my ingredienti. *A recipe of me, as it were: my parents and their parents, my children, all the lovers, and friends and confidantes, and the great blessing of fulfilling work—as close as skin, thoughts embraced and tangled together.*

Oh, but wait. We have jumped over my story, one now nearing its end.

So let's go back ...

1
ITALIAN GIRLHOOD

My father Eugene took my brother Rudy and me to children's movies when we were young. But, after watching previews for the "other stuff"—adult movies—that's all I wanted to see. My dad was assistant postmaster in Milford, Massachusetts, and the State Theater was across the street from the Post Office. Whenever Mom took us to Milford to visit Dad at work, I made a point to check out the marquee and peek at the posters of the Coming Attractions. Gradually I began a campaign to go to the movies every time they changed the feature. I lobbied hard and May Orr was selected as my guardian.

May was a dwarf with a tiny bump on her back. She had very straight dull brown hair cut like Prince Valiant and a wide smile with blunt square teeth. She and her mother, an immigrant herself, were English—my mother Anita, after thirty years in America, always defined neighbors by their national origins. The Orr ladies lived up the street without Mr. Orr, who must have died, or left years before, in the smallest boxy house I ever saw. The few times

I went in to visit the house was always too warm, and had that ripe, stale scent of radiators in the winter.

Movies with May always happened on Saturdays; Sunday was for church, and huge meals, the weekdays for school. My father and I would climb into his Ford coupe and drive up the street to pick up May. Then we rode in silence to the theater.

May and I were both short, with low blocky bodies; I smiled a mouthful of braces, she, an uneven grin. We could have been mistaken for classmates except that May must have been either twenty- or even thirty-years old, and I was ten. Her presence ensured that no old men with raincoats or juvenile delinquents would approach, or so believed my parents.

I don't think May talked much: I cannot remember the sound of her voice, although when she did speak it was usually to ask me what I wanted from the candy counter—"Nonpareils, please." I doubt that May lived in a world of conversation, although neither did I; in my world, talking was often confused with shouting. In her habit of dramatizing herself through words, my mother often embarrassed me, but May never did.

May gave me privacy and silence so that I could be with my thoughts about movies, about how beautiful they were. There were no paintings in the Porotti house—just immaculate blank walls. As I sat next to May in the dark I basked in the luminous color being beamed out from the carbon arc lamps burning in the elevated and inaccessible projection booth; in those days before the advent of xenon bulbs, there was fire behind the film.

Movies gave me a way to think about becoming a woman even though I was still quite young; I remember paying only twelve cents for my admission. It was while I sat in a darkened theater with May that I began to think of movies as giving me a way to figure out my life. Although, as I grew into adulthood, I kept volunteering for emotional tumult, I was also always looking for the calm, and ninety minutes spent in quiet before a screen could give me that.

Even at my young age I knew that May was not going to have a big life. In looking back across so many years, and assessing how things turned out for me, I can now see that May embodied for me a sense of lost possibilities, especially those possibilities that were now being figured for me so powerfully on the screen. And what I saw there were huge, beautiful bodies, women not unlike my mother: Anita had pale skin, a heart-shaped face, nice breasts, good legs—she looked stunning in clothes. She was sexy, and she knew it.

Watching *Jeopardy*, I hissed at morally ambiguous Barbara Stanwyck when her husband, played by Barry Sullivan, was trapped under a flooding pier. Next week, I chewed my nails, anxious that Doris Day in a non-singing role could out-maneuver her sadistic husband Louis Jourdan in the chiller *Julie*. Doris makes it, and returns the following week as Ruth Etting, honky-tonk-then-Ziegfeld singer married to the brutal gangster Moe the Gimp—James Cagney burning up the screen—in Charles Vidor's *Love Me or Leave Me*. I was collecting data, locating the skills and strategies a woman needed for protection of the self, and for the management of the not-to-be-lost or misplaced husband. On the cusp of dating, I noticed that adult women always had husbands—to run to or from—and that *her* work was never as paramount as *his*.

Not all my movie pleasures were damsel-in-distress vehicles. I was devoted to historical pageants, and Jean Simmons became my ego-ideal—I liked her because she was good while also possessing a demure, exquisitely chiseled face and lithe body. I followed her career as much as a ten-year-old could, enjoying *The Robe* with Richard Burton, *Androcles and the Lion* with Victor Mature, *Désirée* with Marlon Brando, *The Egyptian* with Edmund Purdom, and, most of all, *Young Bess* with Simmons and real-life husband Stewart Granger playing Elizabeth I and Thomas Seymour. Charles Laughton and Deborah Kerr—an unlikely marriage—were the royal parents.

Sexuality in movies—like Marilyn Monroe's daring performances in *Niagara* or in Joshua Logan's *Bus Stop*—was a curiosity and a slight embarrassment. Monroe's body seemed cartoonish, and her vulnerability too raw for my raised-on-American Bandstand sensibility, whereas high-quality women's weepies with Anne Baxter enticing priest Montgomery Clift to unnamed sins in Alfred Hitchcock's *I Confess*—to these I was in thrall. In my Miss Smarty-Pants girlhood, I questioned the authority of the Catholic Church in baby steps by seeing movies forbidden by the Legion of Decency.

Films were my obsession and perhaps seeing Douglas Sirk's *Magnificent Obsession* sealed that bond. There was a narrative perfection in playboy Rock Hudson blinding widow Jane Wyman with his sports car and becoming a brilliant surgeon who gives her back her sight. And then he falls in love with her. Did life happen like that?

Luck with men came down to how you looked. I wanted to appropriate Doris Day's blond hair, Jane Wyman's clearly defined features, Anne Baxter's hourglass figure, and assorted limbs and body parts from starlets like Rita Gam—legs—and Pat Crowley—perky smile and flip hairdo. From Mercedes McCambridge and Barbara Stanwyck there was nothing needed.

As May and I continued our weekend excursions, I began to notice that many people went to movie matinees and saw little of the movie. Making out was big time; I wondered if I was missing something. Roving bands of teenaged boys prowled the aisles looking for alluring faces and thoracic cavities. Boys and girls sat together every week, the girls all wearing the uniform—a V-necked sweater that delivered what it advertised.

I began to wear my red Orlon to the Saturday matinee. My hope was to be chosen by a boy, if not on his first pass through the audience, then on the second sweep. May concerned me because I worried if we were selected in the dark by two boys, the one who got May might offend her or be frightened by discovering her hump. But I kept wearing the red V-neck as well as the men's style chino pants, sewed by my mother from her endless supply of material kept in a hope chest that smelled of mothballs.

One Saturday, I went to see John Wayne and Maureen O'Hara in John Ford's *The Wings of Eagles*. May could not go. I was now twelve, and my mother had begun worrying less about the danger to me and more about the money spent on May for her admissions and babysitting time.

Richie Speroni walked past me. I recognized him—he was considered cute, the '50s term for good-looking. From the Italian gossip-network, I knew he was older, a little wild. Desirable and inevitable. His father had divorced his mother and left her to raise two boys alone. His steady date was a non-Italian prude named Cynthia Anderson who didn't make out at the movies but who consented to ride around in cars. I had secretly been practicing kissing on the couch in our basement with close-ups of Stewart Granger and Jeff Chandler in the pages of *Photoplay* magazine.

Richie asked me if I would like to sit with him. I moved to the chairs at the back and settled into a cluster of silent boys and girls. All eyes were riveted on the screen. Richie never spoke. He put his arm around the back of my chair, and, gradually, his hand made its way to my left breast, where he ran into a handful of Orlon and Maidenform cotton. He squeezed away with side trips to the safety of my shoulder; he also began stroking the area below my throat. No hands inside the bra; perhaps that was one of the rules.

I was terrified that someone would see me, and more importantly, becoming very hot and light-headed, I was missing the film. I also knew that my cousin Billy was a close friend of Richie's younger brother—what a disaster that information exchange would be. When Richie started to kiss me I deflected his dry, tepid attempt, mostly because I was afraid to cut his mouth with my braces. The encounter was quickly becoming tiresome; I just wanted to be away from him. Then I realized that Richie's other hand, nestled in my crotch, was attempting to finger me through my homemade trousers.

I saw Richie at the Soda Shop a few weeks later. He didn't speak and neither did I. When I was sixteen, sleek and trim, I met Richie Speroni at a Whitinsville Record Hop and went parking with him. He didn't remember me, and he still kissed "terrible."

What I was doing with Richie was "forbidden," according to my mother. And it did alarm me, although not because of her prohibition. It alarmed me because someone already had his hands all over my body, not a boy my age, but a grown man. And while I was intuitive enough to keep the actions of the adult a secret, Richie's fumbles in the dark stopped with the swat of my hand.

I have no wish to see my story as an abuse narrative. I was, however, compelled by movies far too advanced for me, and perhaps because my child's body was being asked to respond as if I were a woman. Mine is a story about yearning, for love and touch, surely, but above all a longing for something larger, more filled with life, than it was possible to find in the culture where I grew up. Movies were not a screen but a window, a view with the promise of a way out.

May and I resumed our movie-going after the incident with Richie; I much preferred her company. A movie screening was too important to waste on unsure adventures in the dark. She and I came to cherish movies without talking, absolute silence, no chit-chat. To be a handicapped young adult woman in the late 1950s was about not calling attention to yourself. If May had ideas, aspirations, she did not share. On those Saturday afternoons, she seemed happy to be out of her house and a spinster life with no exit. I am not sure that she had been to school.

I forgot about May, though I remember her as a guest at my high school graduation in 1962. Then, in March of 1969, my mother wrote:

> *First of all bad news. May Orr died yesterday afternoon after a Breast Radical operation. Her heart gave away shortly after the*

operation. Her prognosis was very poor, so possibly this was the best way. God rest her soul in peace.

By the time I received the letter about May, I had gotten out of Milford. May was never presented with such a chance, although she had helped to give me mine. Now, holding the letter in my hand, I knew that it was only a chance, and that the thing about getting out of towns like Milford is not the initial getting out—the trick is to not get pulled back in.

February 2017

"Nonni, what's a beatnik?"

I was sitting in my daughter Courtenay's house in Richmond. My nine-year-old granddaughter Zoe and I were about forty minutes into *Funny Face* when she asked me the question. *Funny Face* is a cupcake of a movie in which a gamine Audrey Hepburn plays a Greenwich Village bookseller resisting the make-over force of a Paris fashion magazine. Fred Astaire, as a Richard Avedon-inspired photographer, and Kay Thompson, channeling Diana Vreeland, are generals in the battle to transform Audrey into the Quality Woman. It's a comedy. And a musical.

A few weeks earlier, Zoe had told me she wanted to be an actress, specifically one that "sings, and dances, and is very beautiful." Zoe, already very beautiful, is working hard with after-school classes on the song and dance skills. Deciding that she needed an Enrichment Program, I became her teacher in a thorough survey of the great Hollywood musicals. She requested—having just seen Emma Stone in 2017's *La La Land*—no unhappy endings.

The first week we watched *On the Town*, MGM's 1949 delight about three sailors given twenty-four hour leave in New York City and the girls they meet and love. Triple threat—Gene Kelly dancing, Frank Sinatra singing, and Stanley Donen, along with Kelly, directing. For all the punning lyrics and industry jokes, *On the Town* bathes the world in post WWII innocence—though Zoe thought the ending, where the sailors have to go back on the ship, was "*almost* an unhappy one."

After assurances from her mother that she had seen the big three—*Singing in the Rain*, *The Band Wagon*, and *An American in Paris*—I had encouraged *Funny Face* as the next movie.

Little did I realize how much had changed in the American musical between 1949 and 1957.

First up were some bold new ideas about women. Believing herself "funny looking," Audrey's Jo works in a West Village book store and wears very loose, asexual clothes, a style that American women would not embrace until the 1970s after Woody Allen's *Annie Hall*. Jo believes in "empathicalism"—a homebrewed philosophy spouted almost exclusively by pipe-smoking men wearing beards, turtlenecks, and corduroy. They hang out in Parisian *boîtes* where jazz and *apaché* dancing backdrop their portentous conversations. At one point, Jo, dressed in black sweater and capris, demonstrates her beatnik affiliations by dancing to African drum music. That's when Zoe asked her question.

"Nonni, who are those men?"

"Oh, they're probably beatniks."

Never realizing I wouldn't be able to come up with a compelling answer, I fumbled through a description of beatnik clothes, folding in a riff on American-in-Paris jazz musicians Dexter Gordon, Kenny Clarke, and Lucky Thompson, and then drove myself off a cliff by talking about dharma bums and Jack Kerouac.

Zoe smiled tolerantly through it all, twisting her long caramel-colored curls into a big girl ponytail, just like the one Audrey wore. Then we were back on track: Audrey is spirited out of the *boîte* by an Astaire who woos her by partnering with an umbrella and a trench coat. They are dancing their way into love. The beatniks were the bad guys, the movie implies—let's stay away from them. As the story ends, Audrey and Fred twirl from the Chateau grounds onto a small raft and float downstream into marriage.

I WAS ELEVEN when I saw a preview for a film called *Lady Godiva*, retitled *Lady Godiva of Coventry*. The poster showed a naked Maureen O'Hara covered only by the longest auburn hair I had ever seen. The Catholic Legion of Decency had it on their list. And so did I. But how to see it?

Godiva of Mercia is married to Leofric, the oppressive Earl. When she asks her husband to repeal the excessive taxation on his Coventry tenants, he refuses and challenges her to ride through the streets naked. Only then will he grant tax remission. Clothed in nothing but her hair, Godiva rides through a town empty of all its citizens except for one man, a tailor known forever after as Peeping Tom, who watches and is blinded for his voyeurism, either by God or the townspeople. The 1955 film starred O'Hara with George Nader as the Earl and Victor McLaglen as Grimald. The pale coral and ochres in Universal's Technicolor print were inspired by Pre-Raphaelite John Collier's painting of Godiva.

On this particular Saturday morning, my aunt Martha calls me.

"Ann Marie, how ya doin'?" Martha and my mother have mastered the colloquialisms of New England. My grandparents, even though they are in grocery retail, retain thick, almost indecipherable Italian accents, but Martha and Anita can now pass as native speakers.

"Fine, Auntie, do you want me to get Ma?"

"Nah, honey, I have something to ask you. Would you take Barbie and Billy Boy to the movies today? For the matinee. I know you like to go to the pictures. Bring your brotha' Rudy too."

I am speechless. I know that *Lady Godiva* is playing at the State Theater. Today. I cannot believe my good fortune.

"Of, course—sure. Send them with plenty of snack money." Already plotting how I will distract the youngsters—Barbara and Rudy are eight, their birthdays three weeks apart, and Billy Boy is only seven—I firm up a plan to bribe them with candy.

My Dad is as always the designated driver. He and my brother and I pick up Barbara and Billy Boy and drive to the theater where there is a long line buying tickets, mostly of parents with children.

And then I see the shocking news. *Lady Godiva* is playing, yes, but only in the evening. Today's matinee feature is *The Wizard of Oz*, which I have already seen—and dislike. Alas, the die is cast, I have my charges for the afternoon, and off I go into two hours of misery.

I hated the shift from the homey-melancholy black and white of Kansas to the Technicolor Oz. Everything becomes suddenly too much, the flowers too bright, the sky too blue, the leaves too green—the greenery of bad science. And on this Saturday afternoon I had been looking forward to seeing a woman let down her hair. Instead, I was forced to watch as a young woman, pretending to be a girl, put it up in pigtails. To this day I have no idea how *Lady Godiva of Coventry* looks, or what it might have given me. It and I never crossed paths again.

AT HOPEDALE HIGH I was a dutiful student. Mrs. Stearns, the school librarian, eventually took me under her wing and gave me a part time job filing books. I have always loved reading because it carries me away, but it wasn't guided reading, mostly historical romances like *Dragonwyck* and *The Winthrop Woman*. Seeing that there was less interrogation from my parents if I earned good grades, I worked hard to secure them. After ending up as the class Valedictorian, I gave a fiery speech on corruption in state government.

Teacher-Nurse-Hairdresser: those are the careers projected by the girls pictured in my high school yearbook. In the fall of my senior year my English teacher put me in touch with a recruiter from Marietta College, and I attended a tea in Franklin. It turned out that the hostess was recruiting as much for her sorority as for the school, but I accepted the eventual offer anyway because it came with free tuition—and because Marietta was in Ohio, not Massachusetts.

My high school summer job working at Hixon's Ice Cream Stand was also my best. Seven or eight girls stood behind tiny screened windows just big enough to pass through cones, a sundae, or a shake. I wore a little white dress made from a crinkled acrylic material. When it came to stains, worse than chocolate was black raspberry. Even more dangerous was whipping up a frappe, the New England equivalent of a shake: put in too much ice cream and you'd have an explosion. The job came to an end when our beloved boss Freddie moved to Oregon after he was burned out by the mob. The "goodfellas" wanted to build a McDonalds on Hixon's busy section of Route 140, but he refused to sell.

Work got me out of the house. But I also liked the ice cream stand because you had to be fast, you could not make mistakes, and as a result you came to feel important. At fourteen, this dynamic was irresistible.

I made a good friend over the years spent at the ice cream stand. The friendship was not instant. David Z. was hired by Freddie as a manager, which meant he did not have to wait on customers or do much cleaning. His responsibility was refilling the ice cream bins during service, resolving the money at the end of each day, opening and closing, doing the heavy lifting, being in charge. Although David Z. was a year younger and came on board after I had, he was seen as my boss, and I did not understand the "why" of that status. It pissed me off, and I suspect I tormented him with sarcastic jokes. He was awkward around girls, a solitary guy and clearly not an athlete. But within this unpromising beginning, I think we both saw the inner nerd in each other, the smarty-pants factor. So we hung out a bit, I stopped sniping at him for his lack of cool, and he became my partner in years of cinematic curiosity. Together we got serious about movies—*The Pawnbroker, Days of Wine and Roses, Splendor in the Grass, The Misfits*—as high school drifted into college and he went off to Penn State. Usually we drove to the Shopper's World screens in Framingham, and the ride home allowed time to unpack what we had seen. It was my first experience of intellectual conversation. Meanwhile, I dated guys who played sports and were happy to make out with me.

WHEN I WAS a girl, my grandparents Ardelia and Cavi used to drive into Boston to the Exeter Street Theater in order to see Italian language films. I asked to go with them to see *Bitter Rice*, but my mother answered with a firm, "No. That's not a movie for you." The film had been advertised with pictures of female rice pickers standing with their skirts hiked up in water-filled fields. My mother had come across an ocean to keep me out of that field.

Anita Molinari arrived in Milford when she was thirteen. The men who worked for Nonno at the sausage factory taught her that "shit" was the word for "hello." When I was a kid, my uncles tried to teach us Italian swear words.

I have no idea how much she was chased around.

She grew up in The Plains, Milford's Italian ghetto. There were open sewer drains; friends in elementary school still used an outhouse. Mom's schooling began slowly, and slogged on until she graduated from high school at the age of twenty-six.

Meanwhile, she was Cinderella, a life of cleaning and sweeping at home. Everybody lived in the three-story white house on Main Street; my mother didn't move out and into an apartment on Congress until her late twenties. I believe my grandmother threw her out after she had gone to nursing school; Nonni didn't want to associate with a daughter whose work allowed "touching men."

My father Gene was a neighborhood boy. He was more interested in my mother than she was in him. They were married in January, 1944, and I came along in December. Anita was thirty-six when I was born; it was a late marriage for both of them.

My father spent the war working for the Army Postal Service in Washington, DC. When he came home my parents moved in with his mother, and that was a disaster. My mother hated Nonni Porotti and she hated her

Cesare and Ardelia Cavigioli, Martha, Anita, Johnny, Carlo, and Pia Molinari

back. Anita got us out by buying a poorly built tract house on Mellen Street in Hopedale. It was the house I grew up in: two bedrooms—Rudy and I shared—a living room, a small kitchen and breakfast nook, a basement and a garage. Eight years later, my parents bought a generous wooded lot, also on Mellen Street, and my mother built her American dream home—a stucco three-bedroom, one-and-a-half bath ranch with a finished wet-bar in the basement.

My Aunt Martha was four years younger than my mother Anita. The sisters lived out their lives in Milford and its suburb Hopedale, small towns south of Boston, and the distance between their houses was never more than a few miles. They raised their children together—Barbara and Billy were more like a younger sister and brother to me than they were cousins—and all of us shared the cottage at the Cape for a month every July. The sisters' attachment was strong, even profound, and may have been the most significant emotional bond in their lives. But it had not always been so, and this was because Anita and Martha met each other for the first time on the boat taking them to America.

Ardelia, my maternal grandmother, was born in Emilia-Romagna in 1882 and had five children between 1902 and 1911. Johnny, Pia, and Carlo

Anita and Martha, 1940s

were followed by my mother Anita in 1907. Martha was born in 1911, and soon thereafter Ardelia discovered that her older husband Enrico had liver disease.

So she left. She located care for her dying husband, and her children were scattered to the homes of various relatives. After arriving in America Ardelia found work as a ladies maid in Boston. What she also found was freedom from childcare and a desire to be a woman of business. Her partner in this enterprise was a rough character who, having knocked around various continents, oceans, and personal disasters, settled with Ardelia in Milford. Always a ladies man, Cesare Cavigioli—known to us as Cavi—was not dazzled by my grandmother's plain beauty. What led him to the altar were Ardelia's unsentimental views on hard work and family and her ultimatum that he marry her before she would bring her five children over from Italy. The priest advised this, and Nonni was reunited with her children.

Cavi had a shadowy past. Confessions shared with my cousin Billy have him fleeing a prospective bride in Bergamo and creditors in Genoa when he jumps a freighter to Argentina. In the land of cows, horses, and meat processing, Cavi lands a job with Hormel as a gaucho—there are pictures of him on the grassy pampas, with wide chaps and a stately mount, smiling at his good luck. His next journey brings him to the Chicago slaughterhouses and work conditions out of Upton Sinclair's *The Jungle*. Along the way he contracts a case of syphilis, probably in rooming houses doing double duty as brothels.

When he and Ardelia settled in Milford, respectability enveloped them like a cocoon. Their property included a large three-story house with two kitchens, several parlors, many bedrooms, a sun-room. The extensive garden held grape vines, roses, tomatoes, border flowers, herb beds. There were several other buildings within the corner property, the most impressive being a sausage factory with the word "Cavigioli" carved in Roman capitals on its granite façade. Cavi's meat products—sausage, luganega, salami, plus fancy cuts of pork and veal—were butchered on the premises and sold locally at the 170 East Main Street address. For customers further afield, there was a fleet of delivery trucks.

When the war came Cavigioli refused to submit to government meat rationing dictates and was sent to Danbury Prison for six months.

CAVI MAY HAVE married Ardelia but he never really settled down. This was confirmed every Easter when Miss Marguerite Pianca—my French tutor *and* my father's high school French teacher—brought the Easter Lamb Cake.

For the nap-inducing holiday dinner three generations gathered at the East Main Street house. The meal seemed endless, and began with an antipasto featuring thinly sliced homemade salamis and prosciutto. I loved the pickled porcini and especially the morel mushrooms gathered by Cavi in nearby forests. Pia, the Pasta Queen, served up her cappelletti in chicken broth. Or Ardelia might stir up a risotto with chicken livers. There was the roast leg of lamb, solidly cooked, and stuffed with garlic and parsley. Then came the drama of dessert.

My mother made eggnog pie, a lovely, gravity-defying chiffon. Torrone nougat and panettone came in the mail from Milanese relatives. And finally, the cake.

Miss Pianca's Lamb Cake was a several-egg yolk *genoise* assembled into the shape of a kneeling sheep. Its sturdy white frosting was generously showered with coconut. Licorice jelly beans for eyes, candied cherry for the nose. Around the edible lamb's neck was a silky ribbon with a bell that all the cousins found irresistible. Ding, Ding. We could not leave it alone. Eating a piece, you got coconut all over yourself. No wonder I was chubby.

Miss Pianca dropped off the cake before Easter dinner. Cavi would greet Marguerite warmly and my grandmother would thunder out of the room, voicing an unmistakable "Che puta." Turns out in the old days, Cavi and Marguerite used to rendezvous during those trips to Italy taken by Cavi to visit his relatives, and Marguerite would just happen to be there, touring with her brother.

We kids just loved Miss Pianca's baked goods. Her specialties appeared for all Catholic Communions and Confirmations—again sponge cake buried in inches of Seven Minute White Frosting with a doll (not edible) baked in the middle of the cake. And for ordinary drop-in visits, there were *farfalles*, fried dough butterflies dusted with walnuts and drizzled with honey.

Miss Pianca was one of my donor figures. She tutored me in French as she had my father, and I scored a 650 on my SAT Achievement test. Doing well in a language mattered then because the two professions every father wanted for his daughter were either airline stewardess or UN translator. Even though I knew I wasn't tall enough to be a stewardess, I indulged my getaway fantasies by starting a novel about three American girls who are hired by the airlines to travel to England, France, and Italy. I wrote a page or two and that was the end of it because, from my personal life, I had no imagination of what my characters might do besides meeting a guy and getting married.

My grandparents quickly adopted the essence of American business: devise a job, and then hire someone else to do it. Though they employed many locals, usually men, to do the butchering, the arriving children were immediately put to work, with schooling a distant concern. Pia suffered more than the rest. She found first grade humiliating and quit, staying home to play the maid to my grandparents until they found her a suitable husband. Carlo, apprenticed to my grandfather, became a fine butcher, although reading skills might have later helped him advocate for himself when he was victimized by his ruthless wife Ida and son, Carlo, Jr.

When I was a young girl, Anita often sent my father and me to Uncle Carlo's with a shopping list. His butcher shop was in a big barn, connected to an even bigger space by a huge noisy sliding door—the slaughterhouse, I presume. It was on the edge of town, a place I thought of as far away because

Cavigioli Packing Company, Milford, MA

of the unmarked dirt road. I don't remember animals around the property, or meat carcasses hanging in the shop, but they must have been there. This was long before I thought about what I ate; I was still enjoying my grandmother's *minestrone alla trippa*, clueless about the American name for its central ingredient—cow's stomach.

So, no, I didn't know what *trippa* meant. There were lots of secrets hiding behind the Italian words my parents never taught me. On the other hand, in the crossing they had made, many things must have gotten lost in translation for them as well. Cavigioli and family may have set about creating their own version of Italy in the little world they lived in, south of Boston, but it bore small resemblance to the beauty and the menace of the Italy I would someday discover.

Ardelia's brood left Genoa in December, 1920 and arrived in Boston in early February, 1921. Martha and Anita formed a bond on the crossing that lasted until their deaths. What must that experience have been like? At the moment of reunion after eight years apart, did my mother even recognize her sister, a babe in arms when they had been separated?

I think about that coming to America. Two Italian women are hired to accompany the five children on the old troop ship. Because the seas are rough, all the passengers are confined together in steerage, where there is constant danger of dehydration from vomiting or from contagious disease. My mother often screamed when she was startled, so there must have been lots of screaming for Martha to deal with. Martha remembers being nauseated for the entire trip. As for my mother's memories of the voyage, she never spoke about them, except once to say that several passengers had died and it was hard to avoid seeing people's tacky behavior—"tacky" was her code word for sex.

On the day of my cousin Barbara's first wedding, Ardelia turned to her and said, "A woman who has children is a fool." I suspect it was an emotion that came to her late in life. When Ardelia comes to meet the boat to collect her five children, she greets them as an elegant matron, dressed in a long sealskin coat, her head covered in a black hat with ostrich feathers. At eight years old, Martha is virtually meeting her mother for the first time. Cavi and Ardelia have pulled out many stops for this extraordinary homecoming: drifts of snow, which the children have never seen, cover the street, and there is a sleigh with a team of horses to drive the kids around Milford. All that stands in the way of this family reunion is the USA Department of Immigration mandatory three-day delousing of the Molinari children. Later, Martha tells her daughter that her days in Italy with her kind aunt Barbara were the happiest of her life. Anita, too, speaks glowingly of her temporary home in San Felice sul Panaro with Uncle Paul and Aunt Lucy. After leaving Italy, she never sees them again.

Once Ardelia and her new husband set up in the big house and in their meat provisions business, it seemed as if the actual Italian childhood of my mother and her siblings was replaced by a society much cruder and more grasping than the one they had left, although one also safe from poverty and hunger. Perhaps Anita's generation had gone through so much change that it was simply tired out; its members displayed, in any case, little interest in the Italy left behind. The archaeology of that gone world was going to be up to me to explore, and it would turn out that there were two ways in: food and movies.

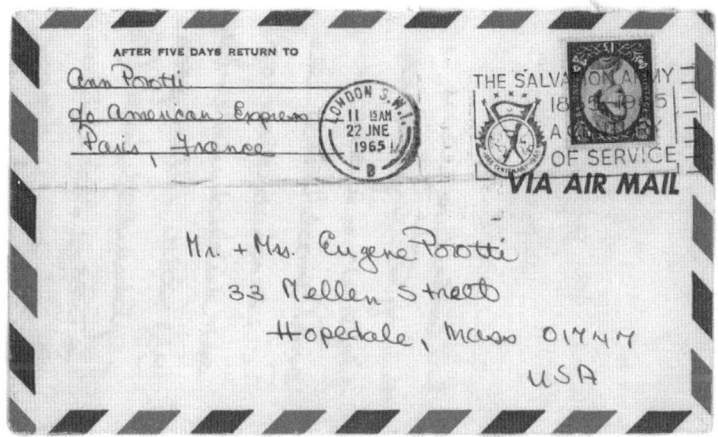

2
RUINED

July 6, Nice France, 1965

Dear parents:
    I bought a bikini, a little white knit one with tiny red strings. It was expensive, $15, but I plan to get a lot of use at home from it. Also, I'm sewing a Villager label in it so I won't have to declare it at customs.

In the summer of 1965 I went to Europe for two months and wrote two dozen letters home. London, Paris, Nice, Milan, Florence, Rome, Copenhagen, Norway. I came at this trip sideways with two very different donor figures guiding it to life. My college roommate Jean Helmle and her family had hosted an AFS student from Norway, and Jean wanted to visit Else in Vestnes. But there was no way her parents would let her go alone. Then, after a not-my-fault car accident with my father's treasured Ford Fairlane, there came a settlement generously in our favor. Plus, Nonno Cavigioli, hearing that Italy was included in the trip, invested in my fantasy with hotel accommodations in Milan and a cash stipend. A visit from TV's Michael Anthony of *The Millionaire* could not have surprised me more. I needed a passport. Luggage. And clothes.

Cavi may have had a shadowy past, but the grandfather I knew was a wealthy man with a neighborhood of beachfront properties on Cape Cod and money enough to take my grandmother to Miami each winter, or back to the old country, as Italy was called. Years ago I found Cavi's travel suitcase at the Cape cottage. It was a hand-woven wicker rectangle with a sturdy handle and a convenient side-opening compartment. Still wired onto the handle was a destination tag reading "Cavigioli-Genoa." I now use his suitcase as a place to store my hand-knitted sweaters. Whatever my grandfather's bad habits might have been, he believed in world travel as a maker of souls.

LET'S BEGIN WITH what happened in Milan:

July 10, 1965. I am staying at the Hotel Rosa on Piazza Fontana, just a few steps from the Duomo. Rooms have been provided courtesy of Cavi's nephew Carlo Cavigioli, who works in the hotel as a manager, but for this weekend he is away on vacation. Our arrival has barely survived the initial uninformed chaos: "Who are you? What letter of introduction?"

It is Sunday and I am determined to visit the church alone: Santa Maria delle Grazie, and the convent which contains Da Vinci's *Il Cenacolo*. That morning the world's most famous and ill-conserved painting knocks me out with its palette of pale blue and peach and grey. Damaged over the centuries by humidity, this fragile tempera on a composite of plaster, wood, mastic, and gesso has also been hit by the war. Allied bombing destroyed one of the walls of the chapel, and on this day, few protections appear to secure this treasure. And still, dignity and everlasting joy pours out of it and into me. A bombed-out church with a profound painting—it does not seem like a safe environment—and yet I stay, moving around carefully.

Not all of my lingering in the church is about being alone with *The Last Supper*; in my walk down Corso Magenta, I have been followed by a soldier. His method is to advance, make a little small talk in Italian to which I answer *non capisco;* then he holds back and stays behind me. But he does not go away. And there is no one, not one soul, on the street. Church, family dinner,

I guess. I am thinking about how long I have walked, wondering if there is an alternate way back.

My thoughts reel back to a movie seen a few years earlier on a date at the Milford Drive-In. Vittorio De Sica's *Two Women*. Sophia Loren and Eleonora Brown are mother and daughter, fleeing the Germans at the end of World War II. They hide in a bombed church. The mother is unable to prevent either of them from being gang-raped by Moroccan irregulars. These were "friendly" soldiers fighting with the Allies who nevertheless turned on the liberated populace.

He's there outside the church door. I begin to walk with a purpose and he gets closer and speaks again, this time touching my arm. Suddenly coming toward me is a Milanese mother with her younger daughter. All my energy goes into a plea—*aiutami per favore, signora!* She must believe I am sincere; I am wearing a modest A-line skirt with a sweater set, not provocative apparel. But I fail to connect, she waves me away, and I am left with the too-close-for-comfort soldier who keeps suggesting and smirking in Italian.

If I had had more experience in Italy, perhaps I would have seen it coming. Because this is the Italian male way, circa 1960 and then some. Always talking to you, touching your arm—and those braver will grab your ass, or your crotch, or show you their penis. But that comes later. Now, this soldier stalks me and I am terrified, at the edge of tears.

I head north toward the Piazzale Cadorna, beyond which I see a grassy hill and a giant castle. There is still no one around; Sunday in Milan or nuclear war?—The abandoned streets reminded me of a scene in Stanley Kramer's *On the Beach*. In fact so much of 1965 Milan is careworn, broken, closer to post WWII neo-realism than the Technicolor Italian Economic Miracle.

I arrive at the Castello Sforza, where the access bridge leads me to the women's bathrooms, *le donne*. And safety. Hot and flushed with fear, I wait for a long time, then I emerge. He has gone. I calm down and walk back to the Hotel Rosa. I never mention this to Jean, or to my parents in my letters home. A part of me believes that I caused this to happen by walking alone in Italy.

JULY 13, 1965. I am alone in the Stazione Centrale di Santa Maria Novella, the Florence train station. Jean and I have just arrived from Milan, and she has gone searching for clues about the location of our *pensione*. A quick, second-class trip, standing in corridors blocked on one side by suitcases and on the other by American college students. We have been warned that the lecherous, ripe-smelling Italian men with octopus-hands like to stake out American girls on the Florence-Rome trains.

Hunger gets the best of me, but, it being Italy, there is a counter with hot food. Words on a chalkboard list the offerings. "*Gnocchi, per piacere,*" I mutter. And moments later, for a few *lira*, a plate of white, fluffy little edible pillows modestly dressed in the sweetest tomato sauce joins me.

I eat them standing up. Five minutes max, and my plate is clean.

"The most delicious thing I had ever eaten in my life"—that was how I remembered it. I could not know then it was to become a benchmark of taste and cooking skill in my life. Eventually I became the unofficial Gnocchi Queen, maker of the standard potato gnocchi with Yukon Golds, and, later Russets, as well as ricotta gnocchi, where cheese replaces potatoes, flour continues and sometimes spinach steps in too. An outlier, semolina gnocchi is twice-cooked—first as a porridge and then cooled, stamped out with a small drinking glass, and baked in layers to resemble Mediterranean roof tiles. Parmesan and butter rain down and melt into a delicious skin. All other gnocchi are imposters.

Here's your basic recipe. Tools you will need are a potato ricer and a bench knife.

1½ cups of all purpose flour
1½ pounds of Yukon Gold Potatoes or Russets. No colors.
Boil potatoes whole until easily pierced with a fork.
Drain. Peel quickly. Rice onto a wooden board. Knead a cup of the flour into the mound of warm riced potato.
Add flour as needed. When the dough comes together, divide it into six pieces and roll them into sausage lengths—about one inch in diameter.
(Rescue moment approaches: if you have any concern about the integrity of your dough, cut several one-inch lengths from one roll. Drop these test pieces into boiling water; if they float to the top and hold their shape, you are good to go on the rest of the batch. The fix, if needed, is plus or minus flour.)
After forming your rolls, cut into 1 x 1.5 inch pieces. Lightly dust the gnocchi and a long-tined fork with flour. Then flip each segment off your floured palm as you mark it with the tines of the fork. Resist washing your hands. Use a bench knife to move the

gnocchi onto a tray. *Freeze those gnocchi! Please do not skip this step!* Store loose frozen gnocchi in a zip lock until ready to use.

SO I ATE my days through Florence. Staying in a *pensione* where both breakfast and another meal were provided, I worried, "Are we eating too much, can we pay our bill?" But I kept drilling through the delicious Tuscan cuisine, with gnocchi at every turn. We ate lunch at the Student Mensa for 300 *lire* (about 50 cents), often returning to my beloved train station for pizza that cost a little more than a quarter or risotto for twice that much. Enter the Era of Four Meals a Day.

From my letters, Florence appears to be the genesis of a fantasy of return:

> *Don't panic, Dad, about my studying in Firenze since I won't be getting married until I'm 25 or so, I plan to come back to Europe, maybe to study art history in Florence, maybe a Master's Program.*

From my careful response and my eventual promise to study Library Science so as to be able to earn a living, I sense that my parents were in full-blown WTF is she talking about. As much as I loved the student-y, boho vibe in 1960s Florence, my affection for Renaissance art was lukewarm and would never stand the test of graduate school. What I had fallen in love with was Italian food. Head over heels. And I never got over it.

JUNE 26—JULY 2, 1965, Paris. My note to Anita and Gene includes the words "Paris is marvelous" four times, the way Audrey Hepburn would have said it in *Funny Face*. To Fred Astaire. "Take the picture, take the picture," she urges, running down the Louvre staircase.

I glance through my shopping list of art and architecture seen—Tuileries, Sacré Coeur, Jeu de Paume, Notre Dame, Pantheon—and gifts to be purchased—a bikini for cousin Barb, prints from the Louvre. There is a serious survey of perfumes named Joy, Bellagio, l'Interdit, Crêpe de Chine, as if they were philosophies to study.

> *I have been shopping at the bookstalls on the Left Bank ... Jean and I know Paris rather well. We walk the Latin Quarter (alias Left Bank) ... creatures of habit in our new home.*

At the end of this flying-high letter I list our itinerary through mid-August. Nowhere does the word Copenhagen appear. And yet, on July 24, there I was writing from Copenhagen, extolling the Danish self-service laundry techniques allowing me to clean beer stains from the white pique skirt I can barely wear given how much weight I have gained in Italy. Rome had proven so impossible that only touchdown in Copenhagen could revive a girl's spirit.

What did I think Rome would be? Endless hours on the Via Veneto in pursuit of La Dolce Vita. Looking for Anita Ekberg bathing in black satin and ermine at the Trevi Fountain or jaded Marcello Mastroianni joyriding with paparazzis. But those were activities for Italians; what do American girls do in Rome? In July. At night. The major impediment was navigating an unmarked Inland Sea of Roman Men. At every corner, down this *strada*, and that *viale*, *dappertutto* on the sidewalks, *i vitelloni*: crowds and gangs of men with nothing to do except hoot, whistle, sing, touch, expose, and grab. And since it was nighttime, only American girls had the freedom to wander unescorted.

After a week I was finished with this town. As I wrote my parents:

> *God do I hate Rome. The city is so lovely but ... it's resting on its laurels. So hot, and the people are so crooked. Yesterday, Jean and I were lamenting our fate to be here until next Wednesday, when after a few glasses of wine, I marched to the SAS office (my third visit) and got our flight to Copenhagen moved to tomorrow. You have no idea how happy we both are. I am never coming back to Rome.*

That night, we celebrated our good fortune and went to the movies. *The Great Escape*.

"Fantastic, "I wrote, "I got very homesick—even though it takes place in a Nazi prison camp and was probably filmed in California—but then I read your letters, and realize what a lucky girl I am. I miss you guys."

The Great Escape was the only movie I saw during my summer away. The museums of Paris had turned my head to painting and enlivened my hunger for art. At the Jeu de Paume, I took a chance and bought two prints for my parents, both by Claude Monet: *Houses of Parliament* and *Woman and Child in a Field*. When I got home I had them framed at a fancy shop in Framingham and then hung them in our bare Hopedale living room. The paintings opened a doorway out; perhaps I thought they might burn holes in the wall.

In their deepest fantasies, lucky girls traveling to Europe in the 1960s could hardly not have been influenced by *Three Coins in the Fountain*. Hugely successful, the 1955 movie follows three American girls working in Rome— Jean Peters, Dorothy McGuire, and Maggie McNamara—as they toss coins in the Trevi and hope to find true love. A secretary wins her boss Clifton Webb, an honorable spitfire tames Italian wolf Rossano Brazzi, and a sweet miss lands prince Louis Jourdan. As a life-lesson, this modern fairy tale runs circles around contemporary travel marketing with its reliance on swim-up bars, thread counts, and rewards points. I confess to seeing *Three Coins* many times before going to Europe. And I believed it all might happen to me. But clearly it was not going to happen in Rome. Arrivederci, Roma.

> *Dear parents,*
>   *The flight was great. SAS jet, great meal. We met this divine, wealthy Philadelphia lawyer on the plane. He said he wants to feed and chaperone Jean and I around Copenhagen. Fine with me, too bad he's pushing forty, he's such a great catch.*
>   *We arrived finally at the Danish tourist bureau at the RR station where—because all the hotels were booked—the agent put us in a private home. Mrs. Hoffman is divine—$2.80 per day with breakfast in our quiet, bright, cheery twin bedroom. And happiness —we can use the bathtub when we want. In Rome with its 120 degree heat, you have to pay .50 more to take a shower in a $3.50 room. After a week of sloshing around in the bidet, the tub was a miracle last night. Mrs. Hoffman sent us to a neighborhood restaurant, and the waitress helped us order economically. That would never have happened in Rome.*

> *Dear Anita, Euge, + Rudy:*
>   *July 30, Copenhagen. Be prepared for an absolute tome. Wednesday was the greatest day of this entire trip (rivaled only by that day in Florence with the Yalies). I called Bill, the 36 year-old bachelor lawyer. He offers us lunch at the Royal Hotel (most expensive divine place in Copenhagen.) Then to Den Permenente, a furniture*

store. Because Denmark is a socialist country, the government controls all the industry, even the breweries. The store is a conglomeration of ceramic and wood with furniture from all the Danish craftsmen. Everything has the government (Parliamentary vote) approval on its attributes of taste and high quality. Fabulous place—sort of expensive. 'Uncle' Bill dropped a fortune on Swedish crystal, goatskin rugs, porcelain, silverware and teak tables. I bought you guys a foot-long lemon board for serving cold cuts, pizza, and a companion cheese board where the handle flies out and has a stainless blade. They stack. I shipped them to you; total 22 bucks.

Next we went with Bill to an artist's home, Per Damen. We sat around drinking Tuborg beer. Bill had bought a wood carving from Axel Hansen, another well-known Danish artist. It was so great just sitting around drinking and talking. Mr. Hansen's son Benje, a history teacher here in Copenhagen was with us. He speaks great English. We all ended up at this divine artist's tavern Tuborg-ing away. Danes certainly drink a lot of beer ... constantly.

That night, Bill and Margot (a nurse friend of Benje, divine girl), Benje and I and Jean and Harold (44 year old friend of Bill's from Phillie who popped into town) went out to dinner and then dancing at a 'neatsie' nightclub. (Danish nightlife is incredible—goes on until 5 in the morning.) Benje and I had a marvelous time—we ran the conversational gamut from politics to art, socialism to morals. Danes think like Swedes—free love, rationalized love—it's an admirable philosophy but a little too uninhibited for Americans. Jean in the meantime had a problem with Harold who forgot she was a young innocent not his usual 35-year-old European hooker. He groped her so we called the evening to a halt. I had a wonderful time with Benje.

Thursday, Jean and I had a Finnish Sauna—courtesy of the lecherous Harold; it's a cold shower, followed by ten minutes in a dry hot room (180 degrees), repeated and the grand finale, a massage. Divine. We kissed Bill good bye, promising to visit him in Philadelphia, then we went out with Benje and Per for afternoon Tuborg-ing. At night, Benje took me to a great student Tavern where we drank from big mugs and sang into the evening. He's such a handsome darling.

> Tonight I took Jean to Tivoli—my third appearance this week. It's so lovely at night with all the fountains and lights. Dragged her to the Dance Hall where we danced with all these strange Danes and Swedes who wanted our addresses in America. One guy said he's coming over to Boston in 1968 and he 'wants to meet my parents so he can ask for my hand.'
>
> Tomorrow is our last day in Copenhagen. We see Margot, the nurse, for tea in the afternoon; then I have a dinner date with Benje. I want to come back here really soon.

NORWAY. THERE IS only one letter written from Norway, although we stayed there nearly two weeks. These were bucolic, restful days of picking raspberries, mowing the grass, and riding a kid's bike on gravel roads. The big news was that I had gained eleven pounds—I was up to 122, and nothing fit. I was reduced to wearing my stretchy French bikini as underwear, and my only available dress was a baby-doll cotton mini with a high waist and great fullness around the middle.

Jean's AFS 'sister' Else lived north of Oslo in Vestnes. My memory is that we took two days by car to get there, switch-backing around various fjords. I was dazzled by mountains rising straight up from the water, and a little carsick. We stayed in a Norwegian hamlet with Else's parents who spoke no English but communicated instead with a generous Call to Cream involving six dairy-rich meals a day. These were hours spent without museums, or shopping, or boys to chase; it was a sweet, calm ending to a transformative summer.

THE MOST BITTERSWEET memory of my time away is from an evening in Florence.

On July 14, Jean and I are chased by Italian soldiers onto the Ponte Vecchio and its nightly open-air party. Listening to a band, we latch onto two American guys. Jim and Fred, recent Yale grads, seem happy for the company and take us to a bar. After exchanging good nights, we walk back to our hotel and there, waiting at the door and conversing in charades with our hotel manager, are Jim and Fred.

We leave Florence in their 1965 VW bug and drive high above the city to Piazzale Michelangelo. There we step out of the car into a grand panorama:

below us a ridge of spires, domes, and covered bridges leading the river toward the distant Tuscan hills. Jim Moore and I talk into the night about Boston politics, whose art is best, are American women feminine, his upcoming new life at Stanford Graduate School. At sunrise he and Fred are off to Venice and Jean and I to Rome. Once I had seen the European Adventure as a great way to meet new guys; now I am beginning to realize that I am in possession of a runaway-train mind less interested in "being attached" and more in conversation, ideas, intelligence. In my arrangement with Jean, I have felt sometimes like the man, marching into hotels, bargaining for rooms, dining like a frugal traveler. If I don't do it, my upper-middle class, Lacoste-shirted, Cheever-suburbanite roomie will not have a clue.

I know now, looking down over the lights along the Arno, that I can never go back to my life in Milford, never work another summer job at the needle factory, never spend time with my stalker hometown boyfriend. It is going to be next to impossible to get through my last semester at college. Europe has ruined me; I am ruined.

3
MEETING CHIEF

Someone once asked me—now that I am past seventy—"What was the turning point in your life?"

"For me," I answer, not quite believing I am saying it, "it was meeting Chief Gordon."

Francis Guthrie "Chief" Gordon III and I met in Charlottesville, Virginia in the fall of 1966. He was a rising senior at the University; I was a floundering graduate student.

Chief has been gone from my life for almost forty years. But he left a lot behind. I know that he was here from the seven books by Pär Lagerkvist still sitting on my shelves, books that I have dusted but never opened. I know that Chief was here from the Wagners missing from my stack of opera LPs. He left behind the house in which I still live, at 115 Rothery Road. There are of course our two children. And perhaps more than anything else he left behind the art of leaving—long before he really left.

I arrived by bus in Charlottesville during a huge snowstorm that blanketed the entire mid-Atlantic. I thought I had come to the balmy South and was wearing brown Capezio flats with loden-green knit separates. There were the obligatory nylon stockings and a camel car coat. Now, in a foot of snow, I had to walk the mile from the Greyhound station to Mary Mumford Hall—none of the taxis were out and about. The town was paralyzed.

After my transformative summer in Europe I decided to rush to graduation and managed to complete my course work at Marietta College in December of 1965. My dream had been to go on in Library Science but, since they did not accept students at mid-year, I decided to attempt an M.A. in history. The night before my GMATS I was a drunken bundle and my scores showed it. Somehow UVA let me in anyway—my college advisor had successfully extolled an undergraduate record far stronger than my test results.

At the Dean's office, Edward Younger smiled at me across the table and said, "Welcome to the University of Virginia, Miss Porotti." When he said my last name, he pronounced the "o" as in "rope," the way people now mispronounce "risotto." The interview involved running a familiar gauntlet, like modern-day Homeland Security but with a different kind of body scan. We worked out a list of classes and then, as I was walking out the door, he added, "Good luck—you are very attractive."

For a lot of women this works—you are allowed to play with men because you are good-looking. Later I was to cause a stir when I showed up in Alderman Library wearing a pair of jeans. I was cruising the carrels, looking for books on French playwrights, when someone saw me. Women were required to appear in public spaces only in skirts or dresses, so I was hauled in before the Women's Dean, who reminded me of the rule.

I quickly came to see that history, at least history as it was being taught at the university, was landlocked. At the end of that semester a kind professor said, "History might not be the graduate program for your interests." He suggested English. That department was then presided over by Fredson Bowers, a famed bibliographer. The interview with him took less than five minutes. After staring at my grades and test scores he glanced at me and said, "I cannot admit you into the English Department. You are not qualified to be a graduate student at this university."

So I walked across the parking lot to Minor Hall and signed up with the Department of Drama. My final resting place at the university made a kind of sense, because I had arrived hoping to study Eastern European literature, especially the work of Czech playwright Karel Čapek. But then I came across John Osborne's *Look Back in Anger*.

The play was a huge hit when it premiered in London in 1956—it felt like a break with everything that had come before.

Alison Porter comes off as both passionate and helpless. She absorbs her husband's anger because she loves him, and perhaps I thought, "I guess that's what you do, if you are a woman. You just take it." But I saw myself in Jimmy Porter too. It did not seem to me that he was the strangest man on the planet. Not since Hamlet had someone on the English stage been so willing to say, "My life sucks!" When it came time to attempt an MA Thesis, I set to work on Osborne, but I eventually burned the unfinished project.

I did find a supportive figure in Roger Boyle. While taking his playwriting course I ran across an arrogant trio of graduating seniors, and a man named Chief Gordon was among them.

It was assumed that because I was a girl I could sew. And I could. I became not only one of its graduate students but the Drama Department's seamstress. My first big job was to costume Eliot's *Murder in the Cathedral*. Working away on my portable Singer, my hands developed cuts and sores as I turned out twelve sets of muslin tunics and dyed—in my bathroom sink—tights. I can still see Chief prancing around with the other murderers in the UVA chapel. At the time, I was not the least bit interested.

Over the following months I dated a lot of younger guys and also began relying on amphetamines. I was out there in the wind with too much choice and all of it unsatisfying, repetitive: school, work, guys. My roommate Marcia Bonnell occasionally joined my path to ruin. Though making fewer bad decisions than I did, Marcia did make the spectacular purchase of a 1963 Triumph TR-3 convertible, a roadster, styled for trips to self-discovery with plastic window screens instead of glass and a very muscular stick shift. During spring break, she and I drove it to Yellow Springs, Ohio, via New Orleans, where she had friends from undergraduate days at Sophie Newcomb. Mostly I remember sleeping rough and evenings drinking at the Napoleon House, corner of Chartres and Saint Louis. I drove "TR" north, following the Mississippi River to Memphis where the wipers quit mid-downpour. In Ohio, Marcia and boyfriend Don put me on a Greyhound back to Massachusetts. It's hard to remember why I headed home to see my parents. Maybe I wanted to prepare them for my exit from graduate school and a return to Massachusetts. Unequivocally, I had nothing going on.

Travel shakes me up, for good and bad. My attempt to get home stalled in the Pittsburgh bus station from not enough cash to buy a ticket to Hopedale; they didn't take checks, credit cards not invented yet. I fell back on Dean Younger's assessment of my looks, and politely asked several people waiting if I could write them a check for cash. Most said "Yes," and soon I had the necessary twenty dollars.

Back at school, I distanced myself from the pills and most of my course work, but not the guys. One night I went to a party and began dancing with Chief and we realized we both like R&B oldies.

The *Griswold v. Connecticut* Supreme Court decision legalizing birth control pills did not arrive until 1965. Before that, it was our unsentimental Time of the Diaphragm with Mary McCarthy's *The Group* as narration. The previous year I had jumped on the pill bandwagon but had stopped after the New Orleans trip—part personal clean-up, part health concerns over side effects. Yes, spring was in the air, I was having adventures, and Chief was one of several.

It was a beautiful April. Chief was playing Hamlet at UVA's amphitheater, his friends director Ed Stern and actor Chris Leahy also in the production. Things happened pretty rapidly after that. I am a sucker for smart, and Chief was not only a voracious reader but a passionate moviegoer.

Chief desperately wanted to study acting at Indiana University but, even though he was admitted, his mother refused to pay for it. He had also applied to and was accepted by the UVA law school. Around this time, Chief began talking about getting married—he seemed oddly compelled by the idea.

He would say things like, "If you don't marry me I'll just marry someone else because I don't want to be alone."

Chief was tall with curly dark hair though much of it was already streaked with grey. He was full of self-confidence, boosted by a huge cackling laugh. Always acting, he liked to do different accents, and, on a later car trip with my parents to Massachusetts, he managed to speak the entire time as if he were in a Noël Coward play. When my Dad quietly asked, "What is he doing?" I answered, "Oh, he's just playing." He was a great buffer for me; he took the focus on himself with his polite theatrical behavior, and my parents barely noticed I was in the room.

By the time Chief graduated in May I had agreed to marry. My parents reluctantly drove down from Massachusetts to meet him. Judging by the contents of the following letter, they must have put up considerable resistance to our plan. The letter is postmarked May 27, 1967:

Dear Mr. and Mrs. Porotti,
   It is not, I hope, too late to pull some order out of the chaos of the last few days. It is most certainly true that Ann and I want to marry before the end of the summer, and it is not true that we are totally unreasonable in our dedication to this plan.

Chief goes on to describe Charlottesville as "a very lonely place" for a single man and makes a case for the society provided by the "Law Wives' group here at Virginia." But these considerations pale in comparison to what he calls "the real crux of the issue:"

   Because I care for Ann—and love her—I am very much afraid for her. I am clearly a highly-prejudiced observer, but I do not honestly believe that three more years of single life will do her one single scrap of good. I think it is only her intelligence and sheer force of personality that have kept her on an even keel this year. Before I began dating her, admittedly not long ago, I had been watching, almost in horror, as she went through a succession of disturbing, turbulent relations with students here at Virginia, none of whom were her equals in mind, character, or talent.

He then takes up the question of "Why so soon:"

   The strain of a three-year engagement, the forced propriety of our dating, the restless irritation, all these factors are likely to become extremely dangerous for two basically erratic personalities like ours. In order to preclude the possibility of a disaster that will send us both back to our old ways, I think the shock treatment of responsibility in marriage is the ideal remedy.

He closes by asking for my parents' blessing and signs the letter,

>   *Sincerely,*
>   *Chief Gordon*
>   *(actually Francis Guthrie Gordon, III).*

In reading this letter again, I am touched by Chief's almost parental concern. As for my experience with UVA men, some of Chief's claims may have been prompted by reading the infamous graffiti in the Minor Hall Men's Room: "Why Doesn't Chief Gordon Marry a Virgin?" I only came to know about the scrawl from Frank, a Drama graduate student, openly gay when few were.

By the time I met Chief, I had already learned something that the guy who wrote the graffiti had not: If you give it away, they go away.

At our engagement party that June in Northern Virginia, Chief's parents, Katheryn and Francis the Second, put on the suburban dog, with black waiters and multiple blenders whipping up daiquiris. Katheryn loved my quiet father Eugene and plans went ahead for a Labor Day wedding. Then in August I went to see the local gynecologist for a check-up, and perhaps to restart birth control pills. I confided to him that I had been losing weight, even after quitting cigarettes, and that my periods had sorta stopped.

He examined me and said, "No need for birth control pills. You are three months pregnant."

I must have looked horrified because the doctor then said, "Unless you don't want to keep it. And I can help you with that, but it must be soon."

The bride made her wedding dress. It was high-waisted, Empire, silk *peau de soie*, and it concealed a four-month baby *in utero*. She wore no illusion veil. Those in the know were me, Chief, and my Maid of Honor, cousin Barbara. Eugene and Anita hosted the wedding in their Hopedale backyard: she fought with the caterer, he worried about his lawn. Wedding photos are absent from that day, but a family friend Joe Petrone filmed the event in 16mm: the church mass at Sacred Heart in Milford, the buffet dinner, and a long receiving line in which I see my grandparents Ardelia and Cesare, my uncles Bill, Johnny and Duffy, and in a white suit Sonny Dagnese, a local Mafia figure. I wore a white mantilla Cavi had requisitioned from Milan; the rum drinks were replaced by a fountain of Asti Spumante.

With Anita, you never quite knew what you were going to get. There came a point soon after Chief and I had married when I realized I had to tell my mother and father that I was expecting. In the autumn of 1967 I was teaching fifth grade—geography and history—at William Morris Elementary School in Greene County, Virginia. But this being the old days, pregnancy and public school teaching were combinable only until the start of the second trimester, and I was already very far along by the end of October. My acting assignment at school was to pretend to be "lightly pregnant" until the Christmas break so as to retain my job.

Chief and I hatched a plan. We would drive in our new but ridiculously unsafe Mini Cooper across the mountains of West Virginia to Lexington, where my brother Rudy was a sculpture student at the University of Kentucky. Spend the weekend with him, tell him about the baby coming in February, and most importantly enlist his help in informing Anita that her daughter had been knocked up before marriage. Because Rudy and I knew that this was Anita's favorite pillory: for every young woman in our community who delivered a baby earlier than nine months after her wedding, my mother impulsively commented, "Another shotgun wedding, rush job." Now, it was happening on her doorstep. Didn't matter that I was married, twenty-three, and employed.

Over dinner the three of us decided that Rudy would call Anita first and tell her about the incoming baby, softening the news, and then I would phone an hour later, and, with luck, she would be calm, almost grandmotherly. We thought we had synchronized our telephone calls but forgot that the coming Sunday was the beginning of Daylight Savings Time, "spring forward, fall back."

When I dialed Hopedale at the agreed-upon hour of seven in the evening, and began casually talking about being pregnant, my mother had not yet spoken to Rudy, who had failed to take note of the time change. She exploded, yelling "you whore, you *puta*," ending with "I never want to see you again." Then she hung up the phone. Shocking but not surprising; her temper tantrums were legendary.

There was radio silence until the holidays, when Chief and I drove north for a visit brokered by my father and neighbor Emily Carracino. Anita never apologized for her outburst, she just moved on to the next set of emotions, which appeared to be enthusiasm, and anxiety, for the coming baby.

Ian was born on a cold February 7, 1968, in the era of lonely childbirth. As the wife of a UVA law student, I had university health care; all prenatal and OBGYN visits were covered in the clinic. The baby was delivered by Chief Resident Dr. Hedgpeth. My waters broke after a tumble at Minor Hall, the drama building; during the night, I flooded our bed and was advised to go to the hospital. Admitted, and given an epidural, I spent five hours yelling my head off in a room by myself. Eventually that tiny baby—five pounds, ten ounces—popped out. No one held my hand, or put ice chips on my dry lips, or fed my groaning tummy snacks. I might as well have been lying in an open field.

My little papoose and I went home to more cold. Canadian air mass, the TV said. Chief and I were then living in a converted gas station called Twin Pumps, a cinder block structure located south of town on Route 20. When I got the baby home, the kerosene heater was not working. In the midst of this domestic crisis my mother arrived to be my nurse. "Pipes are like babies," Anita had written us, after hearing about our freeze-off, "they need to be kept warm."

My mother worried a lot before things went wrong but was great once they had gone wrong. During the week she spent at Twin Pumps, she was like the imaginary figure a postpartum Charlize Theron conjures in *Tully*, always helpful, always there. She woke me in the night to nurse the baby, made warming tea and toast at every feeding. Dinner came early, before dark. Until we went to sleep the oven door was always propped open. Chief used a blow torch to thaw what we thought was a frozen fuel line, except, turns out, the heater had been clogged with wood pulp by the previous tenants. Anita slept on a narrow sofa that unfolded into a bed with spinal unfriendliness. Despite her efforts, some mornings when I woke up I had produced my own Creamsicle; the overflowing breast milk had frozen on my nipples.

During the Twin Pumps years, Anita wrote me once a week. Her news spoke of deaths like my auntie Mary Ianzitto's from reproductive cancer; family disagreements with her brother John; a seven-year sulk between her and her sister Martha. And sewing projects. She was making a world of plaid clothes for Ian, a car coat for my cousin Barbara, a gown for herself, which, she confessed, "had lost its appeal." Where would she be going that she needed a gown? Sewing was her work; the nursing career had evaporated once Rudy and I were out of college, and then my father died. Occasionally she worked as a housekeeper for a wealthy bachelor who might have been more than her boss. "I might have done some tacky things," she once said to me, smiling coyly.

THE ACTUAL TWIN Pumps—concrete platforms where gas was purchased in the past—were long gone and not part of the house proper. We lived in what was probably the old store connected to the gas station. The craziest home building detail was the variety of floor treatments: one room had wide pine boards, our bedroom had cement with rubber tile, the baby's room was only sub-flooring and had to be heavily rugged in the winter, and the kitchen was a huge space with buckling sheet linoleum. But there was an ancient six burner gas stove with a decent oven. Cooking was a good distraction.

I worked from the Rombauers' *The Joy of Cooking* and Craig Claiborne's *New York Times*. My party dish was Country Captain, but, having no idea what a curry was, this rendition tasted like a bland chicken stew. One weekend I volunteered to make pizza for a party and Chief invited his entire law class. "We're going to have a party—everybody come out!" I made dough but it didn't rise and, after, producing three circular crackers covered with tomato paste, I vanished into the crowd.

I cooked because we had to eat, but it wasn't until 1973, when my former roommate Marcia gave me a copy of Marcella Hazan's *The Classic Italian Cookbook,* that I recovered the pastas and the risottos of my youth.

Just the other day I found some swatches of fabric that reminded me of another way I spent my time before opening my movie theatre. I made my children clothes, especially upper body things. All in vivid seventies colors—one piece of acrylic knit has white ducks on an orange ground. A photograph from the Cape shows eight-year-old Ian and six-year old Courtenay holding hands, the two of them sporting three different plaids.

"Porotti" was what I had been called in Graduate School. Once married, Chief began calling me "AG", or, if he were writing me a note, it might begin with a sweet "Dear Mum." Birthdays often required a hunt to find your gift; one year he penned a five-stanza poem to guide my search. Here are the closing clues:

We can all make merry'o

When you have looked where once the stereo
(One was weaker)
Kept its old grey speaker.

> Now that you have found your prizes
>
> I hope some are surprises
> You know of course that they mean too
> Happy Birthday—I love you.
> Chief

Getting poems like this was nice; the problem came when the theatrical sentimentality went off the rails. In the beginning Chief was very tender and content; my black and white photos of our life in the Virginia countryside look "happily hippie." But, somehow, he developed a swagger—it was as if he went to swagger school.

IN 1969, AMERICA'S summer of love, eighteen-month-old Ian and I lived poolside at a patio apartment complex in Westwood, California, while Chief, after two years of law school, worked as an intern in downtown Los Angeles at the law firm of Kindel & Anderson.

Ian and I shared a pleasant endless summer. We strolled every inch of the leafy UCLA campus and found the local Ralph's Market, later a midnight destination for Elliott Gould's Marlowe in Robert Altman's *The Long Goodbye*. We shopped hip vintage stores for me and found ice cream for Ian. On days when I could borrow the Mustang, we drove down Sunset Boulevard. It was not glamorous anymore, but I was looking for photo equipment, not movie stars. I found my first 35mm SLR camera, a Minolta with a fast f-stop, 55mm lens, and 135mm telephoto. The weekends saw trips to Huntington Beach with a fellow intern from Ohio, and even further afield to the San Diego Zoo where my camera caught all the wild things, especially Ian. Westwood was one of the best exhibition platforms in the country: we saw *Midnight Cowboy, Easy Rider, Medium Cool, Alice's Restaurant*. And perhaps—Swedish director Vilgot Sjöman's 1967 film was just getting its US release—there is a vague memory of seeing *I Am Curious Yellow* in Santa Ana while visiting a fun Republican couple from the office.

My bikini top got lost to strong waves at Emerald Bay in Laguna. I'd never before seen a gated community. Chief grew more frustrated with corporate law. He disdained the conservative politics and grew sufficient facial hair to be denied access to Disneyland. He prided himself on being the target of a running joke at The Firm: "Chief only eats Red Sauce." Commies, not chiles. Up in smoke, I would say, his dreams of practicing law while pursuing a Hollywood career in the off-hours.

Chief did have one more card to play. On the drive back to Virginia we turned north to that foggy urban beauty, San Francisco. There Chief "tried out" for but was not cast by Melvin Belli's celebrity law firm. Belli put us up at the Fairmont, and once again, me and the toddler strolled the daunting California hills.

My first and only cross country car trip came late that August, five days in our 1966 Mustang, with Ian nestled—the last one in, first out—among a TV and kitchen appliances. These are the vistas—desolate Great Salt Lake, Wyoming plateaus, borderless Kansas and Nebraska horizon, steamy Missouri river towns.

After the summer in California, I found a night job working at The Gaslight, an early fine dining restaurant in town. I was the first woman hired at John Tuck's West Main Street establishment; the place was otherwise manned by elegant black men. I became a waitress and then rose quickly to bartender/manager. I loved the place: a dark, high-ceilinged room with antiques and found objects, like an old bicycle, covering the walls. The work got me out of the house and I could boss around flirtatious men while tidying the daily business and accounting ledgers. Luckily, my sweet Ian enjoyed our daytime circuit of errands: bank, post office, the Ben Franklin 5¢&10¢. Tuck seemed to smile at having a very pregnant female manager; my daughter Courtenay was on the way. He liked being a cultural trailblazer.

I still have a luncheon menu from The Gaslight signed by film director Frank Capra, who had been making a UVA appearance. The most expensive item listed, "hot or cold English Prime Rib, Rice Pilaf with horseradish or imported mustard," is priced at $3.50. Frogs legs also appeared on the dinner menu and they came in frozen, avoiding too much biology.

One of the memories Chief left behind was his participation in a court case. In his last year of law school, Chief began his work with local attorney John Lowe. On September 30, 1969, Lowe fought and won a case at the Virginia Appellate level, *Kirstein v. Rector and Visitors of University of Virginia*. It was a victory affecting many lives, including mine.

Albemarle High School graduate Ginger Scott wanted the best in-state college education available and came up against an unpleasant surprise when

she found the doors of Virginia's quality public universities almost entirely closed to women. The all-male College of William and Mary allowed her a mere taste of what it had to offer for one semester. After a summer session at all-female Mary Washington College in Fredericksburg, Scott balked when administrators claimed that women were better served at sister schools. She was tired, as she said, of getting the "bureaucratic run around and the flat nose from the university." "I had to defend my action and it changed me ... All I could say was that I wanted an education." So she sued for entrance to UVA.

Initially Ginger Scott was one of four female plaintiffs in an ACLU case against the University of Virginia. She then became the only plaintiff when the other women feared they would lose their tuition payments if they lost the case. In a newspaper article, Scott said that both her mother's death in 1969 and her limited income from working as a secretary prevented her from going away to another school.

I know now that there is supposed to be a glass wall between lawyer and client, but even as a third-year law student Chief liked to make friends with the people he was working for. But it turned out he was also working *with* Ginger Scott; Lowe had hired her as a secretary after hearing of her plight. During the period of her legal representation, Ginger was, as a result, often in and out of our house. A slightly disheveled but determined blonde, Ginger was smart and without pretense. She was definitely not privileged. She and her shaggy boyfriend were textbook counter-culture: a green and white Volkswagen bus; aviator glasses; a wrong to right. Later, after the case had been won, I bought their bus.

Despite all the glamour that came from winning the Virginia Scott case, Chief still longed for an acting career. Through law school and beyond he starred in four or five Virginia Players shows a year. I was left at home at night with the kids. Did I feel abandoned? Perhaps. But it turns out that I liked being alone, although it took some years before I learned how to use the time. I had, in any case, little choice but to adapt to my husband's comings and goings. As Chief kept looking for a life on stage, he dreamed, I followed, and our lives were about to take a remarkable turn.

Ian and Courtenay at Rothery Road

4
BUILDING

In my files, there's a letter, dated 1972, from my high school friend David Z. He has recently visited my mother. "Anita tells me that you're moving to Indianapolis for a year beginning June," he writes. The letter must have been mailed during the time when Chief was still hoping to follow his friend Ed Stern into a career on the stage.

Stern, a friend from undergraduate days, was a founder of the Indiana Repertory Theatre, and Chief had every intention of joining him there. We took a winter family vacation—kids, too—and the most memorable part of our train trip to Indianapolis was a detour to Columbus, Indiana, where the Cummins Engine Corporation had invited architects like Eero Saarinen and Robert Venturi to build out the town. I was entranced by this sudden eruption of line and form, one devoted to both public buildings and private residences, in what felt like the middle of nowhere.

Plans for the move to the Midwest did not go so well. One of Stern's letters invites Chief to take part in a show scheduled for December, but the

From Charlottesville Redevelopment and Housing Authority, March 1966: "Appendix D

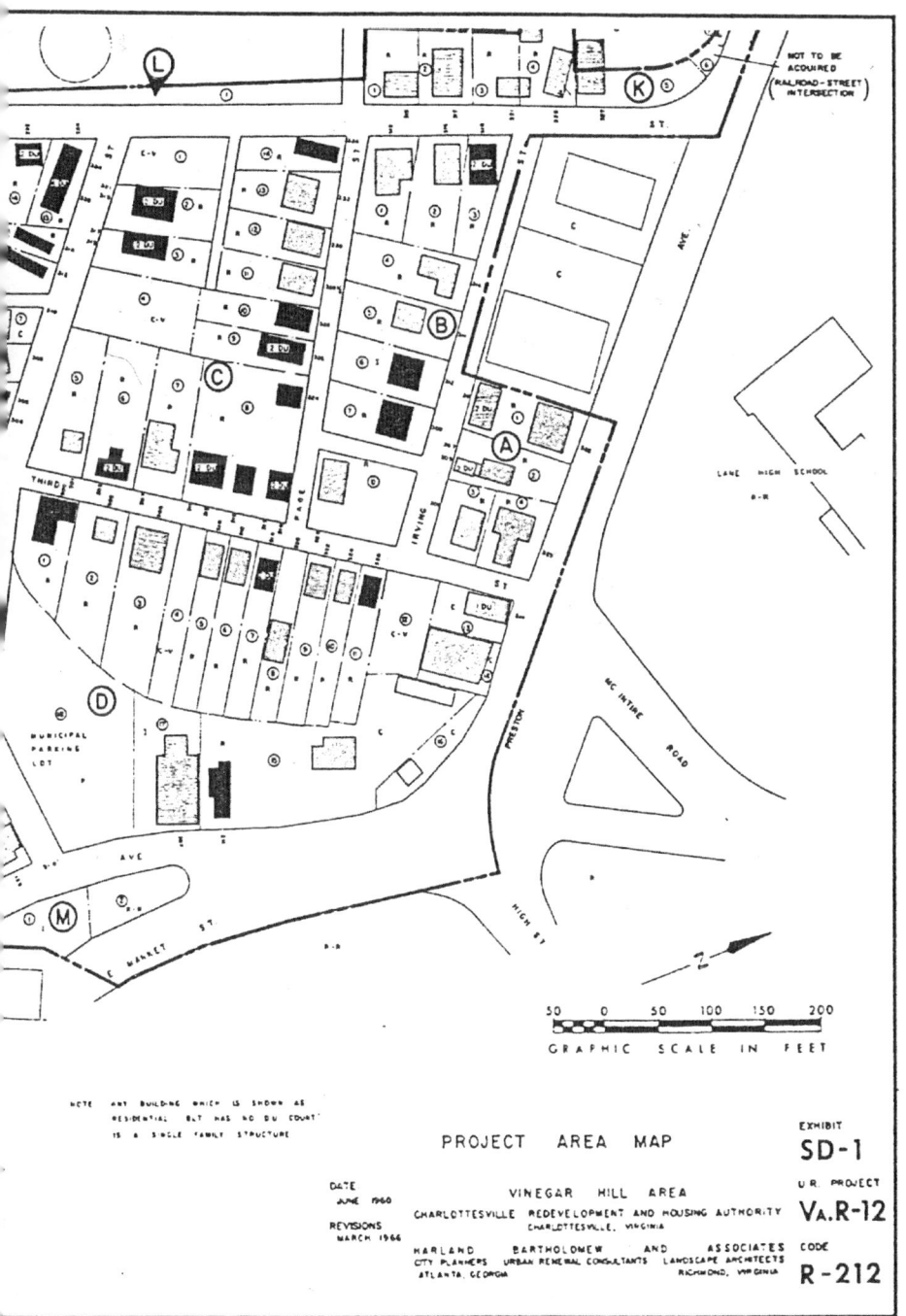

diagram showing standard and substandard housing on Vinegar Hill before renewal."

entire letter is a coded let-down: "I don't know where we stand ... I wouldn't count on it ... it's hard to say what will happen ... I still would want you to come out sometime." Our one reconnaissance to Indiana remains a trip I remember fondly, given Stern's lively arts space in the Atheneum Building and our sidebar to the village of Columbus, but Chief lost his hope for a professional acting career on the little roads that led to Indianapolis, and the upshot is that we began talking about opening a theatre of our own.

In the early '70s the BoHo dream was to own a bookstore or a restaurant or a movie theatre. We thought it would be fun to own all three. So we began looking around Charlottesville for a place to buy, and then, one day, Chief came home and said, "Honey, I found something." And there it was, a small property with three spaces; two of which were currently empty, and the other rented by Jarman's Motorcycle Shop.

The building Chief had located was called the Symington Garage. It straddled both Old Preston, a westerly tangent of Charlottesville's downtown Main Street, and Market Street, a street parallel to Main. It had been built in two phases: the Old Preston piece, a two-story triangle, faced with stone and brick, came first and was meant to sell and service the early twentieth-century automobile. Later, when cars got bigger, a three-thousand square foot showroom was added to connect the older space to the more commercial Market Street.

When you stood looking at the front of building you were standing on a dividing line. To the left was the heart of Charlottesville's white business district. To the right was a grassy slope called Vinegar Hill. The slope hadn't always been empty. Originally known as Random Row, the Hill was settled by Irish families in the early 1800s. African Americans began moving into the area after the Civil War, and the Hill eventually became the center of black life in Charlottesville. The neighborhood was filled with thriving businesses like Inge's Store, along with solid brick homes as well as a number of unpainted clapboard buildings without indoor plumbing. When in the late 1950s the city decided to engage in "urban renewal," some 130 buildings and 158 families were relocated to public housing. One hundred and forty of these families were black. As a *Daily Progress* headline later recounted, "Renewal Meant Blacks Had to Move."

Then, for almost two decades, nothing happened. When you gazed out and up over the long-demolished Hill, it looked like an urban prairie, a tribute to the inertia that seemed to have enveloped the entire downtown area. A history of Albemarle County published in 1976 put it this way: "Center of bootleg activity and vice it was, but the hill most assuredly was much more vibrant in its former guise than it is today, now merely an expanse of bare ground stretching like a no-man's-land, perhaps to be the site of the downtown business district's last stand should the upstart shopping centers mushrooming a few miles to the west ever launch an all-out-attack."

DURING OUR URBAN survey the Gordon family had been given a tour of the old Paramount Theater on Main Street, which had fallen on hard times. Chief and I and the kids were walked through the gothic, decaying structure by a lawyer friend named Ted—later Judge—Hogshire, with whom we had shared our desire to start an art house cinema.

Built in the 1930s as a luxurious movie theatre, the Paramount is a huge space with a lovely balcony and probably seven or eight hundred seats. But in those days a river ran through it; there was water flowing everywhere and we had no heart for the renovation required. It took over thirty years for a consortium of donors and forty million dollars to bring the Paramount back to its original glory. I am happy for the Paramount, but I have never been a non-profit girl.

On the day after Chief told me about his discovery, Ian and I climbed into the Volkswagen bus and drove over to see what I was up against. Little did I know that it was a drive I would take as many as six times a day for the next thirty years.

I drove down Rothery Road to the intersection with Route 250 West. Had I turned left the asphalt would have taken me across the Blue Ridge, through the Shenandoah Valley, and on into West Virginia. If I turned right—which I did—it brought me to within one block of the Grounds of the University of Virginia. We drove across Route 29, up alongside Jefferson's Rotunda, the center of his Academical Village, and turned left on Rugby Road. Rugby took us past Mad Bowl where students rolled in mud every spring—*Playboy* rated the grain-alcohol-fueled bash the best college party in America—and into the heart of Fraternity-land. A right turn on Grady Avenue, and we were driving past big ramshackle buildings that would soon house UVA's first sororities. It was now a straight shot to the new building.

I downshifted as we coasted through one of Charlottesville's oldest surviving black neighborhoods. As always, there were people crossing Grady

to get to the Lucky Seven. As Grady merged into Preston, things became more industrial; there was the large brick Monticello Dairy Building, Settle Tire, and beyond that the Coca Cola Bottling Company, the town's most beautiful Art-Deco structure. Where Preston becomes Market Street, we came to Lane High School. We stopped, crossed the intersection, drove up the steep hill, maybe fifty yards, and pulled into a small parking lot.

The address was 220 West Market Street. It was a fifties-style cinderblock building, with a dozen twelve-foot windows facing Market. Below the windows, panels of Schuyler, Virginia quarried soapstone decorated the exterior façade of the building. You entered through a pair of heavy one-inch thick glass doors. The showroom was huge, fifteen-feet high, and was filled with shiny motorcycles which were occasionally driven across the fading green rubber tile floor. The business was moving to a less urban location but it was still a bustling center of activity.

"Mom, look at all the helmets. Do they play football here?" Ian said.

"Not exactly. Helmets are what you wear when you drive a motorcycle," I replied. "Don't you remember, I had one when I bought that small Honda."

Ian's eyes widened. "Was that the one Dad drove into the house at Twin Pumps?"

I tried to stifle a smile. "Yes, honey, but he wasn't going very fast. He was trying to learn to drive the Honda—but turns out he had never even learned to ride a bicycle."

"This place is cool. Like Santa's Workshop. Except the elves have long hair," he countered. "Like Way Out Welding, Uncle Rudy's shop."

From the back of the cavernous space, someone revved a bike, silencing our conversation. Just enough head-rocking distraction to make me wonder if I still knew how to put one foot in front of the other.

The physical space was almost identical to the Biograph Theatre in DC, also converted from an old auto dealership. I had visited owner Al Rubin weeks earlier, and gotten some do's and don'ts. Rubin and his wife Susan had been on M Street at the edge of Georgetown since the fall of 1967, and their programming of classy foreign films, edgy counterculture views, and porn for lunchtime was both practical and inspirational.

David Levy of the Key Theatre in DC and the Charles in Baltimore had also generously shared his adventures about life as an independent cinema owner. After my appointments with exhibitors like Rubin and Levy I also sought out some face time with film distributors in the DC region, from single offices like Ross Wheeler and Cinema V, to United Artists and New World. These companies would eventually decide which films I could play.

IN THE SAME year we located our entertainment center, we also bought the last buildable lot near the university for $8,000 and began designing a house. It was a completely improbable project—although, as it turns out, it is the house where I still live.

The project was improbable because the lot consisted of a steep hill that ended in a wetland and a creek. The unpaved road to the house was an undedicated street. While anything situated on the site was going to be tricky to build, we were, however, only a few minutes walk from the university's central grounds. And the lot happened to be shaded by a poplar forest, a virtual cathedral of tall, straight century-old trees.

My grad school friend Marcia Bonnell had married architect Don Whitaker after his return from Algeria, where he had designed slaughterhouses in the Peace Corps. In the summer of 1972, Don and partner Larry Linder set up an architecture business near New Haven, Connecticut, with Marcia and her freshly minted Harvard Business School degree running the office. The product on offer to us was "the smaller more personal house that remains probably the most challenging design problem encountered." Guided by West Coast architect Charles Moore, Don and Larry were "attempting to work for corporate clients who pay well, god bless them; yet have enough time for smaller projects about which we care, and on which we spend proportionally more time as we develop more worthwhile ideas."

Both men avidly embraced the challenge of designing a modest space for fifteen to twenty-five thousand dollars. Ours would eventually clock in at thirty thousand, plus two or three thousand for the design and supervision. After receipt of a beautiful 3-D model of our future home, Chief and I signed on, expecting construction on our project to begin by the scheduled October 15 date.

What Don ended up giving us was a three-story tree house that cascades down a hill. You park on the street—it was finally paved in the late seventies—and then enter the house by walking over a wooden causeway that spans a sharp incline. When you come in the front door you are on the second floor. Stairs lead down to the bathrooms and the bedrooms, with more stairs outside taking you down into the yard. It's all glass and angles—over forty windows—and a ceiling that slants upward from the front door at a slope of thirty-degrees. When you sit at the dining room table you are looking out at an elevation twenty feet above the ground; you are up in the trees.

Construction didn't go so well. Charlottesville was a city of brick houses done up in one of several approved conservative styles. The only contractor who answered our calls was a California transplant named Rip Hewitt who was tossing up casual wood frames at Lake Monticello in Palmyra. In order to support a structure that in Bangkok might have been built on stilts, we had to pour huge concrete pilings. But the yard was so muddy the cement truck got stuck and had to be towed out. The trickiness of the design took more time than Rip had estimated and he went bankrupt before the house was finished.

In order to cut costs the entire place was sheathed in 4x8 pieces of Texture 1-11 redwood siding which, in Charlottesville's humid and rainy climate, acted as pipettes. And there were no gutters—this was to preserve the "modern" lines. So the house began to melt.

Seven years after the house was finished I had to seek out my first loan

The Rothery house

as a divorced woman. I went to see a kind banker who figured out how to advance me the $10,000—an astonishing amount in those days—to buy the shingles and the labor it would take to do the job. Shingles were what I knew from my New England girlhood and it turned out they were to hold up well, although ours remains the town's only house sheathed in *white* cedar.

The house was also so poorly insulated that in the first cold winter the pipes routinely froze. Many of the pipes actually ran under the house without any insulation at all. We hired a plumber and he moved the pipes to the insides of the downstairs walls, where they can be seen snaking around the corners of various rooms to this day.

But I would build this house again in a heartbeat, I so love it and its light-filled rooms. I'm not sure how I got the building bug, but it may go back to my grandfather Cavigioli. On Dr. Bottero Road, formerly sandy Comfort Road in Dennis, Massachusetts, Cavi built at least six scrappy houses on the ocean-facing street. The duplex he built across the street from our cottage he named the Maryann, but we called it the Chicken Coop; he told me that

I was the namesake and I reminded him my name was actually Anna Marie. But the rationale for all this building was the ocean and endless beach a few steps from each front door; the landscape, not the number of rooms, held your attention. It's possible that when I married Chief I chose someone with a building jones not unlike my grandfather.

IN 1973, WHEN Chief came home with the news about 220 West Market Street, I was busy raising two kids and overseeing the construction on Rothery Road. We were clearly now doing two things at once, but I had time on my hands, time to pick up the slack on both projects.

We paid $30,000 for the entire property on West Market. In order to finance the renovation, we sold limited partnerships to investors, some family, some friends. Partnerships went for five thousand dollars apiece. Chief promised the original investors and their offspring free movies for life. Twenty-five years later one of these investors who had long since been paid back was still sending his adult children past the ticket taker without having them stop to pay.

We owned the downtown building for several years before construction even began. As Chief wrote a friend in the summer of 1974, "the film theatre hurtles forward at glacial velocities. We have final drawings but no bid yet. The theatre will open just about the time the three sisters get to Moscow." We finally did secure a bid for the renovation from Stockton Creek Builders and incurred even more debt after signing a construction contract with them for $93,000.

When you build a movie theater you are building a public assembly building. It turned out to be a fortress with steel supports, no balconies, lots of codes to obey. The biggest challenge was to find enough space for both a lobby and a projection booth. This was all before the days of handicapped accessible and panic doors. The net result was my ending up with an office about four-foot square with an open wall, like a tiny opera box for four people.

The old showroom space was filled with metal posts that held up the roof and were clearly a problem for our sight lines. Remembering the infamous Janus Theatres in DC with a pole in front of half of the seats, we opted to replace the posts with a big expensive steel I-beam.

The showroom had a level floor. But the floor of a movie auditorium has to be raked. In order to accomplish this, the builder terraced the floor by constructing a series of staggered wooden forms. The forms were filled with gravel and then covered with a thick layer of concrete. After the addition of a skim coat, we were able to screw in the chairs. The result was a rake that fell four feet from the back of the auditorium to the screen. I loved marching down that pleasant incline and became so used to it that when the house was blacked out I could walk it in the dark.

We decided to hang a silver screen. From the seats, a movie screen looks solid, maybe even dimensional. But a silver screen consists of a woven fabric-like material coated with a substance that makes it luminous—and you can roll it up. You hang it in place with grommets and hooks and eyes to stretch it tight.

We bought the building in 1973 and opened the theatre in 1976. Meanwhile, Chief's uncle Charles agreed to co-sign a $100,000 SBA construction loan; our original investor money was quickly gone. Once everything borrowed had been spent, I broke out my Sears card, and charged the carpeting, the popcorn popper, and the ice machine. By 1980, the interest rate on the loan had risen to twenty percent, but by then it was too late to turn back.

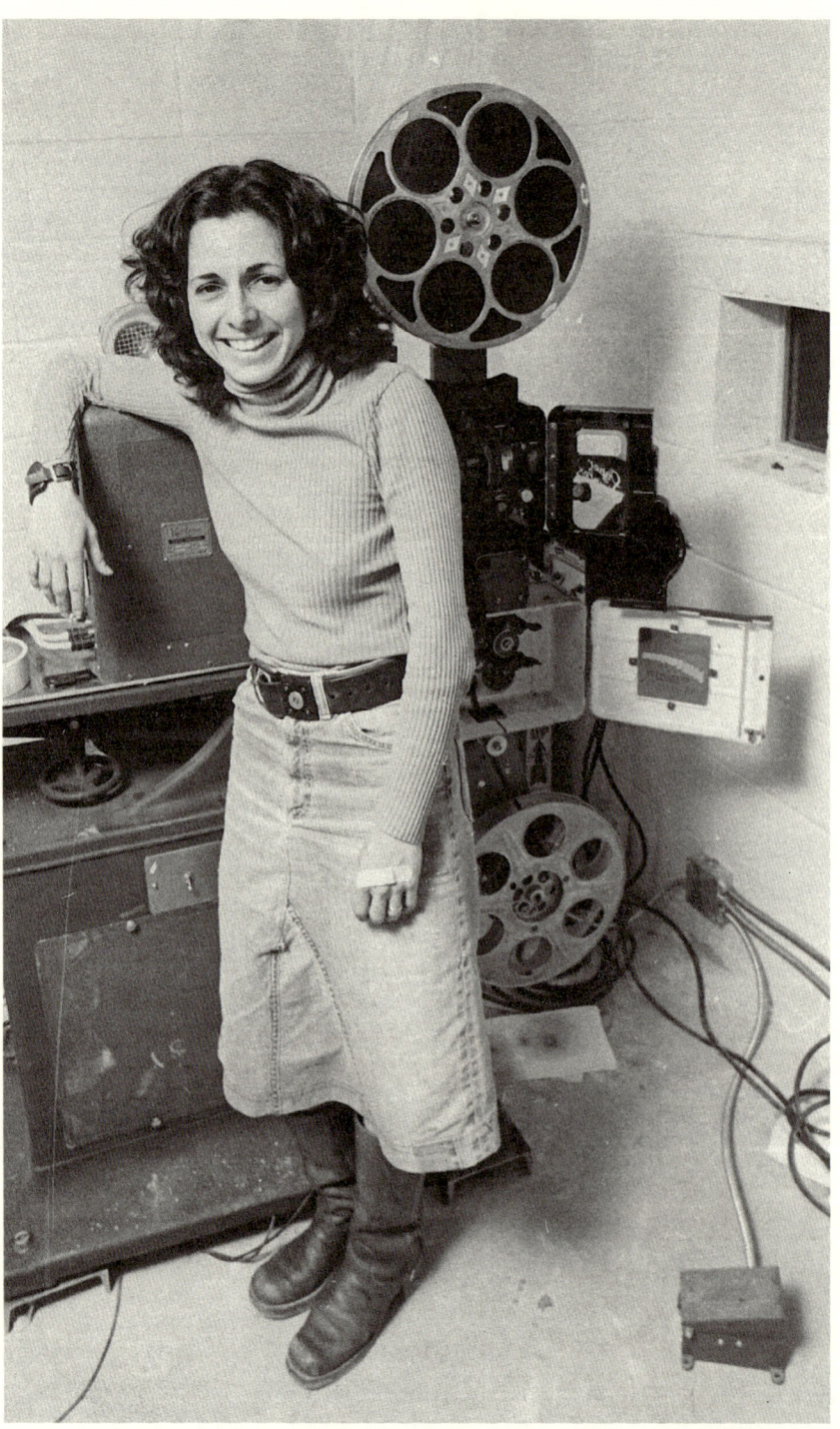

5
WOMEN IN LOVE

Valentine's Day, 1976.
    We were only a few minutes into the first reel when the film broke. In my movie theatre. On Opening Night.
    Earlier that afternoon I had gone home to change and when I got back to the theatre the lobby was so crowded I couldn't get in the door. At that point, the evening looked to be shaping up as a success. By seven o'clock two hundred people had gathered. We got them seated and cranked up our two projectors, which had arrived late—very late, around five that day. We had purchased them from a sketchy outfit in New York City. They were Simplex Projectors. These well-worn machines ran film in twenty-minute intervals. When you got to the end of a reel you did a changeover, hoping to hit the pedal at just the moment when a series of dots appeared on the upper right hand corner of the screen. The impact of the foot shifts the visual and the audio to the other projector. While the second projector does its work, you thread the next reel onto the first machine. In a film of two hours length, there can be as many as five changeovers.

It turned out that nobody was using a Simplex any longer and within a few years we had changed out almost every part of each machine and rebuilt the innards.

But on opening night I knew none of this. I had hired two projectionists, Steve Waller, a local film animator, and David Minckler, a graduate student in English, and they were supposed to take care of things. They had both worked with 16-millimeter projectors at Wilson Hall, across town at the University of Virginia.

Before the film broke there was an earlier problem that only became clear when I slipped into the auditorium to check on the sound. The glass portholes between the auditorium and the projection booth were open—the construction company had been unable to finish and install the windows. Standing there in the dark, I could see the stream of light pouring through the glassless opening and hear the rattle and whir of the projectors as they now become part of the movie soundtrack.

We had sent out invitations to our big night and when people arrived they were wearing bell-bottoms, velour, and lots of beads. The postcard/

invite featured a curly-haired Charles Laughton playing the lyre in a Roman toga, a still from *The Sign of the Cross*. While people milled around in the lobby we served chocolate cake and champagne. Celebrity-obsessed friends had rented searchlights now beaming all over Charlottesville.

Whenever I imagined running something, I simply opened the doors and began doing it. Unlike my husband, I did not have an Opening Night gene in me: my passion was for movies rather than for the glamour surrounding them. But for Chief Gordon, it was always a big party. Once everybody had found a seat he got up and gave a speech in which he introduced our limited partners but forgot to thank our builders from Stockton Creek. Then we began to roll the film.

We were screening *Swing Time*. Arlene Croce had been promoting the Fred Astaire/Ginger Rogers musicals in her *New Yorker* dance reviews, arguing that *Swing Time* was the best of them all. Directed by George Stevens, who later made *Giant* and *A Place in the Sun*, the movie had songs written by Jerome Kern. I loved *Swing Time* after seeing it at Wilson Hall because it had a down-home feel. In the title dance sequence Rogers wears a simple black dress with a Fortuny pleated collar. We paired the 1936 musical with *Made for Each Other*, a contemporary comedy, Jewish girl meets Italian boy and sparks fly, with comedians Renée Taylor and Joe Bologna.

Film is heavy. In those days films arrived in octagonal metal cans holding three twenty-minute reels, so picking them up, day after day, put muscles in my arms. But the movies we were showing had been treated badly: the leaders were broken, the tails were destroyed, the color was gone. They had been stored in overheated warehouses or run by incompetents who left big scratches across hundreds of frames. Now, with the rise of the art house, people were clamoring for prints of classic movies, and many of them were unplayable.

It's no wonder that our film broke. We soon learned that you didn't just put a film up on the screen without inspecting it; you spooled each reel through your bare hands to remove the dirt and fuzz and to repair the offending frames, or tried to fix the problem with a glue-splice that had to be done very carefully or it would unglue itself when you ran it through the machine. If that happened, the projector began chewing up the film, like a meat grinder.

As I stood there listening to the clatter of the projector, I noticed another problem. "Why is that movie all over the walls and the ceiling?" It turned out that we had not inserted the aperture plate—this is a framing device that cuts

Film cans

off the edges of the image so as to make it conform to the dimensions of the screen. This was one of the many parts of the projector I was going to need to learn about.

After the film broke, Dave Minckler stopped the machine, and, treating the projector as if it were an over-grown and more dangerous sewing machine, pulled down a long length of film and rethreaded. On with the show.

We had rented *Swing Time* from Ajay Pictures, run by Arnold Jacobs, the sole distributor of the Astaire-Rogers musicals. Jacobs was known for heavily used prints and down-to-the-wire shipping arrivals. His films were also expensive: we paid two hundred and fifty dollars for *Swing Time* and had to cover freight, in both directions.

Jacobs couldn't hold a candle however to the dreaded Toho Films freight lady who sent her Samurai films out days late, in busted-up condition, and imperiously refused to refund any guarantees. In a moment of frustration and revenge, I once returned a film to Mrs. Toho—Overnight, Special Handling and C. O. D. "How do you like those costs, Mrs. Toho?" After that I was forever on her black list.

Countdown to opening night was complicated by the arrival of KG, my mother-in-law. Katheryn Gordon was six feet of blonde self-confidence who made herself useful by firing the desultory cleaning crew and vacuuming the newly-laid cobalt blue carpet free of spackle particles, a task she completed fifteen minutes before the doors opened.

Katheryn had decided not to put any money into the venture. My husband's uncle Charles did come through however with $5,000. A personal injury lawyer in Hampton Roads, his motto was "A black man's pain is worth as much as a white man's." But everything about him was white—his suit, his Cadillac, his pinkie ring and Billie, his platinum-haired wife. Unlike my husband, he did not think of himself as a man trapped in a lawyer's life.

The creation and lifespan of Vinegar Hill Theatre would end up being an intricate collaboration of family, friends, and many essential employees. As I wrote this book, I often asked for stories from the past: when I couldn't remember any "lightness" about opening night, I quizzed Ian and Courtenay for celebration details. Ian remembers:

> Opening night for Vinegar Hill Theatre occurred on a week after my eighth birthday. I remember people I was accustomed to seeing as slovenly now all dressed up, with wide ties and party dresses. I also recall the candy display, and how it must be sampled; it was always going to be Halloween. There were Sugar Daddies in the case. I knew from prior investigating at local 7-11s that Sugar Daddies had mini-NHL and NBA trading cards inside them. I remember getting a couple of Boston Bruins and New York Rangers that night.

Swing Time showed at eight—with a brief delay, and *Made For Each Other* was scheduled for ten. The eight-pm, ten-pm, and midnight shows on weekends were an early experiment that was dropped when we discovered that audiences wanted a seven and nine pm starting time.

COURTENAY, TWO YEARS younger than Ian, mostly remembers her father's dinner jacket:

> My parents seem surprised when I say I remember very little about Opening Night. It was over forty years ago, I think to myself. Memories when one is five are more about blurs and fleeting images. I do remember feeling short. For some reason, in my mind I'm thinking my father may have been wearing his famous "Rick's" white tux for the opening of the theatre, but I may be combining my five-year-old memories with later nights when *Casablanca* played and he worked the ticket booth. Then again, maybe I'm combining the nights when he was working the door at Fellini's, but that's what your mind does

when you're trying to remember something that happened when you were five.

When Ian talks about the crowd being all dressed up I recall that months before opening night I bought a dress pattern. Very Easy Vogue. A brown gingham, Gypsy skirt with three tiers, increasing in fullness to my calf-high boots—I needed to be careful getting into the Mustang. I topped it off with a yellow peasant blouse with huge wrist-length sleeves and a ribbon-tied neckline for pulling down off the shoulders.

But it really didn't matter what I was wearing. Vinegar Hill Theatre would go on to become a center of Charlottesville's downtown life for twenty years and survive as a business for over thirty, but on that terrifying night I spent most of it hiding in the projection booth.

IN THE DAYS after our disastrous opening night it seemed as if no one came to the movies. On Sunday, February 15, we grossed $108.50 in ticket sales. On Monday, the total dropped to $22.75. We didn't top two hundred dollars in tickets until the next Saturday, when we opened *High Noon* and *Johnny Guitar*. And our concession numbers—in the early days we were collecting tax, which accounts for the odd totals—remained downright pathetic: on one night, I have written in a figure reading $5.54.

Initially the price of a ticket was $1.75, but you could get it down to $1.25 if you bought a card for ten admissions.

The long green ledger sheets with the handwritten entries tell a revealing story. The daily grosses for each film appear, at first, in Chief's handwriting. About three months later, in May, I have taken over.

By the summer of 1976 a few patterns become more or less clear. We have hits, and we have bombs. With more bombs than hits, the ticket takers begin to say things like "Oh, they stayed away in droves." For all of February we grossed $1531.50.

Our expenses, as far as I can remember them, were considerable. The mortgage was $1000 a month. Film rental was calculated by the distributors at a rate of 35–40% of every gross. Freight, with those terribly heavy octagonal cans, ran $150 to $400 per month. Air conditioning bills were high in the summer, and gas heat with our all-plate glass lobby was exorbitant. Other expenses included advertising in the *Daily Progress* and the production

and bulk mailing of three thousand schedules every few months. Our projectionists received $8.00 per hour; candy chicks and dudes made a few dollars less. As the manager of the theatre, I received $150 per week.

We were two months in before we had our first big hit: Bernardo Bertolucci's *Last Tango in Paris* and Ken Russell's *Women in Love*. Each movie portrayed a male character in a sexual and emotional meltdown. Ian, aged eight, recalls watching a few scenes from one of the movies and then censoring himself to the safety of a broadcast of a UVA basketball game. On the second Saturday in April we topped $400 in ticket sales for the first time, and the total for the four-day run of the double feature made up a quarter of that month's revenue.

It was difficult to avoid the conclusion that our audience liked sex.

In May, three weeks after Bertolucci and Russell had come and gone, we opened *King of Hearts* and *Harry and Tonto*.

King of Hearts played in the mid-'70s at Boston's Central Square Cinemas for five years, but I had never taken the trouble to see it. Chief and I didn't think to book the movie until David and Ellen—about them, more later—came along and said, "Oh, you have to play it."

King of Hearts is set during the First World War in an evacuated French town where there is a bomb that needs to be defused. The only people still living in the town are inmates in an insane asylum. The inmates come and go as Alan Bates, a private in the British army, attempts to neutralize the bomb. In French. With subtitles.

I did not get the movie; I am not fond of movies about crazy people and have never been able to re-watch *One Flew Over the Cuckoo's Nest*. In my blurb for *King of Hearts* I did however concede that, "if the world were perfect many people believe this film should be called the best ever." Over the first weekend in May, the double bill of *Hearts* and *Tonto* grossed $1,378.50. When we brought back *Hearts* in October and paired it with *The Go-Between*, we enjoyed the biggest night of the year, taking in over $800 in tickets and $100 in concessions.

In the attendance wasteland that followed February into midsummer, there were a few moments where our financials brightened. We came to depend above all on a movie from Jamaica.

People call it Jimmy Cliff's *The Harder They Come*, but the film was actually directed by Perry Henzell. Roger Corman, King of the B movies and early sponsor of Martin Scorcese and Brian De Palma, presented the film. But the real deal was the music. Once that blues organ kicks in on "You Can Get It If You Really Want," what you really are is carried away.

Cliff plays singer/songwriter Ivanhoe, who would rather be a free man in his grave than live like a puppet or a slave. His record will only be played however if he pays. So he begins dealing ganja, kills a cop, goes underground, and becomes a folk hero whose music is heard everywhere.

The film is anything but a big dope party. It is instead a profound look into the beauty and pain of black lives. Once I had booked it, I knew I did not want to be limited to putting up old movies so as to make people feel good about the past. And I suppose I watched the film as an allegory of my own life, the would-be-independent entrepreneur up against the big corporate swallow.

We first showed *Harder* as a late show. And we did that two more times. What we netted from each engagement made enough to pay me $300—half of my monthly salary. Then, in July, we put it up on a double bill with *Black Orpheus*. The pairing of the more literary Brazilian film somehow worked to poeticize Henzell's movie for our audience, and people did come out in droves. The place was so crowded that the fire marshal showed up to see if we had people sitting in the aisles. We did, we made them get up, and then they became "standing room only." By 1983, Vinegar Hill Theatre had screened *The Harder They Come* fourteen times.

Ian has vivid memories of the weekend on which we first showed the movie:

> *I was hovering around the theatre building when a friend of the family came up and said, "Hey, Ian, Virginia just beat NC State in the ACC Tournament!" In the second grade I had no concept of the ACC basketball tournament, no idea what that guy was excited about. But on Friday, March 4, a couple of theatre customers cornered me with uncontrollable giddiness. "Hey, Ian, you're a basketball fan?" the bearded grad student asked, "Well, Virginia is beating Maryland! They're going to the ACC finals if they can hang on!"*
>
> *The next night most of Charlottesville was glued to the TV as the Cavaliers went on to beat North Carolina. It was the weekend big-time sports came to Charlottesville, and the beginning of my obsessive fandom, a passion often pulling me out of great movies when I had to check a score.*

Fortunately for us, by the time we put *Harder* up on the screen, a little before midnight on Saturday, the basketball game had ended and Jimmy Cliff's gangsta odyssey was the after-party to the UVA win. In spite of our damaged print, we grossed over two hundred dollars. As Ian likes to say, "It was the night my parents discovered capitalism."

We quickly learned that a month needed to have only two or three big weekends to make the theatre viable. A pattern began to emerge: selling out is hardly the point, but no-show shows are to be avoided. Moderation gets the OK, so we started booking films with an alliance of art and accessibility. What will our audience try? All kinds of foreign films, or just certain countries? Are some genres, like horror, to be avoided? And if so, does that mean that we have more women than men in our core attendance group? A Jill Clayburgh movie turned out to be a guaranteed draw, while only eighty-one people showed up on the weekend we screened Sam Peckinpah's *Pat Garrett and Billy the Kid*.

There were some movies that simply didn't work. For *Memories of Underdevelopment*, a Cuban film about a middle-class man stranded by revolution, the ledger total reads "$0.00." Here is the original blurb:

> February 23–25, 1976.
> *Memories of Underdevelopment* 1968. First Run. Tomás Gutiérrez Alea directs a modern masterpiece—a diffident bourgeois fails to adjust his lifestyle to the Castro regime. On everyone's Ten Best of 1973—when it was finally released in the US. With a cameo appearance by writer Jack Gelber and the Guantanamo Naval Base.

I remember the voice-over of the disaffected Cuban intellectual hero saying, "the sign of underdevelopment, in people as well as in countries, is an inability to establish links." Something was being expressed about the intersection of the political and the emotional, that movies are not merely visual pleasure, that they reach out to a wider world. Only connect.

Memories reappeared Wednesday—Thursday, January 19–20, 1977, on a double bill with Gillo Pontecorvo's explosive *The Battle of Algiers*. The $386 box office was an offering at the High Church of Cinema; we were not giving up. And one final time, from April 22 through 24, 1979, we matched *Memories* with Gutiérrez Alea's complex slave uprising epic *The Last Supper*, and the box office totals grazed $400. Maybe our audience had too much on their cinematic plate; that two-month schedule featured both a New German Cinema and Iranian Cinema series in addition to the Cubans.

It took a little less than a year for things to really take off. By early 1977 our average monthly grosses had risen from $5,000 to $10,000. Concessions were running at about fifteen percent of ticket sales. We were out of the woods and I began settling into a daily routine.

I wake up at 7:30 and get the kids off to school. After bowls of Fruit Loops and Coco Puffs they catch a bus on Cameron Lane. Chief and I have coffee and a quick bite. He is off to Lowe & Gordon by half past eight; by nine I am at the theatre.

I count the money from the night before and walk down the mall to make a deposit at Virginia National Bank. In the early days, we have matinees, so I will be opening the doors by 12:30. The matinees turn out to be a huge failure. One thing making them an ordeal is the condition of our projectors, which often break down. As the day wears on, each show falls a little further behind.

On top of this we don't know how to build in enough time between each show and so we run them back-to-back. It turns out that a break of fifteen minutes is a minimum and, for a big hit, even more time is needed. It's in those minutes you make your nut by selling popcorn.

No one comes to help until thirty minutes before show time. The candy chick—or dude—then brews coffee and works the popper. I find myself walking to Reid's Market almost daily to buy butter; later we claim the luxury of a milkman when I discover that Monticello Dairy will deliver butter and milk to the theatre door.

One of my tasks is to clean the bathrooms and vacuum the carpet, which is quickly gathering Pepsi stains. These are the days before paper cups come with lids.

At first I do not operate the projectors. But I am determined to learn and my debut projection performance is a matinee of *The Garden of the Finzi-Continis*. For the showing I wrote the following blurb:

> *The Garden of the Finzi-Continis*. 1973. Vittorio De Sica's elegant late film with Dominique Sanda (the blonde from *The Conformist*) and Helmut Berger as rich, decadent siblings in a lush, sorrowful tale of the persecution of Jews in Fascist Italy. Magnificent romantic score by Manuel De Sica —& uncredited Bill (*Rocky*) Conti—and cinematography by Ennio Guarnieri.

The film opens with credits in soft focus, so on my maiden voyage I'm not sure I have a problem, but, as the reel keeps unspooling, the movie still looks like soup. I am terrified but, luckily, I find the fine focus knob and quickly rescue the audience from a blurry screening. A few minutes feels like hours.

Mastering the lens takes some time. The lens is a cylinder separate from the projector itself. Once the film is threaded into the machine the lens is inserted into the projector. We had four different lenses, each one geared to a different aspect ratio.

Movies are wider than they are tall, and there are several different "wides." CinemaScope has a 2.35:1 aspect ratio. This means that every frame in the film is almost two-and-a-half times as wide it is tall. So a CinemaScope frame looks like a mail slot. A film shot in VistaVision is less wide and has a 1.66:1 aspect ratio; European and Japanese filmmakers often used 1.66:1 as their default setting. Classic Hollywood movies made before 1950 were usually shot in 1.33:1, so they look to be almost square. Since the mid-twentieth century most American movies have been shot in 1.85:1, a wide, all-purpose aspect ratio.

Three factors control the dimensions of the film image: the distance between the screen and the projector, the aspect ratio of the film, and the projector's lens, which adds on an anamorphic adaptor if the film is in CinemaScope. Films are meant to be shown using the lens appropriate to the aspect ratio, but when we opened the theatre I had a minimal grasp of the issue. The result was that we sometimes showed contemporary films in 1.33:1, thus squeezing a wide image into a fat square-ish frame.

Even when you have the right lens, there is still the problem of focus. In order to focus a movie, you insert a lens into the projector to a prescribed depth. At that point you have achieved what is called "gross focus." Fine focusing happens once the titles appear on the screen and the lens can be calibrated by hand.

The lens sits in front of the "intermittent" and the film. An intermittent consists of an apparatus with a gate that holds the film firmly in place as it passes through the projector. Behind the film itself is the light source.

When things are working properly, the film moves through the intermittent, the xenon bulb—or the carbon arc in older machines—shines through the film, the lens magnifies each frame, and the image is cast on the screen.

Once the movie is going I stay with the machine. When a reel ends, I do a changeover and the movie is now moving through the second projector. Then I rewind the already-shown reel and set up the next reel on the first projector. There is only time to pee or to grab a quick cup of coffee.

On any given day the kids drop by after school. By the time the evening show begins, Chief arrives to sell tickets and I drive the kids home and make dinner. Then I return to help with the nine o'clock show.

It took me some years before I came to understand what I needed to know about work. Not the nuts and bolts of the daily operations but work in the sense of a way of spending my life.

I always liked working and had been at it since I was fourteen; work allowed me to get out of the house and to be in charge of something. Now I had a something of my own. I quickly became scared to death that my new life project was going to fail. And I was also determined to figure it out.

What did that take? Identifying the ways in which it could fail. It could fail from having no customers and hence no money. It could fail from my not learning how to keep a ledger or stock a concession stand. The projector needed to be mastered. As did repair, but I was to find the help for that. It could fail from my not having sufficient energy or a vision of our business.

Sometimes, during all the *sturm und drang*, the theatre felt like my only balancing mechanism, although it took me a long time to honor my job as being as valuable as the M.A. degree I didn't get. What became very satisfying, in the end, was making something. Everyone has the right to develop a self through work that is deeply loved, but not everyone is fortunate enough to do so. I was often astonished at having ended up with a wonderful job.

"WHY DO YOU live a New York life?" one of my employees once asked me. "Because," I answered, "there's so much to do." He was referring, I now understand, to what looked like my unstoppable momentum. I can feel it even now in the sentences as I put them down, a sort of manic rush. Was I aiming toward something, or running from it? I acted like a woman with a wind at her back. I think I sensed then, during the years when I was getting everything up and going, that there was still something more, and that I had not yet found it.

I found work before I found enduring love. But I kept looking for love as hard as I could, sometimes in and sometimes out of my marriage. The few letters saved from Chief profess a depth of feeling I now find a little remarkable. "I love you," I write to him from the Cape, "I'm a shell of my former self without you." And he, after the event of some injury, can write, "You are so utterly exquisite it hurts me terribly when I disappoint you." Such sentiments did not always hold, and we both ended up turning elsewhere. Our marriage really began to come apart when my father fell ill.

My father was a deep but an unknown person. He was dark, like me, an olive complexion with curly black hair and an aquiline nose. Eugene Porotti was quiet, even reserved, but he never learned to exploit the power of his own silence, and, as a result, he was often overlooked. He was strict but did not stand on a grievance, and yet he had, I think, plenty of things to regret. He had won my dazzling, high-energy mother, but her attentions seemed to be elsewhere.

When his younger brother Rudolf was accepted to Northeastern University in Boston, my father was already hard at work at the Milford Post Office. He had hoped to go to college after high school but he had taken a postal clerk job to support his recently widowed mother. Once Fing—that was my uncle's nickname—was accepted to college, his brother Eugene decided to pay his way through school. My uncle died young of the same cancer that would take my father and before I had much of a chance to know him, but one thing I do know is that my father helped to give Fing the life, however truncated, that he had. Still, there hovers about the story of both of the brother's lives a sense of lost possibilities.

Like my mother, my father's strongest emotional tie may have been to a sibling. The letters to Fing written during the war have an eloquence, given my father's taciturn nature, that surprises me. They wrote mostly about concerns for their mother Caroline.

Over the years, my father used his Kodak Brownie to take many and often the same pictures of my brother, me, and himself. We are seen admiring the current Ford coupe, measuring the snow fall, sitting on a dusty front stoop. Neither my Dad nor I smiled much, but Rudy was the jolly subject.

Although I don't remember much father-daughter bonding, there was a regular outing for us during my preteen years. Once a month to the "torture chamber," as I called it.

My overbite was pronounced and a source of teasing at school. Anita found an orthodontist in Worcester who said, "Sure, I can fix the kid's mouth." It required the extraction of several perfectly good teeth before we achieved "a balanced bite."

My father drove me to the dentist, forty-five minutes travel each way. Dr. Perfect Bite would tighten all the metal in my tiny mouth so that for weeks the barbed wires cut the insides of my cheeks. After the appointment, Dad and I went to lunch at a diner in Upton or Grafton off Route 140. I bet he liked being away from the Post Office for the day, but he never talked much. Or at all. Maybe he ate sausage and eggs; my construction project tolerated only tomato soup or something similar.

It was a sweet quiet day that we had together at a time when my regular life glowed with turbulence, a day repeated once a month for four years, and then my smile was brilliant.

Anita Molinari and Eugene Porotti, Wedding Day, 1944

Eugene Porotti retired from the Milford Post Office at sixty and within two years he was dead. During his brief retirement, he was unlucky in trying to convince my mother to travel. "Why would I want to go to Jamaica," Anita said. "Where's that?" He still wrote me terse letters about the weather, his lawn, my mother's excessive use of long distance. They came to visit for Courtenay's first birthday, April 11, 1971, and, after dinner, he complained of indigestion. My mother blamed the broccoli and other nearly raw items in the Chinese food I had made. Daddy spent time in the sun playing with the kids but he looked bad—pale, fatigued, without hope. I tried to take photos, but he hid his face. After a week, they drove the twelve hours back to Massachusetts and almost immediately he went into the hospital for tests. My mother cried all the time, but she wasn't sharing the information.

One night she did call to say that they had operated and removed three-fourths of Daddy's stomach, half of his colon, some small intestine, and nodes on the pancreas. Blindsided by this, all I could think was, "Please don't die and leave me alone with her."

Daddy got well enough to go home and eat small portions. Family talk was about which bland foods he could tolerate, inspection of his twelve-inch abdominal scar, and my plans to go to Europe with Chief. Yup, hard to believe, but we had scheduled the trip before the operation and we were still going.

Fourth of July weekend, Chief and I flew back from England to chaos in Hopedale. My brother Rudy and his girlfriend were living in one of the three Hopedale bedrooms, the kids were being kids, my mother seemed at the edge of sanity. We left as quickly as we could and within a couple of weeks Rudy called with news of a new plan: maybe a second operation to remove the pancreas, more cobalt treatments. I flew back in August to be with my father. By myself.

In the last days he was ninety five pounds shuffling through the house in a maroon robe, pouring a shot of Johnny Walker Red for men from the Post Office who came to visit at the kitchen table with the plaid oilcloth covering. He used to say that no one had told him he was going to die. In the afternoons, I would go into his bedroom, watch him sleep, listen to his breathing. Sometimes I was sure he was dead but later he was resurrected, to continue trying to eat, his brown eyes glazed over like grey fish eyes, a prisoner from the concentration camp with a disease that he never admitted to having. I visited and made him vanilla tapioca pudding. I thought my potion had magic powers and could heal him.

When he died after so many days of excruciating pain, and after his retreat into the afternoon naps where he seemed to die, only to come back when we called him to dinner, I understood that he had been practicing.

Daddy, Daddy—are you OK? Mostly he didn't answer but he always woke up while I was in his room.

He died a couple of days after I left the house.

I always wanted to tell him as he slept, as he flirted with his coming death.... What did I want to tell him? Something to erase what I had done to anger him when I was a teenager, to tell him how much I loved him then and now. But that had never been our way, and it seemed wrong, and selfish of me, to impose that on him, to make him help me with my need when he needed peace.

These were the days when no one said I love you every time they hung up the phone.

I hoped he knew I loved him because I was present, and we had grown comfortable together in the last five years of his life. That was all the tidying up I got.

The wake was not real. He wore a suit, with rosary beads in his hands, lying in a box like a wooden puppet with too many flowers, and in a room with a noisy board floor. I failed as a mourner because I could not stop crying, could not moderate my grief. My mother, more gracious and controlled than I'd ever seen her, was so at ease in that world of immigrants, people often violent, but on this occasion, their behavior was a practice of calm, comfort, and help—lessons I had not learned.

I went to my father's grave to make sure that I knew where he was because at his funeral they had left him in his box, uncovered. I stared at the grave, a mound of brown dirt, absent grass, and watched my children play among the tombstones. It was early September. I have always refused to remember the exact date.

WHEN THE KIDS and I flew home from the funeral a week later, it was Chief's mother who picked us up at National Airport. I was dark, black inside, and very annoyed at having to make small talk with Katheryn Gordon.

Not being able to count on Chief emotionally became a recurring problem. His response to my father's death—"I can't come to the funeral," Chief said, "I have to work"—revealed a growing carelessness about the pain of others. He liked grandiose, somewhat manic gestures, like optioning Poe's Restaurant on The Corner and then not paying for it. But simple helpful things—like putting together an assembly-required child's cabinet on Christmas morning—these eluded him. "Oh, I can't do this," he said, throwing up his hands. I hovered over the wooden pieces, realizing I must learn to work with tools.

"But what did you really feel about Chief?" people sometimes ask. I think about the question a lot. Perhaps I am unwilling to admit that I was in love with Chief. I was compelled by what we were doing together; we had babies and a business partnership. But love? I cannot even say when I fell out of love with him—if I was ever in. Marrying had happened so fast, and he was so insistent, that I went with it all.

I was a person who had many crushes, although it took me a long time to figure out what love was, for me. If I held myself apart from my husband, he was even more skilled at keeping his distance. There was no talk about his personal sadnesses, and so mine also went unexplored. Chief seemed to insist on stylizing his human interactions, as if he were in a play. As a result we became a little like Myrna Loy and William Powell: we performed our marriage, although I didn't do much performing except to look good.

COURTENAY CAME ALONG in Chief's third year of law school. Then my father died when she was sixteen months old and I became a complete wreck; for months I stayed in bed. I was despondent. I had thought that my father and I were going to be close at last because—now that I was a mother—he finally approved of me. I was tied down and wouldn't run around anymore. And then he was gone.

My mother dealt with the loss by having a month-long episode of hysterical blindness. And then she summoned my brother Rudy, in his last year at the University of Kentucky, back to Hopedale, where he stayed forever. Meanwhile, at Twin Pumps, Courtenay was being mistreated, yelled at and ignored. Often left in the crib, the playpen, her room.

What got me out of it? I don't really know. Maybe it was building the house on Rothery Road. Or taking an Italian class. I visited a tall, creepy psychiatrist—I hated him.

If I had to say, at this time in my life I wanted someone to notice that I was really unhappy. I sent up lots of trial balloons and no one seemed to care, least of all my husband. It's not unusual for me to be self-destructive for a while—"Hey world, I'm unhappy"—and then to snap out of it.

But I also came to feel that my husband was tone deaf.

Courtenay did learn to duck her head, and after the bad six months I never yelled at her, but she became skilled at intuiting what had to happen in order to help her Mommy, who was all alone in this project called "marriage." Courtenay knew how to fit in around the pain. She knew how to make my life easier. When I wonder why she decided to become a doctor, the answer may lie there.

ON A WINTER night in 1974 Charlottesville Democratic leader Jane Foster swept all the interesting folks she knew into a room, added cheese and wine, and let the sparks fly.

That night a charming pear-shaped, bald man flirted with me—my Dad had been pear-shaped too, so I was partial to the body type. Peter Bacque was a journalist with the local paper, tall, bearded, witty, with a sense of Cajun mischief. His disheveled appearance made me wonder how he had managed to serve three years in the Army after being drafted to fight in Vietnam. His casual care of self extended to a second story bungalow apartment on Locust Avenue. He smoked cigarettes, he drank, he never exercised. I think he had a collapsed lung from a birth defect.

I was smitten, in thrall, and as they say in yoga, prone to *vatta* derangement. In the beginning, I think Peter enjoyed me, and enjoyed the attention; later I became very needy, and, as Albert Brooks says in *Broadcast News*, needy is never a turn on. I was willing to be treated carelessly, but I also would have said that he was the missing ingredient in my marriage. Was that ingredient intimacy?

Or maybe the problem lay elsewhere. Maybe it had to do with a search for tenderness, although the evidence in a letter from Peter I still possess suggests that there seems to have been not much of it:

> *I feel that you can't touch me, and I want to be touched.*
> *I've told you before that I think of us as two grinding wheels,*
> *eating away at each other in a shower of hot dry, crumbled abrasive.*
> *It doesn't make sense to do that to each other and I don't know*
> *how not to be that way. I feel like I'm being torn away and nothing—*
> *no touch—comes to heal the gashes.*

WE NEVER APPEARED as a couple in public, never went to the movies or even talked about movies. One afternoon, after receiving his pilot's license, Peter took Ian for an airplane ride. It was in October 1978, as Ian remembers:

> *I got motion sickness. Later listened to the NL playoffs, Dodgers*
> *vs. Phillies, in the VW van at the Vinegar Hill lot with the window down.*

What possessed me to suggest such an outing? Ian was famous for getting sick on the Ferris wheel. But I kept trying to work Peter into my life, even inviting him to Cape Cod one summer late in the relationship. My mother Anita met him, liked him. Courtenay recruited him to sandcastle building and racing hermit crabs. He took lovely photos of me that summer. I am skinny and smiling in my black bathing suit. By then, Chief no longer came to the Cape: "Water is for ice cubes," he used to say.

It was a different time, and I want to give you some sense of it. It was a time when many of us found ourselves conscripted into the community property of sex. But that's only where things started: sex may have been the gateway drug, but for me it was always about the dick *and* the brain. In Peter, I was witnessing a man who had escaped a hemmed-in Louisiana childhood and who suddenly found himself starring in a town filled with a constant sense of audition. He had many women, but the appeal was not simply sexual. My relationships with factory guys were just that and nothing more: smoking pot and sex in the woods. But the limits of all that quickly became noticeable.

When Peter came to the Cape, for instance, we did not have sex, and the reason had little to do with my mother and my kids being around. I realized then that I had moved on into another category: there were women he had sex with, and women he did not. Whatever each of us might be experiencing with Peter, we all knew we were sharing him with lots of other women. It was like he was walking all the dogs at once.

Whatever Peter might have been up to, he was discreet. This allowed him to come and go, and to keep me hanging on. He was adept at locating unhappily married women and very good at listening to them. That was it, I guess—the simple need for someone who actually paid attention, who saw you, as the Cape photographs indicate, for what you were.

In maintaining a five-year affair with Peter, I was subscribing to a messiness that was also compartmentalized. We met in the afternoons when it was easy for him to get away from the paper, or late at night after I closed the theatre. One thing Peter did not want from me was any sort of declaration. Like the character in the François Truffaut film, Peter was *The Man Who Loved Women*. The character in the 1977 movie appears to have no work as we know it; his job is to "love" lots of different kinds of women and to be real with all of them. And Peter was good at *his* job. I don't know if he loved me but he got me to love him, and to realize what I was missing.

WOMEN IN LOVE was released in 1969. By the time we first showed the movie at Vinegar Hill in 1976, Chief and I were having all kinds of problems: he was more than tired of facing his life as a lawyer rather than an actor. He would come home and spill out stories about staring out his office window at

Daily sheet, *Women in Love* and *The Go-Between*

nurses walking around in their white uniforms—after eight years of marriage he had little interest in me.

The movie sunk in because I wanted it to sink in. It wasn't a problem that Birkin may be pedaling a goofy ideology; Ursula calls it "an obstinacy, a theory." I wanted the film to be a template for living. In those days, we thought movies were going to save us.

When people in the movie make love, they either wrestle or cry. Otherwise, they talk. It's as if people prefer to make love by arguing. Looking back, I can see that all my eventual chasing after men was also chasing after conversation. I especially liked the very last shot, when Ursula and Birkin are talking about his wanting more and the music hits the strident chord and he says what he says and then the frame freezes on her face and you know they'll be fighting and fucking for the rest of their lives.

Lawrence was perfect for the late seventies moment. When I first read the novel, while breast-feeding Courtenay, I thought, "Wow, this is the book!" All the questions were answered. So many of us were beginning to have big conversations—just not with the right person. And that was the problem— finding *him*. Or her.

The *Women in Love* story culminated on a night when we were showing the movie for the third or fourth time. The film is over two hours long and so came to us in six twenty-minute reels and an additional, shorter reel that contained the last scene and the credits. Except, when this particular print came in, there was no last reel.

I don't remember when I realized this, but I do have a sense that we somehow found ourselves with a movie up on the screen and with a missing final scene. It was at this point that Chief stepped in.

"I can do it," he said. "I've seen it a million times."

"Do what?"

"The last scene. I can act it out."

"You've got to be kidding me—it's a scene in the *snow*."

"I know, I know. No problem."

On this particular Friday afternoon, the screen went dark in the moments after Gerald chases his lover Gudrun to her room. We had no more movie. The lights came up just high enough so that Chief could make his way to the open area in front of the screen. I remained in the lobby explaining to customers that the distributor had not sent us all the reels.

I therefore did not see Chief perform the scene where Birkin and Ursula, bundled in their sled, leave for the snowy trip out of Zermatt. But I had seen the movie so many times that I could have run all the lines myself. I missed hearing Gudrun say to Gerald, "I had to take pity on you. But it was never love."

Nor did I hear his answer to her, "I don't know what you mean by the word *love*."

Perhaps Chief remembered Gudrun's cruel riposte, "Try to love me a little more and want me a little less."

But then how did Chief demonstrate their brutal fight? By stepping away from where he had been standing and turning on himself? Did he say, as Gudrun, "You break me, and waste me and it is horrible to me."

And did he then reply, as Gerald, "You do as you wish. You go where you wish."

The words fall like blows until Gerald mounts Gudrun and pounds her like a rapist.

She gives him his reward: "You are so limited. I could never love you."

"It may be over between us," he replies. "But it's not finished."

I was not there when Gudrun asks for "complete understanding of sensual knowledge." But I was there with her, at least in spirit, because I too was looking for a way out.

The last scene required Chief to play three parts. First he is the poseur artist Loerke and Gudrun in their sleigh, talking about going to Dresden, then he is Oliver Reed, playing Gerald, as he punches Loerke and begins strangling Gudrun.

"I am tired," Chief as Gerald may have said, as he staged the walk away from the lodge and into the snow.

"He should have loved me," Birkin says to Ursula, after they have returned to the scene of the crime. Maybe Chief remembered to say these words, words that might have sounded like an echo of my own, had I not once again been hiding in the booth.

Someone in the audience said Chief did much of the last scene lying on the auditorium floor. I did catch a glimpse of that.

6
THE REIVERS DIARIES

In the fall of 1976, the Gordon family went from just having the father's job to a full-time engagement with the movie theatre. It was not going to go away. And the schedule, our bimonthly calendar of blurbs and photos, had a power in our lives.

It determined what we did on every day of the week. There were "Avant Thursdays" on which we tried something chancy: that September featured the Cuban film *Lucia*, Jean Eustache's bohemian *The Mother and the Whore*, silent classics *M* and *Dr. Caligari*, and Frederick Wiseman's documentary about the Bridgewater, Massachusetts state mental hospital, *Titicut Follies*.

The mid-week permitted many varieties of boutique movie exhibition: October changed lanes into Japanese, and the mid-week titles were *Woman in the Dunes, Rashomon, The Man Who Tread on the Tiger's Tail, The End of Summer,* and *Seven Samurai*.

Meanwhile, the weekends were about survival. August gave up these titles to our Thursday-Sunday drive for sub-run blockbuster hits: *All the*

King's Men and *A Man for All Seasons; Love and Anarchy* and *The Seduction of Mimi; Black Orpheus* and *The Harder They Come; Five Easy Pieces* and *Going Places; Two English Girls* and *A Man and a Woman*. Rinse, repeat.

But we didn't just show movies. We had to watch them. This was a kind of work, too, although it took the form of personal enrichment. We were chasing enlightenment.

Making money was a major part of the deal, of course, but the desire to see and to understand was just as deep an imperative.

There wasn't much time however to talk about what we were seeing: at the beginning, we were screening at least four and as many as six movies a week. We were overwhelmed.

I can see in retrospect the beginnings of structure. One of the things that helped us gain control over our lives was a set schedule format. At the start, each schedule looked different; I still have a beautiful purple poster from 1976. It is detailed with a varnished yellow VHT logo in which the three brush strokes are meant to combine the three letters into what looks like a Japanese character.

By early 1977, we had whittled down the schedule format to a foldable black and white mailer with blurbs of two or three sentences. For the next thirty years VHT schedules graced refrigerators all over town.

And we did have fun with them.

In the early schedules, blurbs were sometimes no more than a sentence in length. The children's film *Ring of Bright Water* was described as follows: "A warm and lovely picture about furry animals who otter know better." The use of puns was quickly abandoned.

Because most of the films we were running we had already seen, it was not difficult to produce a workable description out of old reviews by James Agee or Pauline Kael. We also came to rely heavily on copy from *The Village Voice*. When we surveyed schedules produced by The Circle in DC or The Orson Welles in Boston, we saw that a blurb needed to include the date of a film's release, the name of the director, and, most importantly for our clientele, the matter of subtitles.

As time went on, and as we began to show newer films, the task of blurb writing became more challenging. We were fortunate to discover a publication called *Film Journal*, an industry mag. Once a month its eight pages of synopses faithfully arrived. Most important were the ratings; this was the age of the R- and the X-rated movie. *Midnight Cowboy*, which won the Academy Award for Best Picture in 1969, came with an "X." By the time we were able to show it, the aura of the "X" had however largely worn off.

I tried to avoid writing puff pieces, but I can remember a day when the staff and I were in the lobby, trying to polish off a schedule, and I kept saying, "No, you can't keep calling a movie a "DO NOT MISS!"

Years later, while reading *The Guardian*, I came across my ideal version of a blurb. It was the Italian novelist Elena Ferrante's take on Russian director Andrei Tarkovsky's *Solaris*:

> What struck me and disoriented and frightened me—*Solaris* is still a film that seduces and at the same time scares me, more than any thriller or horror film—was the woman's atrocious deaths and implacable resurrections, her obstinate persistence, the fierce and at the same time self-destructive will not to be definitively annihilated by the beloved man even as pure memory.

LAYING OUT A schedule took a night or two. After the copy came to us in galleys from the printer we cut it up and glued it into columns, with photographs interspersed. We purchased most of our stills from National Screen Service. If I had to guess, I would venture to say that the one face we featured more than any other belonged to Humphrey Bogart.

The schedules were sent out through the US mail. This meant we had to sort and bundle two thousand schedules by zip code and by state. Then we had to generate tallies for the number of schedules in each bundle. I drove my boxes out to the Main Post Office on Seminole Trail, where the bulk mail people checked out our bundling procedures.

When I started to write this book, I mailed my son Ian a set of schedules and he began to send me long single-spaced emails about the old days. His response was a tsunami of total recall. I want to quote generously from the pages he sent me, not only because in them Ian is writing the story of his childhood as well as the golden days of Vinegar Hill, but because it was a shared life, and Ian's voice, like many others, therefore deserves to be heard:

> *Around the age of five, we moved from Twin Pumps, the former gas station we were living in near Scottsville and into our new house*

in Charlottesville. Once in town, trips to the movies as well as the beloved drive-in became more frequent. Seeing Bedknobs and Broomsticks, Patton, Live and Let Die, The Salzburg Connection, among others are memories that one shan't soon forget. I once dated a young woman whose mother would mix herself an extra drink or two at night and watch Patton, and recite the dialogue back to herself as she watched it. Upon meeting her, I was sure I had met my future mother-in-law through some kind of psychic film connection, but no.

CHARLOTTESVILLE, DESPITE BEING a small southern college town, was graced by a number of well-run movie venues, and Ian patronized all of them:

There was the drive-in on Hydraulic Road, friendly symbol of an era gone by. At UVA, Wilson, Newcomb, and Cabell Halls all showed films. The Paramount was an older theater, as well as the Jefferson, which became the Movie Palace. The University Theater was, oddly enough, almost on the UVA grounds. I think Jaws played there for six months. The Barracks Road Theater is where I saw Modern Times with Charlie Chaplin, before which there was a preview for an exploitive horror film called Frogs where animals and the ecology turn on people. I talked about the trailer more than the movie, to the point where my Dad told me to shut up. There was the Greenbrier Theater, closer to Albemarle High School, if you knew the back way. This is where we waited in line at nine am in June of 1977 to see the first showing of Star Wars. Then there was the Terrace Theater next to the K-Mart and also not far from both Charlottesville and Albemarle High Schools. This is the theater where my parents went to see the The Exorcist on New Years Eve of 1973 and the staff called them to the lobby because of some kind of crisis like my sister was sick or something to that effect. I believe my parents were freaked out due to the fact that the movie was so intense, and now they had to deal with their fucking kids at a critical juncture in the film; I can dig it.

Ian and Courtenay at Cape Cod

HALF OF THE screens Ian remembers were owned by a chain called Neighborhood Theaters. And that became the problem. Within a year of being open it was clear that we could not book all the movies we wanted to play, especially foreign titles. Even though I saw them opening on platforms with subtitles in New York City, Washington, DC, and Los Angeles, when I would request a booking date from a film distributor, the films were somehow unavailable. Chief and I had high hopes of playing all the Italian films of Lina Wertmüller during their first-run release, but it seemed we always had to wait six months to a year, and then there was no guarantee that we could have a subtitled print.

Fortitude and fate: that's what this story is ending up being about. I began learning this when Chief and I decided to take on the local monopoly. It turned out that every month or so the theaters in town had a meeting in a hotel room where they divided up the product. All we wanted were the foreign films that nobody else in town was willing to play, but the distributors would not rent to us unless we went through the local cabal. We asked to be invited to the party, nobody returned our calls, and Chief decided to sue.

He filed an antitrust suit against Neighborhood. A revolt by independent movie theaters against block booking was already underway, and we rode the whirlwind. In February, 1977, *Variety* carried the following headline: "All Majors, UA Among 'Em, Using Bids as a Camouflage for Pre-Selected Favorites." The article pointed out that "certain films were committed to certain theaters before they are opened to bidding." Our case made *Variety* too, where it was given the David takes on Goliath treatment.

Out of all the court dates I can remember only one exchange. At some point, either in court or in a deposition, I had said that the distributors only let us have filler. The opposing lawyer looked at me and said, "Mrs. Gordon, what is 'filler'?" Without much thinking about it I responded, "Oh, you know filler is … filler."

We lost, but it was a good way of saying, Hey, there is a new kid on the block.

By 1980, after the case had gone all the way to the Virginia's Fourth District Court, the theater bookers invited me to a meeting at a hotel room in Tyson's Corner. Not knowing how seriously to take this event, I got medium dressed up—a skirt and blouse—but on the way I ducked into Bloomingdale's to calm my nerves and found a luxurious purple with polka dots Gottex bathing suit. Over the years I have bought an empire of smart bathing suits, but this one I kept, a pet article of clothing, long after I wore it out. At the hotel room it was all doughnuts, coffee, and "Hi, how're ya?"—nothing to be afraid of. I said, "We would like to play ——x——." But it didn't matter; it was just like a pat on the head. By then that is, we had found our niche, and we were like a chuckwalla—the more you poke it, the more it expands into the crack where it is hiding.

IAN CONTINUES TO remember:

> Second grade is almost out for the summer when there will be double bills during the week starting at 3 pm, like clockwork every day, plus as an added treat, kids movies play on Tuesdays through Thursdays at 10 am. This led to a summer of all-day movies playing at the theatre, non-stop, starting at nine in the morning and ending after midnight. A movie theatre version of growing up around a ballpark.
>
> When school was out I began helping a friend deliver newspapers in a neighborhood, not far from the theatre. Then I discovered Slurpees from 7-11 and baseball cards, my reward for helping on the route. Back in them days Slurpees were 25 cents, and a ten-pack of baseball cards with dry-ass bubble gum was the same. Just a dollar of reward money for our hard work was a party. To step out of the summer heat at 6 pm and get a Slurpee and a pack of baseball cards was more engaging to an eight-year old than you could possibly imagine.
>
> July 4th, 1976, there was a visit to Charlottesville by her Royal Highness, Queen Elizabeth II. She was visiting Charlottesville due to its new-found standing as All-America City. I didn't know that title changed every year, I thought that meant ad infinitum. Her motorcade was scheduled to go right past the theatre. In the days prior to her visit some magical force removed all the mailboxes and bank clocks in the downtown area—things that you would never assume to be a threat to her majesty's visit. I remember thinking she and first lady-to-be Rosalyn Carter looked alike. Carter also looked like Jaclyn Smith. The shows played on with Top Hat and The Gay Divorcee.

Ian's emails make clear that the tension in his life was always going to be between sports and art:

> *The transition from summer to fall in Virginia weather-wise is spectacular. That fourth Saturday in September was a great day because Craig, one of my Dad's legal aids, took me to the game which was surreal because Martha, his fiancée, was one of the Cavalier cheerleaders. Virginia was playing William and Mary and it was my first trip to Scott Stadium. My lifelong man-crush on UVA football started that day, although they got manhandled by the William and Mary Indians, a smaller school. But I had found the underdog I was looking for. They were horrible—called by ABC Sports perhaps the worst team in college football. They were all mine.*
>
> *Craig bought me a tiny plastic football and I ran onto the field with all the other kids after the game. I learned fast that hanging out can be rough, as some bigger kids took my ball and acted like they*

Chief, Courtenay, Ian, and friends

were going to keep it. This was 1976, no one gave a shit. Everything smelled like hot dogs, Coca-Cola, booze and popcorn. I loved it.

That same weekend the theatre had a double bill of Wuthering Heights, which bored me to sleep more than once and The Lion in Winter, which never did. Half the movie everyone is screaming at each other—another portrait of a marriage—and I had no idea what they were talking about, although John Barry's music was really cool and the plot intense. Later that night on the VHT hillside at dusk with The Lion in Winter soundtrack blasting outside through the walls of the theatre I played with my new plastic ball, imagining imaginary football games to come.

But beyond the tension between sports and art, Ian lived out another one: Charlottesville was and to a certain extent remains a town divided against itself, still fighting out the consequences of the Civil War:

> The beginning of November brought two comedies from the 1950s, while my first presidential campaign took over real life. 1976, it was Gerald Ford vs. Jimmy Carter as Some Like It Hot and Born Yesterday played at the theatre. Charlottesville and Virginia were municipal and state battlegrounds. Election propaganda was everywhere at my school, Venable Elementary, which was a voting place in a hardcore Democratic area. This school was central to several neighborhoods in Charlottesville, including the grounds of the University of Virginia, student housing, commercial apartments, and African-American families who had lived there for generations. On November second, the election consumed our whole day, with kids on both sides wearing shirts and buttons placed on them by their parents. It seemed like my school was 50–50, it really did. Kids screamed at each other, wrestled, got in groups and chanted at each other. I stayed up past midnight, keeping track of the electoral votes on a state-by-state sheet I made up. Jimmy Carter won, as I found out the next morning. California had been the deciding state, and it wasn't called until the middle of the night. The next day at school, one of my best friends, a diehard GOP supporter kid of course, came up to me all woeful and said, "I hope you're happy now, my Mom said now we are

going to have to go to school on the weekends, now that the Democrats are in charge."

I recall getting sick at Halloween that year, a battle between candy vs. my fifty-pound body. Woke up vomiting, after too many Callard & Bowsers toffees. My Mom kept me from school and took me to the C&O for my favorite lunch: steak and baguettes with butter and salad and sugar cubes. Brought me back to life, just in time for the weekend double bill—Mel Brooks' megahit The Producers, *and* The Ruling Class, *which disturbed me all my life.*

Between the holidays came a weekend where we kids were encouraged to stay at the house on Rothery Road. An X-rated film, Inserts, *with Richard Dreyfuss, was going to be playing, so no movie theater for us. Even though there was nothing disagreeable about us watching the co-feature* The Apprenticeship of Duddy Kravitz, *I think the thought was to err on the side of discretion. The same weekend, our house was featured in a home-viewing tour organized by a local community group. The tour consisted of middle- to upper-class homes in the University area. My parents were not at home for the entirety of the tour, which lasted from late morning into the early evening. Upstairs there were brochures, cheese and vegetable platters, along with wine. Throughout the day people would wander in and out of our house. We had our holiday decorations on. With temps in the low 40s, Virginians favored madras blazers and colorful sweaters.*

My sister and I were downstairs, simultaneously watching the Redskins and the Cowboys in a do-or-die game with playoffs on the line, while keeping an eye on the Christmas tree to make sure that the cats weren't going to attempt to ride it to the ground like Slim Pickens in Dr. Strangelove. *In 1975, the cats had successfully pulled the Christmas tree to the floor while my Dad and I were watching the Steelers/Colts first round playoff game. Dad shook his fist at the cats and screamed "Son of a bitch!"*

At some point, the Redskins actually started winning in the hated Texas Stadium. I began hopping and hollering in my room. A businessman, breaking away from the clip-clopping group touring the house, peeked into our open room:

"Are you watching the Redskins game?" he asked, wine glass in hand.

"Yeah, come in," I exclaimed.

Pretty soon we were jumping around in a room made for two little children with bunk beds on each side of it—he had the blazer, the penny loafers, the tie. We cheered as the Redskins put the nail in the coffin and carried head coach George Allen off the field on their shoulders. The amount of activity upstairs as it became dark outside sounded like Santa Claus and his reindeer had shown up at our house and were having a log-rolling contest.

Tomorrow and The Reivers were up next. Both movies were based on works by William Faulkner, still a local celebrity in Charlottesville after his years spent there as a writer-in-residence.

The Reivers was an unusual film for VHT because it was such a seemingly conventional Hollywood vehicle. It was made in 1970 by Mark Rydell (On Golden Pond, The Rose) and could've been a Disney or ABC movie of the week except one character was a hooker with a heart of gold. The lead characters, Steve McQueen and Rupert Crosse (Oscar nomination for Supporting Actor), were dealing with the Deep South of the early twentieth century while being a white and black buddy duo. Based on Faulkner's last novel, reivers Boon and Ned are off to see the world and decide to take Lucius, the young narrator, with them. Some of what he learns is fun, some is painful; their romantic ideal is to live off the land.

The Reivers was a great analogy for my experiences at the theatre in the 1970s and beyond. With this movie theater endeavor, my parents sought to set off on their own adventure, and my sister and I were along for the ride. But the endeavor was also life-giving, it would pay for things, it provided not only the outlet, but the inlet. It was the family farm and circus in one. As a bonus, we would be exposed to some of the greatest art ever made. I was galvanized by the ride.

THE CO-FEATURE WE had paired with *The Reivers* was a movie based on a Faulkner short story, Joseph Anthony's *Tomorrow*:

"Shot in black and white," Ian writes, "*Tomorrow* looks like a Depression-era documentary. It will break your heart. It was one of the first films I ever saw where I recognized my emotional response."

In the movie the Robert Duvall character—his name is Fentry—takes a job at a sawmill about thirty miles from his family farm. He is a man almost without words, very much alone. On Christmas morning he finds a woman lying next to his shack. Her husband has abandoned her. He takes her in, nurses her, discovers that she is pregnant. The baby is born, it is clear that the woman is dying, but Fentry marries her nevertheless. He takes the baby back to his family farm and raises him until he is five. Then the boy's people come for him. Fentry fights them off, tells the boy to run. But the law wins, and the boy is yanked away.

After receiving his email, I decided to call Ian and to ask what had made *Tomorrow* so emotional for him.

"The woman is out of the man's league," Ian said.

When my son said that, I didn't know what he was talking about. "What do you mean?" I answered.

"She's from a different class. Though he marries her on her deathbed, right after the baby is born, that baby will also be out of his league. It's karma."

"Babies don't come with karma, do they?" I said.

I am still baffled by this conversation but I do have a theory about it. I had assumed that Ian's original response to the movie, in 1976, was to the threat of separation—separation of the child from the parent. But now, on the phone, all these years later, he seemed to be getting at something more terrifying: When you have a child, you immediately begin losing it. Karma was just the word he had found to express this.

Ian is now raising two children of his own; he is a devoted parent. Joseph Anthony's film is shot from a father's point of view, and, in watching it, it is easy to feel more for the bereft father than for the repossessed child. Who can say what is harder—being a child or being a parent? Each time in life contains its share of heartbreak, and there are separations involved, inevitable separations. Seeing the movie as a boy of eight, Ian may have felt one thing. But, in writing to me as he was turning fifty, Ian seemed to be substituting a later emotional response for an earlier one. There is often a gap between how one felt *then*, about a big emotional moment, and how one feels *now*, in the act of remembering, and in our family, it is often through the response to movies that the gap gets measured.

7
TUMBLEWEEDS

In the early days of the theatre, I used to walk with my children after closing time on Charlottesville's downtown mall. Ian called it "wino-safari-land." There were strange derelict patrons at a men-only bar, there was a flop house, people living in single rooms renting week to week, and there was a bizarre set of shops that were just old school. It wasn't changing; you could feel that it could stay that way forever. Or it could just be gone the next day. Charlottesville itself didn't have that sparkle, that edge that said, "Let's have new, let's have different."

Chief buying the building for VHT in 1973 was the first signal that the downtown might be a place to remake, although it took many years to create a buzz cinema. But we slogged along, very much buoyed by our own narcissism. We desperately wanted to create a movie theatre like the Circle in DC or the Bleecker Street/Carnegie Hall in Manhattan. If by the early 1980s it had become good days for us, this was not yet true for downtown as a whole.

Four decades after we opened our doors the *C-ville Weekly* congratulated the city on having been so forward thinking as to have bricked over its main shopping street. A November 30, 2016, cover article reads, "By Design." The subtitle continues: "40 Years Later the Downtown Mall is an International Success Story." The story is all about the forward thinking of mayors and bankers and city planners. The point of the piece is to show how shaky it all seemed, back in the day. A former director of planning and development, Satyendra Huja, is quoted as saying about the mall, when it opened in 1976: "You could shoot a gun and not hit anyone. It was totally empty."

Well, not quite empty. Because, six months before the mall opened, Vinegar Hill was there, drawing people downtown. We were at one end of the mall, on its outside northwest corner, and the C&O Restaurant, which opened in March 1976, was on the outside southeast corner. Huja is right to say that there was not much in between. When I asked my staff members what was moving on the mall, they liked to say, "Nothing but tumbleweeds."

In 1959 the newly-opened shopping center at Barracks Road and Emmett Street began drawing business away from Charlottesville's surviving downtown. After a group of businessmen created the Central City Commission, San Francisco-based landscape architect Lawrence Halprin was invited to join them for a weekend-long *charrette*. Out of this meeting emerged the idea of converting the city's Main Street into a pedestrian mall. On July 3, 1976, the first four blocks of the newly-bricked-over mall were dedicated by the first lady of Virginia, Lynda Bird Robb.

So, it was all a triumph of central planning. But of course, this is not how towns are built. They are built—or at least the new version of Downtown Charlottesville was built—by independent urban adventurers, one dream at a time.

The old Charlottesville had two very segregated downtown business districts. The Vinegar Hill African American neighborhood had been summarily razed by the City in the 1960s. The remaining white business district was concentrated on the eastern edge of Main Street. None of the black businesses lost to urban renewal were invited to relocate into the white downtown. And then, soon enough, many of the surviving white businesses were failing too. But there were those able and willing to move into the vacuum. They turned out to be young people, these pioneers, who arrived in Charlottesville in the late 1960s and early 1970s.

The Mall in the early 1970s

None of us who stuck our necks out on the downtown mall were very self-protective. Moving into this dying space, we risked our money and our untutored labor. It was shabby, and rough, and unsponsored to be in business there. And yet we felt we were building a new world.

Let's take the case of Virginia Daugherty and John Conover. Their story is told in another and a much more informed article from the *C-ville Weekly* called "Hipster 1.0." In it, author Larry Garretson captures the excitement and the pure stupid hope that was ours, back in the day.

In the early '70s John and Virginia converted an old bread truck into a camper and drove out to see America. "We went from hippie farm to hippie farm," John later said. They eventually ended up in Charlottesville, where John had gone to school, and hooked up with an anarchist group called Black Flag Press. Black Flag grew out of the turmoil of the late '60s and was dedicated to undoing the system. "Then we fell in with Chief and Ann Gordon," John remembers, "and we realized it was a business and not a terrorist operation or an idealist operation."

We were happy to be fallen in with because we needed money and John and Virginia needed a place to open a new kind of press. We offered to sell them the back half of our building at 220 West Market, a two-story trapezoid faced in stone. They paid us $18,000 and John and Virginia started Papercraft Printing. Later Virginia served two terms as mayor of the town they had helped to build.

LET'S GO BACK in time a little. Let's go back to the beginning and take a stroll down the Mall, circa 1976.

I've just walked out the door of the theatre and up Market Street a few steps. I turn right through the A & P parking lot and am soon on the western edge of the new mall. I'm walking over bricks laid in a herringbone pattern, and they are of an unusual size, four inches wide by twelve inches long.

The first shop I see is Bibb's Fish, run by Mr. and Mrs. B. So basic, and it smells. Lots of flat, scaley whole fish sitting on ice in wooden tubs. Fish for frying. A little further on is Victory Shoe Store, a long, narrow space with a linoleum floor and filled with shades of beige. I may have bought shoes there for the kids, but am myself presently committed to my Frye boots and a few pairs of sandals. Then comes Virginia Lunch, a place for grilled cheese and tomato soup. In this block of buildings, in 1980, Ken and Betty Jo Mori will create Eastern Standard, the first Asian fusion restaurant on the mall. Just a few doors on is The Brass Rail. There was a bar for *only* men like it in my hometown and I was instructed never to go in.

Facing all this, across Main Street, is Leggett Department Store. A Southern chain, two floors, respectable middle-class shopping. As I move across 2nd Street West I come to City Fish Market, the mirror image of Bibb's except that the man in charge is thin and sweet. A few years later, after Chief and I open a restaurant, I will rely on him for flounder and bluefish. Another eatery, Monticello Lunch, and one, like Virginia Lunch, for years rigorously segregated.

If you want a pair of khakis or a rep tie, you open the door to The Mens & Boys Shop and go in. When Ian was old enough, I bought him flannel shirts there. Directly across the way is the more tony Young Men's Shop. It has the designer brands: Arrow, Gant, Van Huesen. This is Virginia, still really the Virginia of the 1950s, where men wear pink alligators embroidered onto green corduroys and loafers with tassels but without socks.

Just adjacent are two discount variety stores, Roses and Woolworth's. Roses has great school supplies and cardboard cutout pumpkins and witches for Halloween. Woolworth's features the rotating nut roaster under the heart-wrenching amber light, the very color of childhood appetite itself, along with bins of candy—jelly beans, chocolate malt balls, all manner of jawbreakers.

After passing Mens & Boys we arrive at Miller's Drug Store. The floor, a repeating zigzag pattern of black and white tiles, signals an apothecary. On the left side of the narrow space—most of the mall spaces are deeper than they are wide—stands a walnut counter backed by drawers and shelves. In a few years Steve Tharp will convert the space into Miller's Bar and Restaurant. It becomes the first live music venue on the mall and hosts a horn man, John d' Earth, who will teach each of my children how to play the trumpet.

— Oh little town of Charlottesville, how still we see thee lie. —

In a few more steps we come to First Street West. There is a tall bank building on the left, Charlottesville's first skyscraper, its eight stories of beige brick topped off by a huge cornice. On this day it houses the Old and the New National Bank and Trust, but, across the decades, as the churning takes over, it will belong to Wachovia, and, finally, to Wells Fargo.

Duplication of function is becoming clear: we have come to another men's store—Page Foster—another five and dime, and then the Cinema Theater. A fading movie palace, it will be divided into an upstairs and downstairs venue before becoming the Jefferson Theatre, Charlottesville's premier headquarters for the big music tours. I walk past Glassner Jewelers, second in prestige to Keller & George, just up the way.

We have now arrived at Central Place. Here the setbacks create room for summer band concerts and the town Christmas tree. Bracketing one side of the square is the shuttered Paramount Theater. The main lobby is entered under a generous and jutting marquee, while the old separate entrance for African American patrons consists of a door on Third Street. That entrance is right next to Puckett's Barbershop, and its spiraling pole.

Across the way, another bank, Standard Drug, and C. H. Williams, preppy clothing for Virginia matrons. Designer fashion is about to arrive, however, by way of Dagmar Kuttner's New York, New York, est. 1982. A black and white Vivienne Tam dress purchased there still hangs in my closet.

At the corner of First and Main stands the Kaufman Building; it houses Lee's Hallmark Card Shop. Purchased by the Williams family in the 1960s, the space will soon open as Williams Corner Bookstore and will be run by Michael Williams until 1996. If you want to hear locals Ann Beattie or Rita Mae Brown or any other writer passing through town, Williams Corner holds a regular reading series.

There is already a fine independent bookstore on the mall, however, New Dominion Books, coming up on the left. The owner, the late Carol Troxell, will eventually move across the street into the former Wiley's Clothing Store and manages to survive the advent of Borders and Barnes & Noble.

Before New Dominion moved it stood next to The Nook. Opened in 1951, The Nook has it all together: a great grill chef, juicy hamburgers, everybody knows your name. Lots of lawyers and men in ties.

But I have jumped over two important doorways. Behind me, smack dab in the middle of the mall, is Charlottesville Hardware. It is a beautiful, four-story structure—but no one wants any longer to drive downtown to buy a few screws. So the building is soon sold and becomes the Hardware Store Restaurant, for many years the mall's biggest draw for tourists on the way to nearby Monticello. It has the wit to have sandwiches that are named: The Jefferson, The Madison, The Montpelier. One of its sundaes is called "Nuts, Bolts, and More Nuts."

And then there is Timberlake Drug Store. Another former bank building, Timberlake's opened in the early years of the century and continues to sell creams and lotions, although its actual pharmacy business has contracted to a symbolic level. But in the back on the first floor there is a lovely lunch room that serves roast turkey breast sandwiches, thick milkshakes, and chess pie.

We have basically covered the mall, although there is more to encounter, especially Reid's Super-Saver Market, a true if compressed grocery store with a meat counter that only gets better after the store burns down in 1977 and relocates to Preston Avenue. Beyond is a space in which the town will soon erect a new, somewhat modernist City Hall, complete with statues of founding father figures. And beyond that is a hillside that will one day become home to a pavilion—really just a big tent—for Fridays After Five concerts. Bruce Springsteen sings some songs there during Obama's second run for the presidency.

I have a final destination in mind now so I turn right on Fifth Street, walk down a block, and then turn left on Water Street. A short block brings me to the C&O Restaurant.

They have kept the old sign and the name of the railroad station across the street. The C&O, like Vinegar Hill, is not *on* the mall. We are located on one outside corner, they on the other. Both businesses opened in 1976, on a wing and a prayer, and, over the years, the mall slowly filled in between us.

The C&O was the brainchild of Phil Stafford and Sandy McAdams. Sandy was a seller of used books; his Daedalus Books, opened in 1975, still operates just off the mall on Fourth Street NE. Stafford, who loved food and wine, arrived in Charlottesville in 1974. One day he decided to walk into Sandy's bookstore.

"I walked into this room—I can picture this pretty well to this day—and this sort of eccentric looking guy with a beard down to his waist walked up to me and said, 'What do you want?' I said, 'I'm looking for this book *The Art of Seeing* by Aldous Huxley,' and he said, 'It's right over your shoulder.'"

Stafford and Adams got to talking, discovered a passion for food, and bought an old brick building on the eastern end of the old downtown. Using wood from a barn in Crozet they built a cozy bar downstairs. Upstairs, beadboard was painted white to create an austere space for fine dining. One day Charles Barbour, Charlottesville's first black mayor, wandered in. "Man," he said, "this place is foxy!"

Phil and Sandy arranged for their two female cooks to take lessons from Claudine Cowan, a chef from Brittany, and opened the very French C&O a month after we opened Vinegar Hill.

Then they had a stroke of luck. Sandy remembered the story this way: "I made $1,000 a month for those first eight years. Didn't care about money, or watch expenses. We poured big drinks. Jason Bell walked around with a veal glacé that cost more than an ounce of gold and kept saying, 'Would you care for some more?' We would have gone bankrupt except for the Craig Claiborne review. Peter Taylor was teaching at Virginia then, Claiborne had read his stories, wrote to Peter, said he wanted to meet. Once he got to town, Peter took him to the C&O. He raved in the *Times* about us, something like 'The dishes we dined on were few but excellent.' The rest is history. Later, I learned that Peter had planned to take Claiborne to Michie Tavern, for the fried chicken—but it was closed!"

SO HERE WE are, right in front of the C&O's modest—almost hidden—entrance. It's been a short but an intense walk, and I'm hungry. Let's go inside and have my favorite dish, fried calves liver with Dijon mustard sauce.

Ruth and Milton

8
FOUR FRIENDS

Friendship, I have found, is often competitive. But there wasn't any competition with Ruth Drexler. She could be argumentative when there were too many men in the room, but alone, when I lay on her couch while visiting her, in her last years, we were good. By then, she was the elder wise woman, twenty-three years older.

May 1976, during UVA's Graduation Weekend, New Yorkers Ruth and her husband Milton came to a double feature of Ingmar Bergman's elegiac *Wild Strawberries* and *Antonia*, a contemporary documentary about a woman conductor. In Central Virginia mid-May is peony season, but other garden treasures accompanied this floral queen—the Drexlers had just bought an old Amish farm in nearby Greene County with a flourishing strawberry patch. They introduced themselves before the movie and Ruth offered me a crystal bowl filled with just-picked berries. That was, to quote Claude Rains, "the beginning of a beautiful friendship."

Over the next thirty years we traded movie tickets for more strawberries, homemade kimchi, Thai basil, and multiple installments of Ruth's famous "chicken-soup" chocolate cake, a bundt construction covered with thick cocoa icing and chopped walnuts. Even on her death bed, she refused to divulge the recipe.

Ruth and Milton became my exemplary adopted parents, cooking endless Thanksgivings, teaching my kids to fish at their pond, and hosting me and sometimes Courtie during the years they wintered in London. When I would join Milton for a movie at the National Film Theater—and the Drexlers' eagerness for art was as passionate as mine—he would say:

"I heard you, long before I saw you. Pounding the pavement."

"Don't want to miss the credits, do we?" I responded, but I knew that I was in no more of a hurry than they were.

"Get it while you're young," Milton answered.

My diary from a London visit in 1990 has me dashing between the Mongolian throat singer at South Bank's Purcell Room and Dutch Post Office Art at the Design Museum. The favorite movie seen was Jane Campion's *An Angel at My Table*. I found it "a film about becoming a writer, becoming a woman—grief, loss in a world that doesn't identify them."

What Milton meant about getting it while you're young was don't wait until you are seventy-five, which was how old he was when he began his winter sabbaticals. I think he and Ruth were able to keep health issues at bay for almost a decade, and then one winter Milton found himself unable to do his long walk from Hampstead down the High Street through Camden Town to Old London City, and Ruth started complaining about her right hip. The London culture idyll was finished.

Ruth and Milton saw everything that moved. Ruth had very strong and often contrary tastes; while she was happy to laugh her way through a porn movie, she found *Vertigo* downright "demeaning." Milton always liked to sit alone when watching a movie and, over the years, he found his favorite spot. Five rows back, on a left aisle seat at VHT, there is a little plaque that reads, "This is Milton's Chair."

Milton died in 2004, and I read something at the funeral. When I got up to speak I had a hard time not crying, but I got through it. Here is a small excerpt:

> *Milton was a great Dad to me because he encouraged*
> *competence. When I got the gardening bug and built some raised beds*

at the theatre I was throwing down plants left and right ... He said, wait, wait, wait—.

Soil is the key. So I thought ... soil, huh. Dirt.

We went to the city mulch dump and then to various backyards in Greene County looking for the magic ingredient—friable top soil. It was a wonderful field trip; not a lot of talking, some heavy lifting. Later I realized that you could grow your own plants from seed—he showed me the light propagation units he had built to get those tomatoes and basil going early—a very Milton device—a little bit of physical technology and a great deal of common sense. One of these contraptions used the body of an old coffee table and fluorescent garage lights.

Milton loved poetry as much as he did gardening and he read it better than anyone I know, so I ended my eulogy by quoting some lines from a poem by Louis MacNeice:

> The sunlight on the garden
> Hardens and grows cold,
> We cannot cage the minute
> Within its nets of gold,
> When all is told
> We cannot beg for pardon ...
>
> The earth compels,
> We are dying Egypt, dying
>
> And not expecting pardon,
> Hardened in heart anew,
> But glad to have sat under
> Thunder and rain with you,
> And grateful too
> For sunlight on the garden.

We were there at Martha Jefferson Hospital the night Milton died. He was on a ventilator, and his breathing was coming slower and slower. I remember one small but loving thing. Milton was wearing pajamas, and Ruth said, "Look, they're riding up—he must be uncomfortable. Someone, please give them a little tug." Ruth lived for eleven more years.

In Hebrew, the name "Ruth" means "a friend." But the English word "ruth" also means sadness for someone's misery, and Ruth had her share of it.

Her son, an only child, lived in Boston, and he and Ruth were often estranged. My own mother stayed close to home and I saw her during summer trips to Cape Cod. What began with a bowl of strawberries evolved into something profound: Ruth became the movie-loving mother, and I became the daughter she had lost.

Ruth's son Josh was the result of her second pregnancy. She had conceived for the first time a few years before he was born, but there was a problem, and late one night Milton had to drive her to the hospital. The baby—it was girl—was born dead. When Milton came out of the hospital, he walked the many miles home, having forgotten that he had ever driven there in a car.

As my on-site mother, Ruth was careful with me about Anita. "Your mother would have been so proud of you," Ruth said, about one of my risky business ventures. Despite Ruth's solicitude, I never thought, "Oh, Ruth is so much nicer than my mother," and this may have been because they were each the product of a barely contained fury. Ruth never directed this emotion at me, but I recognized its presence and its force in her insistence on hewing to the correct line on both politics and movies.

Milton and Ruth sometimes dropped by the house on Sunday mornings, and, after he was gone, she continued the habit as long as she could. She came to chat with me and especially with Dave—she always liked hanging out with the boys. The talk was about the latest book read or movie seen, and the point was to have a strong opinion. In all the time I spent with the two of them, I never saw Ruth upset with Milton, although he did occasionally emit a small sigh at one of her exaggerations.

In her later years when she was unable to go to the movies with me, I would pay Ruth a weekly visit. Lying on her big down-filled couch, I listened to her reminisce about growing up Jewish at her father's hotel and about being the youngest child and the only girl. She didn't have any unhappy memories; hers was a story of a girl who had been loved and completely spoiled. Milton, I came to see, had adored her and simply kept up the spoiling.

IN THE END I became Ruth's caretaker. She gave me full power of attorney and made me executor of the will. This eventually required me to move her into an assisted living facility out in Crozet. Ruth's bad hip had left her unable to walk and she moved around her single room in a wheelchair. In those last years I kept in touch by letter when away, as Ruth had when in London:

> Miles from home and you, I am extending my summer on the Cape—with seal-spotting kayak drives, and dedicated dunking into the 58 degree waters. When I leave Charlottesville, I twinge a little that this is the last time I will see you. But you are indomitable in your motorized Rhapsody chariot, presiding over all our afternoon sessions—me stretched out on your deep purple Crescent couch. And you dipping into your endless postings: from your sheltered Jewish girlhood in urban tundra Winnipeg, to salad days in post-WWII New York City with war vet Milton—politics, cigarettes, red high heels, and hard liquor.

Despite the wonderful experience with Ruth, it is stunning to realize that during the movie theatre years I often had difficulty making myself real to women. As a result I was happy to stay in myself, alone, for days and days. And I had chosen to put myself in a somewhat isolating position: the loneliness of the long-distance boss-lady.

This is not to say that I have not had strong women friends. Ellen McWhirter was one of them. And I will talk about Ellen, because she was someone I could get down to it with.

I feel troubled that I cannot get past my resistance or my pride or whatever it is so as to be able to reconnect with a lost old friend. There would have to be so much talking to get to where things were really real. Don't we all have people we no longer speak to? And yet Ellen—our friendship now exists only on Instagram—Ellen, I would say, helped to give me my life.

She insisted that, contrary to his claims, I could divorce "that guy" and she showed me how to book a movie theatre. It has to come—the right friend—when you need it.

It all began with a letter without a signature. In April 1976 I received a large packet of movie schedules. The author, Ellen McWhirter, listed her academic resume, including Emerson College and a Colombia University

MFA, plus several years managing and programming, with her husband David, at the Carnegie Hall/Bleecker Street movie houses. Now, the McWhirters were moving to Charlottesville.

David was entering graduate school in English and Ellen was looking to find a job in Charlottesville's film community. The letter was without a signature but who cares—suffering as I was with equipment breakdowns and imminent financial ruin from my arty programming—I was flattered, my intimidation lifted by Ellen's impressive but nonchalant work application. She was clearly smart, hopefully funny, and first aid now seemed on the way.

I invited Ellen and David to come stay at Rothery Road and to check out the town. They came and brought their friend Susan. It was a time when hospitality had fewer special needs. Our house was barely 1000 square feet but we managed: I think Ellen and David slept on the living room pull-out couch while Susan bunked above in the loft. Chief and I and the two kids were downstairs sharing our rooms. And one bathroom.

By the time David and Ellen relocated to Charlottesville a few months later I hadn't imagined how I would employ either of them. But, in introductory conversations over potluck dinners, David talked about the necessity for movie rep houses to establish an audience of regulars and to count on them to fill the seats as opposed to more traditional forms of advertising.

After this somewhat unwanted advice, I hired David and Ellen for very little money to drive around Albemarle and surrounding rural counties, placing Vinegar Hill schedules in every 7-11, Mom and Pop gas station, and all community centers.

"We went as far as Zion Crossroads to the east," David recalls, "south to Scottsville (where I remember vividly the restaurant sign advertising "Crispy Gizzards") and Lovingston, west to Crozet and Waynesboro, and north to Earlysville and Ruckersville. We put up the calendar/schedule on bulletin boards, in little country stores, supermarkets, wherever we could find a likely gathering spot. Not sure that I realize that we saved Vinegar Hill from an early death, but I think we knew we were right about the difference between running a normal theatre and what you wanted to do at Vinegar Hill: for the latter, the regulars are crucial. My experience with the theatres in New York was the template: our audience in some sense trusted our programming, and I think you reproduced that admirably in Cville."

Driving Virginia's summer back roads must have had its soothing rhythms, with meadows of orange day lilies, Shasta daisies, green on green hardwood, insect chatter coaxing you around the next bend. After the summer was over David and Ellen decided to keep driving: "Later we rented a house somewhere down the Scottsville road for a year. The drive was a welcome respite from reading those three fat novels a week, and the theatre led to enduring friendships."

ELLEN (NÉE PETERKOVSKY) was very tall, very skinny, with Vermont accessories. Although I had had a few Jewish women friends, none of them possessed Ellen's intellectual rigor. The woman had a knife in her brain. She was old-school Brooklyn, a character out of *Radio Days*, but the sojourn in her beloved New York came to an end when David was held up in a robbery at the Bleecker Street. They left the city, only briefly, for the peace of the Northeast Kingdom, acquiring there the obligatory plaids and flannels, and then headed south.

Ellen's intelligence was so obvious you had to pay attention. It was a very nervous intelligence, and she could be easily flustered. Once, when she brought film critic Molly Haskell to the university for a speaking engagement, Ellen stood up, gave a lovely introduction, and then forgot her guest's name.

At Columbia she had studied with Haskell's husband, Andrew Sarris, and when David came to the university to study English, Ellen was brought on as an instructor to teach film. Once I asked Reid Oechslin, her former student, about Ellen's classroom technique: she was famous for her shot-by-shot analyses. He described her threading up a 16mm projector and then stopping it cold in order to look at a particular frame.

Ellen liked certain kinds of movies: the world-view inherited from Sarris was divided into the Pantheon, and then the Far Side of Paradise, and then further categories. Every schedule, based on the auteur theory, had to have some of the Pantheon. I was on my way to comprehending that directors are the central thing, but Ellen really glued that theory down. And she knew both the old guys—Renoir, Murnau, Buñuel—and the Young Turks like Minnelli, Sturges, Fuller, Sirk, Ray. Ellen launched my second education in film.

Ellen also explained to me the concept of aspect ratio. I knew that films came in different shapes, but after she handed me James Limbacher's *Four Aspects of the Film* I searched out the lenses and aperture plates so the theatre could exhibit things correctly. Ellen found me Reid Oechslin and

Ellen

Leslie Gossage, two employees who became essential to the technical and intellectual character of Vinegar Hill.

Fall 1977. A road trip in the Volkswagen bus with David and Ellen—we are transporting the projectors to Steve Tanney at Star Cinema Supply, our savior repair place in Hell's Kitchen. All this driving allowed us to enjoy thirty-six hours of the New York Film Festival including Agnès Varda's treasure about female rebellion and friendship *One Sings, the Other Doesn't* and Jonathan Demme's working class poem *Handle with Care* / aka *Citizens Band*.

Ellen was a complete romantic. At the McWhirter cottage on Mulberry Street she often screened movies on the living room wall. One night she did *The Earrings of Madame de....* She confessed beforehand that it was one of her favorites; it's all about seduction and betrayal. She also made sure that we followed Ophüls's long tracking shot, as the heroine dances with her lover. I realized later that the appeal lay in the prolonged, continuous, sweeping movement, like an emotion that could not be stopped.

Was Ellen the one who wrote the blurb for the November showing of *Children of Paradise*? "The most beautiful, romantic film ever made," it reads, "about theatre people, criminals, and a romanticism that should upon occasion consume all of us." Ellen's fingerprints are all over the Fall schedule for 1976; we never would have shown the Carné without her, nor *Wuthering Heights*. She was not infallible, however; at her urging we ran *The Third Man*, and they really did stay away in droves.

Ellen and David were very married. It was important that he was taller than she was; Ellen had a height requirement. She seemed and usually acted older than the rest of us; two of her favorite words were "responsibility" and "relationship." When you were with Ellen, you were on your best intellectual and even moral behavior. It was therefore easy for me to come up with some language about Ellen when she asked me to write a letter of recommendation in 1983. In it I quote Ian, who, after watching Ellen handle a lobby filled with unruly customers, declared her "a master of crowd control. She makes them laugh; Fritz Lang would be impressed."

Ellen liked to drop me into new worlds, and it was a day of discovery on the afternoon she threaded up Vinegar Hill's 16mm Hortson and projected Werner Herzog's *The Enigma of Kaspar Hauser* or *Every Man for Himself and God Against All*. Almost a silent film about a mysteriously quiet and disabled young man in nineteenth-century Germany, the strongest action and emotion came from scenes of waving grass. We were both stunned. *Kaspar Hauser* had won international prizes in Cannes, Berlin, and Chicago in 1975, and the film was now making landfall in the US. It would be months, however, before we could locate a thirty-five millimeter exhibition quality print. For the next ten years, Ellen encouraged me to play every emerging national cinema—not just French or Italian films—but the sexy action films from Hong Kong, and gay cinema from everywhere.

Ellen and I didn't go out to bars together. Our strong discussions in her kitchen might be about one of my boyfriends, like a suitor from the early '80s who used to leave notes at my house that the kids would later find. After reading one note in particular, Ellen said, "Oh this looks like a keeper. This guy really loves you." She could not have been more wrong, but she believed it, I think, because of her deep belief in romance. My romantic life had the appeal of public ardor, a kind of broadcasting of feeling, and Ellen seemed to be moved by it, even though it was all happening to somebody else.

ONE PLACE WHERE I went to find movies was film festivals. In a day in New York or Berlin I could see four or five movies and so return home with ideas for little festivals of my own. On Labor Day Weekend, 1977, I went to the Telluride Film Festival. Located in an old mining town at ten thousand feet up in the Colorado Rockies, the festival was, in its early days, very young, very casual, with many of the attendees camping by the river on the outside of town. I met a guy named Phil Anderson from Minnesota who worked at the Walker Art Center in film; we had a nice weekend and made plans to meet again.

The honorees that year were directors Michael Powell and Agnès Varda and art director Ben Carré. But the big event occurred as part of a program of films billed as "The Erotic Woman." During an intermission, experimental filmmaker Carolee Schneemann carried her naked body onto the stage along with a bucket of dirt. She rubbed the dirt all over herself and then began extracting a long paper scroll from her vagina, reading from it as it emerged. Later Schneemann described her action as a response to a flier advertising the event showing a "pseudo naked man with his raincoat open and no genitals. It put me in an odd state because I considered it jokey and prurient, adolescent, completely inappropriate for a theme related to the erotic." Back in our room, Phil was introducing me to the poetry of Adrienne Rich.

Phil, like me, wanted a life in art. After that first furious weekend together, six letters from Minneapolis arrived in September alone; ours had from the beginning all the intensity of something destined to remain only an epistolary relationship. In his first letter Phil referred to having been through "a limbo of pleasure." He pictured himself as "a professionally spoiled, confused, underemployed, lost film person." He also used the word "stability" in quotes; he was twenty-nine. Me—I was almost thirty-three.

In dating, I consistently had an age-gap requirement. My preferred gap was three to four years younger; although I broke that rule, I never wanted an older man.

I saw Phil only once more, in early October. He walked me down to the Mississippi, a place that he cherished. We took pictures of each other on this cool, fall afternoon, although I remember the river as dry-bed and boulders.

I wrote to Phil as often as he wrote to me, saying whatever came into my head, as though filmmaker Éric Rohmer's *Six Moral Tales* guided my amorous inquisition. And still, be "wild as the wind," I heard David Bowie tell me. At some point I hurled an accusation—"selfishness in you is fear concealed"— and Phil threw the words back at me as part of six densely handwritten pages:

> *This has got to be absolutely clear-cut. I don't want to lose you but I want to respond as honestly as I can. You are two extremes in my experience—the best woman/person I have known intimately (the priority given to your human, professional self, the sexual one being so wonderful that to rhapsodize about it might seem over valuing it. I don't want just a good fuck.) You are also, however, the most unapproachable—far away, meaning intermittent visits, and married. What can I do?*

Later, in the same letter, he added:

> *I am jealous of you. NOT (NOT, NOT), jealous of you and other men, but jealous of: your age*
> *Experience*
> *Secure life, (job house)*
> *"vulgarity," ease of expression*
> *self-made profession*

> *and a few other things I will remember later. I no longer perceive you "as rich."*

One of the funny things about owning a movie theatre is that people do think of you as rich. In fact the original Vinegar Hill Limited Partnership agreement, still in effect when I met Phil, capped the combined salary for Chief and myself at one hundred and fifty dollars a week. Otherwise, Phil's description of me was pretty accurate.

The kiss-off note came in July, 1978:

Dear Ann,

> *Our lives and our thoughts about them are simply just further apart in all respects than we thought. I have a certain milieu here which gives me what little strength I need, and there's no one in it who seems to resemble you. This is not a judgment. I just think that if we actually lived in the same place things would have subsided between us long ago. I really am old-fashioned about a lot of things, especially a "desperate" attitude about the Great Mythical Lover I haven't met yet and probably never will. I actually want the kind of one-to-one stability, calm, slowness that a lot of my married friends claim to be bored with.*

He was a good man, and I wonder where he is.

AMONG THE FRENCH New Wave films, there is an odd duck, an inscrutable pre-*Thelma and Louise* girl-buddy *picaro*, that reminds me of my three-decade friendship with Ellen. It's the 1974 *Celine and Julie Go Boating* from director Jacques Rivette. Clocking in at 192 minutes, *Celine and Julie* can sometimes feel like a too-long bus ride, and explaining the narrative delivers mish-mash thinking. But if you can accept the challenging *Alice in Wonderland* format and enjoy the antics of these women as they check in and out of the Parisian *demi-monde*, freedom and joy are just around the corner.

My real Celine and Julie days with Ellen also involved a film festival—two trips to Cannes in 1989 and 1991. This was during a period after Ellen and David had moved to West Philadelphia and while she was teaching film at the

University of Pennsylvania. There was a course called "Penn at Cannes" which Ellen co-taught with Tony Liehm, a veteran Czech film critic based in New York City and a man thoroughly groomed in the insouciance of Europe's film festival circuit. I think he liked the gig in France, light work and five movies a day. He considered the Penn undergraduates privileged and serious only about their two-week hang on the French Riviera; his favorite line was "run away from that movie," a critical opinion punctuated with cheery laughter.

In 1989 Cannes awarded the *Palme d'Or* to twenty-eight-year-old Steven Soderbergh for *Sex, Lies, and Videotape*. Saw it, climbed the thousand steps, marched the red carpet, no one took my photo, but the buzz and excitement for the film was like a NASA launch. Cast member James Spader won Best Actor too. It was nice to see a local boy make good: while growing up, Soderbergh often saw movies at Vinegar Hill.

1989 was a good year for film. There was Emir Kusturica's *Time of the Gypsies*, with Goran Bregović's brilliant music, and Shōhei Imamura's *Black Rain*, about the social outcasts from Hiroshima. Hungarian feminist Ildikó Enyedi's comic film *My Twentieth Century* won *Un Certain Regard*, and black-wigged Meryl Streep was named Best Actress for *A Cry in the Dark*—originally titled *Evil Angels*—in perhaps her most underrated and unsympathetic performance as the Australian mother: "The dingo took my baby!"

Ellen and I went to a few Q & A's and saw film heroes Wim Wenders, president of the Jury, composer Georges Delerue, and Polish director Krzysztof Kiéslowski, thin, pale, and smoking. Unlike most American distributors or exhibitors who stayed on the poshy Croissette at the Hôtel Martinez, we had cozy lodgings in a French widow's home, sharing an antique bed with impeccable linens and smooth *cafés au lait* for *petit déjeuner*. During our two

weeks in Cannes we soaked up the novel pleasures of Jane Campion's debut *Sweetie*, *Speaking Parts* from Canadian Atom Egoyan, and Spike Lee's *Do the Right Thing*, even as we complained about the obviousness of *Cinema Paradiso* and the vacuity of *New York Stories* from Scorsese, Allen, and Coppola. One night for a change of pace, Ellen and I and a Virginia Film Festival pal put on evening clothes and went to the casino where our friend played a few rounds of *chemin de fer*.

But there was another evening that did not go so well. After a day of sightseeing in Arles I returned to Cannes for a midnight screening. My outfit consisted of a pale green sleeveless top, loose silk pants, and sandals. I was standing on the stairs in the red carpet line when an usher walked up. "*Madame, pas de tenue de soirée*," he said. I wasn't dolled up enough. Briefly mortified by my banishment, I swore at him in English.

On our last trip to Cannes together Ellen and I stayed with the Faustines, Marie-José and Monsieur. He called himself a Marxist but he was also a triathlete and a caring host. I had arrived with a bad sinus infection and spent the ten days with my face over a bowl of homeopathic vapors. Ellen kept seeing movies while I tried to clear my head.

The big event for her was Madonna's *Truth or Dare*. When I eventually saw the film I realized it was obsessed with defining a certain kind of female friendship: "Can I borrow your clothes? Can I sleep with your boyfriend? Can I steal your identity?" The great thing about my time with Ellen was that none of these questions ever surfaced.

9
FELLINI'S

Four years after opening the movie theatre, in the fall of 1979, Chief and I bought a restaurant. It was a way, I now think, of trying to salvage our failing marriage, although no one said so at the time. Instead of trying to get out, we both dug in a little deeper, but, in a letter written that summer to my graduate school roommate and her husband who designed our house, I listed the danger signs:

Dear Marcia and Don:
  There's ten-years worth of news. Experience says you won't get it all. The movie theatre flourishes, is four years old, is the best job I could ever imagine. It must be the words of a sick person indeed, but, quote I never tire of locking myself in a darkened auditorium and looking at the films, preferably alone, unquote.
  Our marriage is hanging in there—having endured several almosts, two interims of psychoanalysis, lots of bizarreness, a

handful of hot affairs on both sides; but things are calm, quiet, and reflective and now seems a good time to assess and respect what worked and what didn't. Ian and Courtie are so wonderful in true sentimental fashion I can bring tears into my eyes by merely thinking about them. The house holds up, and continues to assault all those cautionary architects at UVA with its boldness and up-yours lean approach to decoration. My mother, the immortal, is back to her normal, loving, breakneck speed without the case of crazies that she evidenced after my dad's death. Brother Rudy continues to farm and deliver calves in Hopedale—he visits us once a year with Bobby Iannitelli, his one socialized friend, so I am satisfied that his life at least has some light coming into it.

Charlottesville is becoming a big city—but you still don't have to lock your car. Chief is quitting his law job, and we are opening a restaurant with another lawyer who is also tired of law. Just when life settles down—one of us has to endanger it.

Love, Ann

A few doors up Market Street from the entrance to Vinegar Hill there was a white stucco building housing a Mexican restaurant called The Flat. Judging by the slightly burned surfaces on the food arriving at the tables, the only heating devices in the kitchen appeared to be a salamander and a hot plate. The place had a lovely interior, with cozy wooden booths and a nickel-plated stove in the dining room for cold winter nights. When The Flat turned off its lights, Chief and I were able to buy the building for something around $40K. We did a little work on the kitchen and, on the Market Street side of the building, in big black letters, we painted one word: Fellini's.

What I wanted was to make good Italian food. What Chief wanted was a new stage.

Chief could sell tickets at the seven and nine o'clock shows and then walk up the block and spend the rest of his evening presiding over the bar. He never did quit his law job, however, not until years later.

My friends Jean Dunbar and Peter Sils actually met and fell in love at Fellini's. She was a graduate student/waitron, and he, a Darden School first year, practicing his barfly.

"Chief was a specialist in speaking the unconscious," Jean remembered.

"Whenever I would approach him with a customer complaint, he would say, 'We get raves.'"

When Jean said that, I was surprised. I would have said Chief had no ongoing conversation with his unconscious; instead he used words to sell things, above all himself. He was an intellectual without much emotional ballast, and the lightness of being finally carried him away. Chief went deep all the time—he read the Russian novelists with great passion—but he didn't make the connections. What did Jean mean by "a specialist in speaking the unconscious"? When I met Chief I thought of him as careful with words because he wanted them to work for him, but Jean's comment makes me wonder if, by the Fellini Years, he had lost his filter. And maybe the drinking had something to do with it.

Jean's husband-to-be Peter began hanging out at Fellini's soon after it opened:

"I would arrive at ten or eleven and Chief would be dressed in his usual disheveled white dinner jacket and black bow tie. It was all about that thing he had with Humphrey Bogart. I guess he even hoped people would sidle up to him like Peter Lorre and say, 'Meester Reek.' He always stood behind the bar because from there he could watch the house and the front door. He would be drinking, but was never totally smashed because he was also minding the cash register. I remember him as quite cheerful."

At this point, Jean interjects: "If you drink a lot, you're cheerful."

"Well, sure—of course. Anyway, I'd order a drink and talk to the usual suspects. The more one drank, the more sincere the conversations seemed to become. Eventually the bar would close to the public, but the regulars would stay on and drink until four in the morning, and Chief was still there. Or some evenings, he would go off with a woman to trysts unknown.

"Eventually I got into writing classified ads for Fellini's. I ran them in the *Daily Progress* and Chief paid for them. They appeared in the Classifieds, as if they were a For Sale ad rather than a regular display ad. Someone walked in once because he read 'Pasta Grows on Trees,' or maybe it was 'I Met Her at Fellini's.'"

Peter seemed very pleased with his advertising contributions to the early days of Fellini's.

My duty was as the pasta maker. I worked in the late afternoon, or on slow evenings. Cranking, literally, on a manual pasta machine, yards of egg and flour fettuccini. My favorite task was making our menu specialty, Marcella Hazan's Hay and Straw. Marcella opens her first cookbook with an emotion I share: "It is impossible for cooks ever to give a full account of their debts." My pasta dried on a clothes rack set up in the office, with a clean cloth under it. If I was lucky, I could collect and store separately the dried green and yellow noodles—the hay and the straw—before a staff or delivery person upset the operation.

FELLINI'S WAS LOCATED just a block west of Lee Park. In only a few steps from the front door you could find yourself looking up at the man of marble, sitting on his horse Traveler.

Charlottesville was a town filled with statues. On the campus of the University there were the obligatory statues of Washington and Jefferson. At the end of West Main Street, there was a statue of Lewis and Clark—both of them grew up in Virginia. At the intersection of University and Jefferson Park Avenues, under a stand of white pine, was a statue of George Rogers Clark, "Conqueror of the Northwest". Two or three Indians kneel at the foot of Clark's horse, staring up at him.

Down by the County Court House stands what many consider to be the most distinguished equestrian statue in the United States. The man and the horse are one as they ride to the next battle. Stonewall Jackson, who often camped near Charlottesville, is once again heading North.

It was the statue in Lee Park that was, however, to reopen Charlottesville's unhealed wounds. The town may now be a blue dot in a gerrymandered red sea, but it has not always been a liberal town. It was, for instance, a center of Massive Resistance. Desegregation of the city's public schools did not begin until 1959, five years after the *Brown v. Board of Education* Supreme Court ruling. While the University first began admitting black students in 1955, African Americans comprised less than one percent of the undergraduate population in 1968. Prominent faculty members at the University continued to espouse eugenics and racialist thinking well into the 1960s.

Admission to Charlottesville's movie theatres was also a complicated affair. The Paramount and Jefferson Theaters admitted blacks but only in the balconies. The University Theatre, which lacked a balcony, refused to admit blacks altogether as late as 1961. There is a *Daily Progress* photo of the first African American UVA graduate student picketing the University Theatre under a marquee advertising Gregory Peck and Ava Gardner in *On the Beach*. And my beloved theatre was located in a building next to what had once been Charlottesville's lively black downtown, Vinegar Hill, razed by urban renewal.

In the spring of 2017 the Charlottesville City Council voted to remove the equestrian statue from Lee Park. The vote provoked a Unite the Right rally later that summer, when hundreds of white supremacists and neo-Nazis marched with Tiki Torches on the university lawn and then brought their protest downtown. As the Charlottesville and State police looked on, scores of counter-protesters were beaten and a local woman named Heather Heyer was killed when a man drove his car into the crowd. President Trump refused to condemn the racists, saying there were "fine people on both sides."

I was at Cape Cod during that terrible August. When friends there asked me about the news from home, I fell back on "My news is your news—CNN, Facebook posts." Then, one day, I was trailing my boxer Bruno during an incoming tide. A man and a woman came over to pat him and playfully grabbed his tags.

"How are you, Bruno?" she said.

Then, "From *Charlottesville*?" she added, her voice rising with alarm. "What happened there?"

The tone of her voice said everything, and, in the months following, people began to say, when another demonstration raised its ugly head, "It's just like Charlottesville." Within a year, the name of our town had become a metaphor *and* a hashtag.

"How can it have happened here?" people often exclaimed, as if Charlottesville were somehow exempt from history. But the statues we drove by without seeing knew something we didn't want to know. As a friend said to me in the aftermath of the demonstrations, "It was shocking—and inevitable." She may have been remembering the fact that in 1921 Charlottesville was one of the cities where its business and professional men gathered to celebrate the rebirth of the Ku Klux Klan.

After the white robes returned to Charlottesville, people began to make distinctions between the men figured by the statues. Civil War generals were one thing, but Washington and Jefferson, who during their lifetimes never managed to free their own slaves, were somehow something else. By the time of the upheaval, the most trenchant political commentary was being delivered by *Saturday Night Live*, and if anyone still wanted to believe that "the troubles" could not be traced back to the founders, they would have to go through UVA alumnus Tina Fey: "As Thomas Jefferson once said, 'Who's that hot light-skinned girl over by the butter churn?'"

Ian was always much more tuned in to Charlottesville's black community than I was. At Venable Elementary his best friend was Walter Morton, a kid from West Haven, the projects built to replace black housing that had been urban renewed. In the eighth grade, at powder keg Buford Middle School, Ian dated an African American girl named Ariel and was beaten up because of it. In his junior year at CHS, after a group of black students staged a small riot in the school library, Ian spoke at a press conference and pointed out to a reporter that someone had earlier burned a cross in the student parking lot. His life as a mediating figure continues in Pittsburgh: on weekends he can be heard in The Hill district—August Wilson-land—blowing his horn with Teresa Hawthorne's female-led, black '70s Legacee band.

Ian writes in *The Reivers Diaries* about a day in 1979:

> The new VHT schedule started on Halloween, with a Japanese double bill of The Ceremony and Double Suicide. At school, a bizarre incident took place. The sixth-grade teachers at Buford thought it would be fun to do some Halloween hijinks with us, so they took us out of our regular classes and put us in big groups in some room. They cut the lights and showed us innocuous Halloween-themed cartoons. Then the teachers came out in Halloween costumes to get jump scares out of the kids. A vampire, a werewolf, a witch, and uh-oh, a ghost, dressed in, you guessed it, a white sheet. She was immediately accosted by freaked-out students to the point that she had to withdraw and the event came to an abrupt end. The students I saw went berserk and pulled the sheet off of her in a kind of hysteria. Hindsight gives clear eyes for this panic in the streets; but the school administration then reasoned that we were poorly-behaved students. I would counter that while our collective behavior left something to be desired, the adults should have thought this through better.
>
> The first reason is that most of us eleven-year old kids had seen the horror movie Halloween, which had a scene with a knife-wielding murderer wearing a white sheet. But a better explanation

ripped itself from the pages of local history: her costume looked like a White Knight of the KKK. Half of the students who tore the teacher's costume off were black. All of the kids who tore it off were boys, no Rhodes scholars in the mix, the teacher was female, and more of a benevolent, less authoritarian, yet Southern-sounding white lady, so there may have been a vibe with these kids that they could violate her and she'd do nothing back, which was not her fault, but when dealing with learning-support kids, sometimes all they understand is might makes right, anything else and they are bewildered. It is my contention that the costume was stripped off the teacher not simply by ill-behaved kids, but the costume triggered kids to freak out to the point they felt compelled to burn the village to the ground.

FELLINI'S WAS A success right out of the gate. While we made the same mistakes we had made with the theatre—not enough start-up money and opening before we were ready—one thing we had going for us was that Chief had become a local celebrity. On busy nights at the theatre, when the lobby was packed with customers waiting for the next show, he was famous for bellowing, "Lobby Noise!" Chief loved costumes, and so was perfect for the Humphrey Bogart get-up which he wore nightly to sell tickets or to tend bar. A few months after Fellini's opened, he took a girlfriend to Spain and came home with husband and wife capes. His was black and he wore it boldly with a matching fedora, like Federico Fellini; mine was dark red and so oversized that when I put it on I looked like the killer dwarf in *Don't Look Now*.

We did do one smart thing; we drove to New York and at Cinemabilia in the West Village bought all the Fellini posters we could find. We never considered any name but Fellini's—not Antonioni, not Visconti, not De Sica. And the name proved prophetic.

Fellini's was a riff on all the red-sauce restaurants from the Northeast. We made spaghetti and hot sausage sauce, an exploded pesto invented by one of the Beccas called Fettuccini Fellini—broccoli, walnuts, garlic, and cheese. People thought it was healthy, trail-blazing vegetarian. The wine was indifferent, mostly magnums from California or entry-level Italians. There was an upstairs of great beauty and views but we rarely used it; instead, customers crowded into the wooden booths, each identified by a poster hanging over it. "Two spag-meats at *Dolce Vita*," a waitron would yell, as she dropped off a ticket.

Except for Chief and a bartender, the staff at the restaurant was all female: Brenda, Anita, Caroline, Leslie in the kitchen. A wait-staff of two Rebeccas, two Jills, little Jeannie and tall Jean, another Leslie, two Lindas, a Janet, an Ellen, a Cathy washing dishes and a Sarah in the office. All but one were single women. And then there was me. I see myself as having become a Fellini's girl—willing to be passed around with whoever was getting the girls, going out with guys waitrons were also going out with. But I was also the boss. Sort of.

Fellini's was a hothouse of dateable, available, flirtable girls. Nobody wanted to be called a waitress, hence the word "waitron." There was a big table—a ten-top—in front of the bar, and even before it became a place where people had sex it was contemplated as a place where people could have sex. The table was called "the slab" and, after getting up from it, one had been "planked." It was the beginning of the 1980s, a last free moment before the sexual walls again began closing in, and Chief wandered through this bevy of beauties with the same air of bemused diffidence given off by Marcello Mastroianni in *8½*. He didn't so much want them all; if anything, he simply enjoyed being surrounded. He gave the place an air of permissiveness and people liked that.

ONE HOT SUMMER Saturday I wandered up to the restaurant after selling tickets for the nine o'clock show. I went inside, strolled around, walked back out into the beautiful Southern night. Next door African American men from the Elks Club on Second Street were gathering in their doorway. At the same time, an after-hours party of Fellini's customers was getting underway on the sidewalk. There were boom boxes, marijuana smoke, open containers, all the makings of a block party. Even though the crowd quickly became racially mixed, it would never be called integrated. More like respectful coexistence.

My friend Claudia K strolled up and gave me a hug.

"Where are you going?" I said, having just seen her making out with Chief, back by the restrooms.

"Going home to get a set of clean sheets," she mused, "in case I decide to stay at Chief's."

Claudia never learned to pull her punches. She had been on the road since her teens and kept all her belongings in seven baskets in case she needed to make a quick getaway.

As Ian remarks, "the battle lines were soon drawn." Chief was spending more and more time at the restaurant, and I was left to run the theatre. He was burning the candle at every end, and by 1981 he was living downtown in a house on Altamont Street that he and I co-owned. We had both stopped trying to make the marriage work. And now, instead of sharing one business with a man I was going to leave, there were two.

—cinema—

Theatre on the Hill

Porotti and Oeschlin with The Hortson, a faithful old projector circa 1934.

chooses and books the films and writes up the monthly schedules, they all share in the numerous other chores, like projecting and ticket taking, that

shortly after he and Jessica Lange moved to the area. This brought in a good number of people, most of whom really expected to see them there.

10
THE RECTIFIER

In 1979 a new person came in to my life. At the time he was an undergraduate majoring in English at the University of Virginia. He was to become, over the years, my most enduring employee as well as one of my closest friends. His name was Reid Oechslin.

On a very cold day in the winter of 2017, Reid drove over the mountain from Staunton, where he and his wife Nicole were raising two girls, to talk with me about the old days.

"It happened through Fellini's," Reid remembered. "I came to work there as the weekend dishwasher soon after it opened. So I was there for the beginning of the restaurant but not for the theatre—I only became a projectionist later on."

"Well," I said, "the beginning was Steve Waller and David Minckler, and we had the worst equipment, the worst ever."

"Right, and there were still echoes of your bad equipment when I came on board. Although by then you had ironed out most of your problems. Regular changeovers, two fully operational machines."

"But 1979 is a long time from when we opened. Was John Showalter then on the scene?"

"Yes, you had the RCA service contract with him."

"And George Eitel—he was there too?"

"No, never heard of him."

"He saved my life in the early days. Don't know how I found him. I swear I met him at one of the local movie theatres, or at Monticello Lunch. I recently found a note about how grateful I was to Mr. Eitel. After our disastrous opening he did an all-night projector repair."

"Way before my time."

"So you were washing dishes for a while before you came over to the theatre. And Ian reminds me that you were working with Rob Stoney. 'Reid a book and Rob a bank'—that's what the kids called you."

"Yup—Friday and Saturday night dishwashers. And we sort of went through the getting of Fellini's in motion. Converting it from The Flat, that strange Mexican restaurant. They didn't leave a lot behind, although at one point we found a fifty-gallon barrel of cumin."

When I stopped laughing I managed to say, "Only fifty gallons?"

"No kidding—a barrel forty inches high, twenty-six inches in diameter."

"Didn't know cumin in those days."

"No stove, but they had lots of spice. And holes in the floor and no heat."

"Were you busy on weekends? I didn't actually know, being down the block stuck in the VHT ticket booth."

"Slammed from day one. Because it was a new place. Pretty damn busy, and the kitchen … was figuring out—"

"—How to be a kitchen. At first I was too busy at the theatre to help at the restaurant in any big way. Then I started walking over to check out what was going on."

"That must have been after I had moved over to VHT."

"Right—so I'm trying to remember the first time we met. I think it happened through Ellen. You were in Ellen's film class. She brought you by, we watched *A Face in the Crowd*."

"Yes, a day-time screening. I mean, how romantic—to be able to screen movies to yourself and your friends on a weekday afternoon. You and Ellen had these cowl neck sweaters. You would watch movies with the cowl up over your nose but under your eyes."

"That's right! You can just shove it up over your eyes if the movie gets unpleasant. After years of seeing movies, I ended up with an enormous collection of scarves—more useful than a cowl—to do battle with whatever visuals came my way. But I still haven't figured out how you came over to the theatre."

"It happened on a Saturday night. I was doing dishes at Fellini's and a desperate person ran into the kitchen, and said, 'Does anyone here know how to solder?' I looked up from my tub of suds and said, 'Yeah, I do.' I went down the street and a wire had snapped off from the bulb base of the Exciter lamp. We found a funky old soldering iron and I glued it back together."

"I had a soldering iron?"

"I think that things had gotten so falling apart at the theatre that you *had* to have one."

"Yes, it was so falling apart. As you liked to say—'It's all falling or burning.'"

"A line from Gary Snyder. Got that from Dave Wyatt's lit and landscape class."

"It's funny that you and Ellen each knew Dave before I did."

"I think I took his class in my senior year. We read people like John Muir. One day Dave announced that for our final project we would be taking a hike. Four of us climbed into his Plymouth and drove up to White Oak Canyon. A beautiful spring day. Redbud everywhere. But it was hot on the trail coming down, and when we got back to the car Dave opened the trunk and there were these half-gallons of booze. Each of us was offered a bottle—we didn't drink much, but it felt like we were getting away with something. It turned out that Dave was in charge of setting up cocktail parties after guest lecturers did their thing, and so he kept a stash of departmental liquor in his car for easy delivery."

"Sounds like him. In any case, that night you and your soldering iron saved the show."

"And then it was like, everyone said to me, Yay for Reid. But I still went back to washing dishes. The summer rolled around, and you said I could work at the theatre. By then Leslie had advanced to projection—she was no longer your cleaning person. And I started cleaning the theatre. Minckler was the main projectionist and he was annoyed that I was on the scene."

"I hadn't fired him. Yet. You and Minckler then became the main projectionists."

"For a long time."

"Until he got fired."

"When he dropped giant reel number four of *Kagemusha*. Forty-five minutes gone."

"And then lied about it."

"Yes," Reid said, "he hated me for that too—he connected the firing with a continuous pattern of displacement. Those were strange days—so much more seemed to be happening and usually all at once. You know, every so often I have dreams that I am working in the booth, I'm threading, when stuff goes wrong, things are breaking, and the shit hits the fan."

"It happened a lot. Ian's been talking with Chief about how things started and he remembered a time with *Discreet Charm of the Bourgeoisie*. It came in dubbed, so we called and asked for a subtitled print. The replacement didn't arrive by the time of the first show, so we had to screen the dubbed one, and then the titled one showed up, and we just switched prints in the middle of the movie. No one noticed. No one mentioned it."

"Maybe they went with it. People were like—you put salt on a bird's tail and it calms down." Reid shakes his hand over an imaginary bird. "And movies were so—so beautiful then. I mean, today the delivery of images is very complicated, but we would never suspect that because it all just lands in our lap. We never see behind the curtain."

"Yes," I say with a sigh, "now is something different. The visuals always look the same. Vivid. Case in point—*La La Land* just won an Oscar for cinematography. But it was Photoshop vivid. Primary colors, pumped."

"You would fight vivid in the old days. If you were inexpert you would get vivid, but the true cinematographers and Technicolor wizards like Natalie and Herbert Kalmus were always fighting vivid. Tea dyed costumes to get white, pastels to get soft, even the makeup was adjusted to pale. Sets were used to control the bright and blue of the sky, and the green in trees."

"So the '70s guys were fighting vivid. That seems right. Especially when I remember how shocked I was at the shadowy look of *McCabe and Mrs. Miller*."

"Well, it was shot through a coffee filter by Vilmos Zsigmond. The ethos of the '70s look was all those shades of brown."

"And then there was Néstor Almendros doing *Days of Heaven* and *Kramer vs. Kramer*. A man in love with gold light. And Coppola's Gordon

Willis, the Prince of Darkness. And what about Storaro? He took a different way with Bertolucci—finding velvet texture in saturated colors. As if he were a Renaissance painter."

"Yes," Reid said. "We were really plugged into that and we talked about the cinematographers and designers and composers in the VHT blurbs as much as any of the other qualities in the movies."

"We did. Last night, when I was thinking about you driving over, I was remembering *Chinatown*. John Alonzo's camera work is so—so *gliding*. Then Richard Sylbert's art direction uses all that brown and yellow. And Jerry Goldsmith's instrumentation is just plain insinuating. In the best way possible."

At that moment I think Reid and I were each trying to say that the joy of running a movie theater can come in so many forms—just opening a film can and running the newly-arrived reels through my hands was an excitement. A big night with a full lobby and lines out the door never stopped being a thrill. Finding just the right stills for every schedule was an artistic high. Looking at a movie—mesmerized by the thrill of light swimming through celluloid—this would never be merely a job, not with so much beauty winking at you, day after day.

"You know, Reid, we never did many silent movies—what we loved was sound."

"Music brings it back for people," Reid went on to say. "During the Oscars, when they used a few bars from Georges Delerue's score for *Day for Night,* my heart beats faster, I cry. My work life comes back to me. I showed that to my girls, but they didn't get it."

"Maybe they had to see the whole movie. Repeatedly."

"It's really about the whole artifice of making that shot. I can still see it—"

"The rising up, the crane shot—"

"—And that they are using a different camera than the one on the crane in order to show what is happening behind the scenes. And then you get to see the shot in the viewfinder, on the *crane* as it will appear in the movie. What happens in your mind when you see these two different versions of the same reality is amazing—it's the realization of just how much goes into something that you think of as ordinary in a movie. And the whole time there's that soaring music, with the trumpet reaching higher and higher."

"Exactly—and then Truffaut cools it off by zooming to an ordinary little shot in the viewfinder at the conclusion of the scene."

"It's like tearing a hole in the screen."

We are a little breathless from our memories, so I get up and make some tea. Then I go back to remembering.

"I don't think our early audiences thought in these terms—about technique. They were in an accepting mode, and as long as the flow continued they were dazzled and quiet. It doesn't really matter as long as the motion continues."

"I think I have taken your theory of audience management and enhanced it. About the reactions of an audience to a movie stopping mid-screening."

"Which did happen …"

"You go off screen, and the entire audience stops breathing."

"They do!"

"The faster you can go back on screen, the less they notice—that it even happened."

"We had a month in the beginning where we were running twenty-minute reels, every show with multiple breaks because we had only one functioning projector. This was fixed by the end of March or early April, during a run of *The Harder They Come*. It was astonishing to me that I did not put a gun to my head. We owed so much money. People were very tolerant of our 'learn by doing' initiation."

"It was a new thing. It was an alternative universe of movie theatre."

"Because it wasn't professional?"

"It was like the difference between going to a restaurant or to a friend's house for dinner."

"Which is now kind of the new thing. The idea being that you want to go to a secret restaurant that cooks like grandma."

"I didn't realize that it was that bad." Reid shook his head.

"It was terrible."

"You had the Super Simplexes—"

"Two machines, projectors from the thirties—Pegeen Mike with the green light, and Scarlet with the red light."

"And a third head."

"Right. New York sent us the third head as a reparation during the various back and forth repairs. At one time both Pegeen Mike and Scarlet were in the shop. Eventually we had three heads and two bases. And the two Kneisley Rectifiers."

Reid laughed, loudly. "Ah, the Kneisley Rectifiers, those two little grey boxes on the floor."

"Actually that's the title for my chapter about how you saved the theatre—it's called The Rectifier."

Reid dropped into a German accent. "I vas zee Rectifier …"

I smiled and said, "For a while the chapter title was Read-y Kilowatt. But The Rectifier has more glam."

"The Kneisleys were like little suitcases with handles because, of course, you were supposed to walk around with them."

"And they had a dial. Once I had to do something to one, a man guided me, but—"

"Maybe that's why you had a soldering iron." Reid shifted into an imaginary phone conversation: "Go out and buy a soldering iron, then call me back and I'm going to walk you through the Goldfinger disarming-the-nuclear-weapon-process."

"It was eleven o'clock at night, it was terrible."

He continued his imaginary conversation: "You take the white wire—"

"You can laugh, but I'm on the phone with a man somewhere in the middle of the night. He's trying to tell me how to change a part he has sent me in the mail. Dear Jesus, I thought, I could blowup myself and the building."

"The Kneisleys sucked, and we had them until the mid-eighties. All they were supposed to do was to make the lamp bright. We finally found enough cash to replace them."

"Two or three grand. Did we do that when we replaced the chairs? In 1985?"

"Maybe. The chairs were a huge expense."

"Ten K. But we had a big dance party after we ripped them all out. Slab Dancing on the chair-less raked concrete floor."

"It was the time of *Mad Max Beyond Thunderdome*. I remember because you used a still of Tina Turner and Mel Gibson on your invitation."

"Yeah, and we had the two dogs then—I have shots of Voisine and her baby Sylvania dancing on the slab with the kids."

"I love how we date things and measure the time of other things. Stitch them together with pictures, movie releases, little pieces of paper, like breadcrumbs that tell the story."

"I remember you as a big leaver of notes. Some of the best things I managed to save are the Top Ten Lists. Remember those? Every staff member got to do one, and some people went on for five or six pages, justifying a choice. I was pawing through a folder the other day and found your list for 1987—it's labeled 'A Very Good Year.' Here it is:"

1. Housekeeping
2. River's Edge
3. Tampopo
4. Working Girls
5. Blue Velvet
6. Sid & Nancy
7. Round Midnight
8. Dancing in the Dark
9. Radio Days
10. My Life as a Dog

"The funny thing is," I said, after I finished reading the list, "you couldn't stop at ten. There are ten more movies listed under 'Any Other Year,' and then you indulge in some 'Revivals,' like *High and Low*. You even squeeze in a few more titles by giving away awards for music to *Full Metal Jacket* and editing to *Something Wild*."

I hand Reid the list. "And then of course, there is your designation for worst movie of the year: 'Pee Dog.'"

"Oh yeah, I remember that award category—but what did I give it to?"

"*Sherman's March*."

"Never could stand that guy—Ross McElwee. He's trying to invoke the lingering effects of the war but he keeps being distracted by old girlfriends. I guess it was the smugness."

"I have one more very incriminating document. Remember all the fun we had with customer preferences, especially in candy? None of the concession people could understand why anybody would buy those chalky Necco Wafers. And then one day something in your handwriting turned up, and everybody began piling on."

I handed Reid another yellowing piece of paper.

May 27 A Special Necco Report

Since Joan called in sick today, I did the janitorial stuff. This gives me a special opportunity to write up previously unreleased information about Necco customers: the inside (the auditorium) story.

Necco eaters usually sit on the side rows rather than the center section. Is this a function of their size, their tardiness, their many trips to the concession stand, or what? Who knows. Anyway, they tend to tear the waxed-paper into shreds, or in the case of a small elect, into tiny squares measuring no more than ¼" on a side. This tendency spreads beyond their Necco candy wrapper habits as well—the aesthetic lift from neat squares of gold Cadbury Caramello foil scattered across the grey cement floor is unparalleled in my experience as a janitor.

Necco consumers also consider the wafers themselves to be objets d'art. Objectionable flavors, after being dampened by the tongue, are placed on the floor at the Necco consumer's feet. Overnight, they bond themselves to the concrete with prodigious strength; the next day they have become like pennies glued to the sidewalk by pranksters: tantalizing pastel dots that resist all attempts to pry them up. In this way, Neccos become '50s pastel polka-dots with a dada-istic twist.

P.S. Chief ate a pack of Neccos today!—Reid

"I can't believe I actually took the time to write that," Reid said when he finished his reading.

"But you started something—look, there are four more pages of this stuff—in four different kinds of handwriting! Who's this, do you think?" I asked, and offered him another piece of paper.

"It's pretty clear," I said, when Reid looked up, "that people had lots of time on their hands behind the concession stand."

"Yup—but upstairs in the projection booth we had to stay more or less on the ball. Changeover dots—remember those? Now they're gone with the wind, but back in the day our lives depended on them. You watched and waited by the second machine, loaded and ready to go. As the first dots appeared, you started that machine, and then eight seconds later when a second series of dots flashed on screen, you hit the pedal and changed over."

"You know they've taken the dots off digital prints—although the other night, I was watching a DVD of an old Ann Sheridan noir—*Woman on the Run*—and there they were."

"If I see a dot, I'll have some sort of Pavlovian reaction. My foot will start stomping on the floor, hand twitching. Where's the pedal, where's the motor switch?"

"You remember, we got so careful that we had projection notes for each print: a handwritten note stuck on the shelf, with a push pin, written in Sharpie. The title, the aspect ratio, changeover details, film condition, and how it ends."

"Yeah, the end part was most important because otherwise you might suddenly see "The End" and then a white screen with just the sound of the film running out—which could be heard in the lobby."

"You know, Reid, I can still do the changeover dance. You have your left hand on the motor switch, your right hand on the lamp dowser, your foot is hovering over the pedal. Turn on the motor, open the dowser, turn to the front, grab the focus knob with right hand and the frame knob with left hand, and then hit the pedal. Then you focus and frame."

"Yup—and you have used all the body parts that are moving on your person."

"A little ballet, Charlie Chaplin style." I paused a moment and then I said, "People like to know how a thing is done."

11
POPCORN

Straight up, I hate popcorn. To eat. Nevertheless I always popped with culinary integrity insofar as exploding the kernels was concerned. Palm, canola, peanut or coconut oil for the fire, real butter for the dressing—no Tubs with Heart Healthy symbols—rather, doubled bags, grease-smeared, grocery store browns. When we first opened a large popcorn went for a buck; by the time we closed we were charging five dollars a bag. But the bag was bigger by the end.

In *Popped Culture*, Andrew F. Smith unpacks the romance of popcorn. Maize, he tells us—what we call corn—was domesticated in Central America some eight thousand years ago. Of the 218 races of corn grown in the Americas, eighteen were popcorns. Remains of popping varieties have been found in burial sites in Chile and Peru. Writing in the early seventeenth century, a Jesuit missionary reported that Peruvians toasted "a certain kind of corn until it bursts."

There is little evidence of North American Indians popping corn, but the practice is mentioned by John Winthrop, Jr., the son of the first governor of

Massachusetts, as well as by Benjamin Franklin. By the 1840s popcorn had become a popular snack in the Eastern United States, with Thoreau noting in his journal that popcorn is "only a more rapid blossoming of the seed under a greater July heat."

Movie theater owners originally resisted the sale of popcorn: it was seen as both cheesy and messy. With the coming of the Depression, however, outside concessionaires began leasing the privilege of selling popcorn in theaters, and, at a nickel or ten cents a bag, the profit in the activity soon made itself obvious. Theatre owners started buying large poppers and the aroma of exploded kernels soon began filling theater lobbies.

During World War II sugar was rationed but popcorn was not. Popcorn provided a cheap alternative to scarce and expensive candy, and popcorn sales took off. By 1945, almost half of the popcorn grown in the United States was being eaten in movie theaters. Sales were especially high during Abbott and Costello features; in 1957, Elvis Presley was honored by the Blevins Popcorn Company for his ability to generate high popcorn sales.

Without salt or butter added—and if it is not popped in oil—popcorn is a very nutritious food. One cup of undressed popped corn contains only twenty-seven calories. Popcorn has even been praised as one of "the eleven things that don't cause cancer." But of course movie popcorn always comes with its lovely additives. In 1994, the Center for Science in the Public Interest reported that a tub of movie popcorn with all the trimmings contained more grams of fat than six Big Macs.

Here is my daughter Courtenay, on being a concession person:

> *What my mother remembers vividly about the projectors, I remember about the popcorn machine. I actually still have a scar on my right hand from a burn from that machine. It was a large kettle in a yellowish plexiglass box; at the beginning, we used to use orange-colored flavored oil sticks to pop the popcorn, which I secretly liked better than the healthier choice we later switched to. However, it turned out that coconut oil used to be thought of as bad for you, so we switched. Popping the popcorn was a very specific art. Heat the kettle, drop in the grease, a ladle full of corn, a teaspoon of salt. Pop until done but not all kernels popped or you will burn the corn. Later in life, when I worked behind the counter, I came to realize that the*

popcorn was quite famous around town, as the bus drivers would stop their buses in the middle of a route to get a bag. Usually large buttered. I'd like to think that my obsessive removal of the film of fat and salt from the top of the butter—essentially, I made ghee, I have come to realize—had something to do with its notoriety.

Reid Oechslin, who became The Rectifier of every mechanical device at the theatre, remembers that Marty and Mitch at Victor Products were shocked that we were dumping a pound of corn and six-ounce logs of oil into the twelve-ounce kettle of our Gold Medal Whiz Bang popper:

> That was the only way we could keep up in the early days. Later we dialed back to actually putting in twelve ounces of corn and one four-ounce packet of Lou-Ana oil. We went to extraordinary lengths to keep the Whiz Bang running. You must've picked it for the size cabinet it had (not too big), but it was really undersized and under built for what we were asking it to do. I completely rewired it once because its terminal board was starting to melt. A kettle heat switch only lasted a year. Kettle heating elements would fail at exactly the wrong moment, turning our production from a torrent to a trickle of small, oily, dark kernels. I think we came to think of it as our printing press for producing money—a machine that you definitely would want to keep running when the rest of running an art cinema was so expensive.

Vinegar Hill had a huge lobby, huge, that is, in comparison with the size of the auditorium. We could squeeze one hundred people into it when we had to. The lobby was graced with high, plate-glass windows that faced out onto Market Street. In the corner, by the front door, there was a ticket-selling stand made out of waist-high brick. I stood in that corner for many nights over many years, watching the town drive by. There was also the feeling of being on display.

On our second anniversary an MGM festival was in full swing. It was a snowy, icy night, and we were showing a double feature of *The Fountainhead* and *The Letter*. A patron in a hurry drove up the hill, braked, and then slid straight into the front window. The glass cracked but remained in the mullions.

Vinegar Hill lobby

We hired Charlottesville Glass & Mirror to do the repairs. A few days later I was watching a half-dozen men, working under a broken but intact mass of glass, trying to suction big pieces out of a mullion. Suddenly a section from the top slid down and severed a blood vessel in a man's neck.

The repair work came to an immediate halt. As one of the workmen later said, "The men are so tore-up they can't continue." He offered no further information about the injured man. CGM covered the window openings with plywood and we operated with no view of the street until April.

During the early days I was wired to protect customers and the theatre from all dangers and drunks. I evicted big guys who talked during movies and once took on a crazy man who was trying, in broad daylight, to steal our Mustang. The car was parked in front of the theatre and I looked out and saw someone opening the driver-side door. "Stop, stop!" Chief yelled, as I ran out and yanked on the guy's arm. "Leave him alone!" The man's sweater came off in my hands and he was still in the car, but I scared him enough that he ran away. I was fearless, without blinking; I was protecting the art and our sacred space.

One time there was a man who had been stabbed; Charlottesville's downtown remained, well into the 1980s, a sketchy place. We were showing a matinee of *Chinatown* when the man staggered into the lobby, bleeding from wounds in his chest. David Minckler came down from the booth and took him into the men's room. Once the rescue squad arrived we learned that there had been a fight at Main Street's Virginia Lunch.

In those days people treated movie theatres as dark, shabby places where you could do what you wanted. A crew of old guys had a habit of bringing in a tub of fried chicken; an hour later, there were bones all over the floor. During clean-up we could find everything from dirty diapers, to beer bottles, to composted food. One day Reid went into the men's room and discovered a homeless man asleep in the toilet stall, next to his empty gin bottle.

Most shows went more quietly. A concession person came in thirty minutes before the first show. With luck, the cleaning person had turned on the popcorn warmer to refresh any leftover corn. If the bin was empty, it was time to pop. Then came the set-up of Mr. Coffee. After that you went upstairs, unlocked the safe and brought down the two cash drawers for the concession stand and the ticket booth. Restocking the candy had been done the night before: Hershey with Almonds, Twizzlers, Reese's Cups, C&B Toffees, and the best-sellers, M&M's, Peanut and Plain.

The Coke dispenser had to be checked. The premix, a thick, molassesy syrup, came in an industrial plastic bag stuffed into a cardboard box. A tube from the premix connected with two additional tubes: a water line and a heavy line from the CO2 canister. At the end of the shift there was lots of clean-up; Windexing the glass counters, purging the sugary Coke machine drip, emptying the kernel tray, sweeping the carpet. If there was a new movie coming in, you had to change the sign.

The marquee was a big metal rectangle that faced down Market Street; the bottom was maybe nine feet off the ground. The eight metal tracks on which the letters were hung gave you four lines of information. The letters were black plastic pieces about ten inches high and we never seemed to have enough Z's or E's. You usually put up the sign late at night when it was dark and you were tired and on top of that you had to use a twelve-foot long metal grabber that was supposed to clutch a letter firmly. The top line was a killer: it was far away, you couldn't see, and there was a trick to hooking the grooves of each letter into the metal track. You tended to drop as many letters as you secured during the first try. If you didn't attach each letter firmly—top, bottom, all four slots—you might find your sign blown away by wind the next morning, or hiding in the deadly juniper bushes below.

While I hired all kinds of people to work concessions and to sell tickets, it turned out that a number of my core employees were, like David McWhirter, graduate students in English. The two that have remained the closest friends are Leslie Gossage and Jody DeRitter.

Leslie and Jody were married in 1983 in our backyard. From that day there is a photograph of a smiling Courtenay who, then in the eighth grade, has clearly become tipsy on champagne.

Leslie started out as a cleaning person: "I'd rather do that," she said, "than work for nothing at the library." She quickly graduated to the rank of projectionist and, in 1984, when I spent a year away in Philadelphia, it was Leslie that I asked to manage the theatre. Jody remained a concession-box office worker during his graduate school days, and therefore had to endure the routine humiliations involved in retail:

> I'd been working at Vinegar Hill for three or four years when a crew of students from UVa's Darden School of Business decided to study the operation. They looked over the books and passed out surveys to dozens of audience members, some of whom they interviewed as well. They talked to Ann and probably to a few of Ann's employees, but I wasn't interviewed, so I can't really say much about them or the questions they asked. What I can remember is that when they finally presented their report, we learned that some of our paying customers had singled out the people who sold them popcorn, candy, and drinks as being "rude, surly, and inert." We thought the comment was hilarious, and for the first 48 hours after the report came out, the three of us who worked behind the candy counter talked about getting matching T-shirts, each with one of the adjectives blazoned across the front so the customers could identify us. We ended up not doing that because it turned out that while each of us would have been perfectly happy to be labeled "rude" or "surly," none of us really liked the idea of being called "inert." "Rude" and "surly" sounded like mischaracterizations of the behaviors we used to get a long line of customers into the theatre so that the show could start on time. "Inert" sounded like slander.

While many of my employees did become my friends, I could become a little too involved with some of my worker bees. At least this is a conclusion I have come to after finding the following letter in my files. The letter is undated, but was probably written in the early 1990s:

Dear Ann,

I am very sorry that my neglect in the Celco Credit Union situation came to bear down on you in legal terms. As an employer, you have been especially considerate and I have been grateful for the lengths you've gone to over the past seven years regarding my concerns, financial and otherwise. I can't expect you to continue shouldering my problems with debts and such, especially after those previous times that you helped me out.

The letter continues in this vein and refers to a decision "to release me from the staff."

I still possess a copy of the Show Cause Summons from the General District Court, in which I am commanded to appear on March 25, 1994, at 9 A.M. The amount being charged against me was $1045.34. As a hand-written note reveals, I paid the bill for the garnished wages with check number 11266.

Did I fire him? I really can't remember, although I can say that firing people often had the strange effect of somehow endearing me to them, at least if an open letter dated February 13, 2001, and published in the *C-ville Weekly* is any evidence of the case.

The letter was written by a man named Carol Trainum, Jr., and is entitled "Vinegar Hill Valentine." In it, a self-described "small-town cinephile" recalls discovering foreign films at VHT along with "the idea of having to read a movie while trying to watch it." He is glad we are still around: "seeing a 'David' survive a number of 'Goliaths,' has also changed me." And he duly notes his pleasure at being able, then and now, not only able to watch great movies but "to enjoy fresh-popped corn (with real butter)."

Happy as I may have been to read this letter, I was also somewhat surprised by it, since Trainum, who had cleaned the theatre in the early days, had been fired by me for coming in to do his job on Sunday afternoons while playing White Snake and Black Sabbath at such a volume as to provoke complaints from our elderly early arrivers.

MY PHILOSOPHY OF programming evolved. I came to realize that you had to sit through a certain number of financial disasters—no yanking something if it didn't perform on a weekend. A kind of economic suicide that needed to be accepted. The money losers had to be surrounded by golden geese so that my risk-taking remained modest, while programming continuity soldiered on.

My attitude toward customers also evolved. At first, I was very ashamed when nobody came and I felt this even when our numbers were not all that bad. I could only think of how to fix it and of how not to be in the spotlight while fixing it. Chief usually manned the ticket booth—the site of maximum exposure—and I worked concessions only as a replacement figure. My preferred role has always been Miss Behind-The-Scenes. I solved the problem by becoming a projectionist; I felt protected there, unless I made a technical mistake.

It's striking to remember how much of our lives Reid and I spent in the projection booth. The space was a lightless warren, ten feet deep by twelve feet wide. To get to it, you walked through the lobby, up six stairs, and past the world's smallest office. Once inside the projection booth, there was a long skinny work counter on the left with rewind spindles both manual and motored for 35 and 16mm. This was where we built up the films. To the right, there were three glass portholes facing the auditorium: two of the openings were for our 35mm Super Simplexes, the third was for our Hortson 16mm projector, a machine we used more than you would think. The walls were concrete block and covered with film schedules from ours and other venues and quirky postcards from fans, former employees, bold travelers with cinema on their minds.

Sometimes I did come downstairs. One triumphant public moment came when Leslie Gossage and I organized a movie poster sale. After ten years, we had amassed an inventory of hundreds of posters, all labeled and alphabetized for possible reuse. So we typed up a list, placed an ad in our schedule, and posted a big sign in the VHT window.

We held the sale on a Saturday afternoon before the 3:00 matinee. The offerings were arranged alphabetically by title in boxes in the lobby. People began streaming in and unspooling posters on the carpet. There is a vivid memory of seeing the sexually charged *Blue Velvet* poster in broad daylight, with Kyle holding a swooning Isabella as if he's going to break her. I had kept back a dozen cherished posters like the one for *Going Places*, which now hangs in my bedroom. Miou-Miou stands with her thumb out and her sundress off her shoulders to her waist, although we only see her from the back. Do you think she got a ride? Yes, and in the car was a skinny waif, the family daughter, who wants to hit the road too. She was played by a twenty-year old who grew up to become an actress who never looked her age: Isabelle Huppert.

"I love retail," Leslie said, when the sale was done. We had cleared over five hundred dollars.

While many of my customers became people I called by name, complaints did sometimes arise. When the projectors were down there was grousing about the delay between movies. After we installed our espresso machine in 1991, there were more frequent skirmishes at the concession stand about the wait. Early on we had a terrible air conditioning and circulation system that we could not afford to replace, and on hot summer evenings people said, "It's so close in there, I can't breathe."

The most significant complaints were about the movies. The blurbs on our schedules expressed strong opinions and people sometimes felt misled. If they exited after fifteen minutes and asked for their money back, we gave it to them. But staying in the auditorium for an hour and then leaving? That was another matter.

In 1996, the last year we published and mailed out film calendars, I received a two-page single-spaced typed letter from a disgruntled customer. He and his wife had gone to see the Dutch language film *Antonia's Line*. Roger Ebert had given it four-stars, even comparing it to the e.e. cummings poem, "anyone lived in a pretty how town."

I was very committed to seeing films before I showed them—that's why I went to film festivals. But sometimes we had to write a blurb before seeing a film. We used all the film criticism help we could find: Siskel and Ebert, J. Hoberman, and my moral compass when it came to movie reviewing, Stanley Kaufmann. In our blurb for *Antonia's Line*, which none of us had seen, we described it as "a grand family saga, rich in fabulist and political storytelling, handsome and soothing."

Our customer found the movie "disappointing" and "after 55–65 minutes (not more)," as he wrote, he and his wife walked out and asked for a refund. This was his first objection. "To our great surprise" the letter continues,

> *Vinegar Hill's representative at the theatre would not accept objection #1, on the grounds that the film had been widely acclaimed. Our disappointment in the film was not legitimate, apparently. If I had ordered a pair of shoes described as size nine, and I received size eight, I would not expect the company to object to a refund because the shoes were popular.*
>
> *To our second objection (that the film was not as advertised), we were frankly shocked by the answer of the person I spoke to: "It's Art. You take a risk."*
>
> *We feel entitled to a refund. You may write a check for $11 to _____.*
>
> *Should you choose not to, I feel it reasonable to distribute, off of Vinegar Hill property, copies of the attached "Warning".*
>
> *You have my word that I do not consider such a move out of vindictiveness.*

Those are a few highlights from the letter. From the WARNING, I quote this paragraph:

> *After my experience with Vinegar Hill, the theatre gives me no choice but to conclude that it believes that one filmgoer cannot legitimately be disappointed with the well-received film if it claims to be "art," and that art houses are too good for the usual practice of mainstream cinemas' of refunding dissatisfied customers who leave early.*

I never saw one of the WARNINGS posted. The incident ended with my reply:

> *Dear _____,*
>
> *I have enclosed a check to _____ for $13—reimbursement for two tickets to the Saturday April 20, 1996, performance of* Antonia's Line *which you and your wife did not enjoy, and additional $2.00 reimbursement for the mailing list from which I have stricken your name. Vinegar Hill Theatre cannot afford to have customers like you. Please stay home with your teddy bear and your blankie.*
>
> *Yours, truly, Ann Porotti*

12
THE LONG DIVORCE

"I'm afraid I'll end up like that."

It was Christmas of 1979 and Chief and I were talking in the kitchen, which is where we had our serious talks. It was and is a tiny kitchen—a nine by nine square—so we were less than six feet apart, with Chief sitting on one butcher block counter and me on another, the window and the sink between us.

I had read the newspaper story and had just asked him about George C, a man who had been accused of soliciting a minor.

"So, what am I supposed to say," I answered, "is that a bid for some kind of sympathy?"

"If you knew a person who had what someone might call 'urges,' and yet you wanted to be with him, well …" His voice trailed off.

"The main thing is the lying. I just can't take it anymore."

Then I thought of the moment that fall when I walked into Court Square Tavern and dumped a glass of white wine on my husband's head. Chief looked surprised but not alarmed. Then he laughed. He was sitting with three women. Even at the time, I knew it was the kind of thing that people only do in movies.

"Remember the Bergman movie, A.G? I think you and I will be like that couple in forty years."

"Are you talking about *Scenes from a Marriage*?"

"Yeah, you know, they've been divorced forever and then they end up in bed in a hotel room. That'll be us."

"Let's get back to the topic at hand. I have rented an apartment—it's over on Lexington Avenue. We can share it; we'll split the time between here and there."

Chief nodded but he wasn't agreeing or disagreeing. For someone who loved to talk he could be very quiet. His resistance to anything I might ask took the form of never admitting what had been done. Then he said, "Well, you know, it's going to take a year, at least according to the laws of Virginia."

"A year—what are you talking about?"

"In this state a divorce can only take effect a year after the last intercourse."

"I'll be seeing a lawyer, Susan White, next week. But I really don't get it: why do you want to stay married?"

"But I like it here. I like our life—you, the kids, the cats, the cozy house."

"You like the services, but you always have to go out for more treats."

To this, Chief made no answer. He just smiled.

WHEN IT CAME to marriage and sexual betrayal, I had a learning curve that only I calibrated. I might not have left Chief if he had been more respectful of me and not so flagrant and proud of his wandering. I was, oddly, a public figure, in part because my husband was the local Lab. In his Casanova-ing he would show up on women's doorsteps at two in the morning. Expecting something. Once on Election Day I was voting at my precinct at Alumni Hall and a League of Women Voters volunteer who was handing out *I Voted* stickers told me, very impromptu, that Chief had "dropped by her house" one night after flirting with her at Fellini's. It wasn't so much the betrayal as the public display of it that wore me down.

And, although Chief was busy, I was no slouch myself. At some point in early 1979 my boyfriend bonanza finally caught up with me. Before I could even contemplate a divorce, however, Peter Bacque and I had to be finished with our stormy affair.

One cold day in February Peter stopped by the theatre. I was previewing an Ingmar Bergman triple feature: *Through a Glass Darkly, The Silence,* and *Winter Light.* I came down to the lobby from the projection booth when he showed up. We were alone.

"I'll be moving to Richmond soon," he said. "Got hired by the *Times-Dispatch.*"

I wasn't surprised—he had once described us as "two grinding wheels"—and I knew he had been job-hunting. Now he could get away; numbness and relief for both of us. After he left I comforted myself in the melancholy chamber of *Winter Light*; movies were always my anti-depressant.

But things with Peter were not quite over. A year later he came back to town and tracked me down at the C&O bar where I was drinking with a girlfriend. There was anguish on his face, liquid eyes, slumped shoulders; his mother had just died and he wanted to talk. He needed the tenderness he had once written to me about. But he had been too careless with me, too open about all the others. I had nothing for him, which as I write this, seems so brutal. I sent him on his way and never saw him again. It's easy to look back and to judge myself, now, on the page. But I am trying, as best I can, to avoid the seductions of regret.

Because there was something withheld with Peter, something not shared. I only began to make sense of it when, soon after beginning this book, I ran into an old friend at a Christmas party.

"How are you," I said.

"Fine. And you?" she replied.

"Fine, busy, but I've been writing. And things have come up. From the deep past. Are you still in touch with him? Our mutual friend?"

Her face got that look of sad but slightly fresh pain. And trying to be careful because we were at the center of a noisy room, she said:

"He died. Last year, or a little before. He died alone in his sleep at home."

Then my friend said something else, something wonderfully and terribly clarifying: "I heard he was gay."

In the obituary about Peter I googled the next morning, it was therefore almost comforting to read the following words: "He was a loyal friend for twenty-seven years to Bill W."

YOU MAY ASK, reader, why I tell you so much about my romantic confusion. About all the other men. The answer is simply this: I give it to you because it was the experience of this very confusion, all the relentless searching and the not finding, that made it possible for me to be able to choose, when the chance came.

AND YOU WILL not be surprised that once the romance with Peter ended, I found myself falling head over heels for a different someone; it became clear to me that my marriage was, finally, over. My conversation with Chief in the kitchen was therefore one in which I felt myself backed by a sense of new possibilities.

The new guy presented himself at my cousin Barbara's second wedding, in October 1979. His name was Doug Magee.

But first—this is the moment in the screwball comedy when pages of the calendar fly into the wind and we travel back to May, 1970, when Doug walked me down the aisle of the Milford Sacred Heart Church for Barbara's *first* wedding, to Joe Quinn. I was the lone matron in a sea of single maids all wearing peach; as a nursing mother to four-month old Courtenay, who had recently joined two-and-a-half year-old Ian, my concerns were about milk stains. I knew very little about my escort in the shiny blue suit, who was also Joe's Best Man. Both scholarship boys at Amherst, Doug and Joe had been roommates and athletes. And now, a year out of college, Doug was entering Columbia Divinity School and looking towards a career in social activism; he was also married and the father of a son. Doug and I were the "young parents," our futures somewhat mapped out for us, at the wedding of twenty-something graduate students. I could have used some of their ambition to offset my exhaustion.

Nine years later, on Columbus Day Weekend, 1979, Doug Magee and I met again. He was the official wedding photographer for Barbara's second wedding and had been charged with picking up the Matron of Honor at Boston's Logan Airport. I am traveling *sans enfants, sans mari*. We settled into the three-hour drive north to Tamworth, New Hampshire, where Barbara was to marry Chris Alt. We got down to business, weaving together our personal histories.

"Kathy and I divorced early on—with me getting custody of Tim. Then I moved us to Spanish Harlem in the City. I'm a freelance photographer, a vegetarian, and I've written a book about death penalty prisoners—though the last two don't pay," he chuckled.

The CV on offer from me for romantic seduction included a steel trap memory of hundreds of movies, cast and crew, and intellectual assessments

Barbara and Ann at 1979 wedding

thereof. I thought *that* was the sexy thing. Not all men responded to my knowingness, but when they did, things really clicked. My appearance was not the main entrée, though at thirty-four I looked younger and was confidently bra-less. I didn't get to practice my craft as much as I might have liked in Charlottesville, however, but, wherever I was, the stuff in the head was driving the bus. Sometimes I found it—with Peter in the afternoons, and then with Phil at Telluride—but that day in the car with Doug Magee I fell as fast and as hard as I ever had.

Pulling into the driveway in Tamworth, I thought, "This could be the best evening of my life," high as I was from our talk about Didion, The Band, and Bertolucci.

Around 1 o'clock in the morning, we paused.

A: Uh oh. I think I'm in trouble. Where am I sleeping tonight? Remember—Chris had this elaborate schedule of locals who were hosting us out-of-towners. I'm not supposed to be here. Where are you staying?
D: (Looking out the fogged-up car windows) Down this driveway, I think. Same place as Barb's brother Billy.
A: OK, I see Billy's Datsun. So you have a bed, but what about me?
D: We can stay here. In the car.

There was a month of good times. While Doug went to Alabama interviewing death row inmates for his book *Slow Coming Dark*, his son Tim flew to Charlottesville. Now I was responsible for three kids. Whew!

Doug and I met up in New York and caught a late-night screening of *Apocalypse Now* at the Ziegfeld Theatre. Things went south during a post-Christmas road trip to Maine, where Doug was shooting photos for an article about the elderly poor. Working out of motels in snowy Augusta, we drove around. The electricity from our earlier conversations was nowhere to be found; things got very silent between us and never more so than when I said, "I think I might be in love with you." He replied, "I am not prepared to hear that."

Nights were spent soaking in a bathtub with Jack Daniels, a massive block of fudge from the Old Sturbridge Gift Shop, and perhaps a joint or two. A kinder, gentler *Sid and Nancy*, although that story didn't make it to the screen for seven more years.

In the end, I burned Doug's letters under the theatre marquee while trying to avoid setting fire to my beloved Joan & David suede boots. People at work tiptoed around my broken heart. Months later, I heard Doug had reconnected with an old high school girl friend. Then a package arrived addressed to Courtie and Ian. It was a contact sheet and negatives from his visit back in October, Doug's lovely candids of the kids, the cats, and me, showing unmade beds, an epidemic of hanging plants, the oak kitchen table, center of my casual hippie life. This parcel I did not destroy, but kept it safe.

THE MOMMY-YEARS, that half-a-decade when I was pregnant twice, breast-feeding and chasing after toddlers, had its shock and awe. Growing a child in and outside of your body is the awe, but the shock comes with the loneliness, the boredom, the responsibility. The mommy job description might have read: Must be able to cook, clean, repair, teach, endure. No experience required. Make it up as you go.

I missed the few girlfriends I had from graduate school. During Chief's law school years, Edie King had been my one great pal and I was despondent when she and her husband moved back to Maine to work in state politics. I don't know what I dreamed about, but career aspirations were the distant thunder of other women. You go to college and then suddenly life casts its giant net over you and it's easy to feel lost.

Homesick was what I was. I missed mortadella, hated our vine-ridden forests, and longed for a New England summer. Heat waves and sultry humidity: I had to find the water.

There was a beautiful pond in Fluvanna County that belonged to Betty, a woman Chief had met through the Virginia Players. Betty and I quickly became close. Out at the pond we held impromptu weekend parties, multi-generation affairs with inner tubes, canoes, potluck and pot, warm beer, warmer bad red wine. Girls swimming in fluttery transparent blouses, living out a strange confidence as many of us showed our wares. Betty was a dazzling, indiscriminate flirt, married to Chad, the world's most dour man. She adored Chief, but so did other women, and Betty was also good to me, often caring for my kids when I needed help or just because she liked them.

One day when I was alone at home I received a phone call from Chad. I was sitting on the couch under the big windows in the living room at our incomplete new house on Rothery Road. Chad told me he had proof—

letters—that Chief and Betty had been having a long-term affair. It was being carried on mostly during their lunch hours.

This was 1973, five years into our marriage. And it was the beginning of Chief's lawyerly but disingenuous explanation of his sexual urges. The forever-damaged friendship with a woman I deeply liked now took a back seat to her creepy husband who suggested that I start sleeping with him in order to get revenge.

That evening I drove myself to my part time job at John Tuck's Gaslight Restaurant. Suddenly I found myself on the 250 Bypass, with all the cars speeding past me. I realized my legs had gone numb and that I had stopped driving the car. I steered the old Mustang onto a shoulder and had a good cry before going on to work. What did it all mean? Is adultery also marriage? Do I stay or do I go, and go where? How will I take care of my children?

It's doubtful I answered any of these questions at the time, but I did resolve to ask Chief when he came home if Chad's call was true. "What if you knew someone who did this," he said, through my tears and anger, "but he really loved you very much?" Chief was skilled at speaking of us both in the second person. I accepted his dissembling because I had no other options, and, by my compliance, I signaled that I would not challenge Chief's insistence on what amounted to an open marriage.

At twenty-nine I was sexy and aggressive, but I was also a square. I thought marriage involved some sort of commitment. Then, within a year of Chad's phone call, I had taken up with Peter and believed I had found what I was looking for. Chief and I would carry on, but with increasingly parallel lives.

Five years later, after the break-up with Peter, I tried my best to find a way to love only my husband. Then I ran into Doug, and I was a goner. By early 1980 I had decided to leave Chief, still believing, perhaps, that Doug and I had a future.

As the divorce unfolded, the big issue was custody. Of our two children, of course, but also of the three buildings and two businesses Chief and I owned together. I loved living in the house on Rothery Road and had every intention of staying in it. I had little feeling for Fellini's, but, above all, I desperately wanted to hold on to Vinegar Hill.

It is therefore still a little surprising to remember that I was the one to move out.

I did so because Chief simply refused to budge, as if our strange marital arrangement could go on forever.

The only question to be asked when a relationship fails is simple: What was my role in this? I am the Yes-No girl: it was always easier for me to agree and to put up with something while I brooded about my actual wishes. All my life, I have managed possible harm with initial consent and later dissent. I did this with my parents and their rules, with my abuser, and with my first husband, although Chief's lack of spirit for a fight allowed me to stay in my marriage without really saying either "Yes" or "No."

Whatever else I was doing during the period of our separation, I was determined to keep track of my feelings, as evidenced by pages typed on my trusty Selectric:

> New Year's Eve … packing up the essentials to take over to the new apartment, and listening to Bette Midler's impassioned WHEN A MAN LOVES A WOMAN … a temptation to draw imprecise and easy conclusions. New Year's Day … I woke up in a new apartment, with a sense of complete aloneness—just the plants, boxes and two sticks of furniture and me … I was supposed to cook a turkey with Courtenay, but I overslept … thought it was 11:10 but turned out to be 1:55—when will I learn to tell time.
>
> I barely made it to work on time. Ian was in the projection booth and when I went to hug him, I started to cry. "I miss you so much," I said. "You should have thought of that before you moved out," he said. He seemed worried that the people filing into the theatre might see me crying. More embarrassment about the separation—then he disappeared into the dark movie.
>
> *Camelot* was no distraction. A foolish movie, not about love but about royal whim and the dangerous traditions of coquetry, chivalry, pride, and truculence. Chief told me that I looked awful, and I suspect he was right. Why am I past the point of forgiveness? Why is it different, why for five years have I blanked out what existed and seen only what was convenient?
>
> Dinner at the house: Ian said that my mother called. Apparently she asked him "Where I was" and when he said, "At her apartment," Anita said, "Who's she sleeping with there?" I fell apart on the spot—big tears, bigger pain. The double threat of my mother trying desperately to hurt me, and to do it through my kids.

Chief looked concerned and left hurriedly. I tried to explain that the separation was not so I could sleep with a lot of other men, but because Chief and I weren't getting along the way married people should. I guess I had to tell them that Chief had a girlfriend too. Once they realized this, they realized that was why Chief had been so adamant in telling them that the separation wasn't my fault but that he was more to blame. Ian got very depressed and alert—saying that he knew who it was, someone named Rebecca, that they met at the bar and she had feathers in her hair.

Chief returned, expecting me to leave for the apartment. When I kept vacuuming he said he was going to sleep but within minutes said he was going over to Rebecca's to sleep because he didn't want me having to go over to the apartment at 2:00 am. Looked like a planned exit to me.

There is more of this—but you get the idea. "I hope that this arrangement works out," I went on to write, but I cannot have really meant it, because Chief soon tired of having to spend his evenings watching the kids at Rothery Road and within a month of my moving out I was back and Chief was gone. I had the house. Getting custody of the theatre, however, was not going to prove so simple.

Perhaps Ian ought to have the last word on the decade in which so many of us lived out the long divorce:

> While I was at music camp in the summer of 1981, VHT showed the Arthur Penn film, Night Moves, from 1975, a candidate for being a perfect movie. Alan Sharp's screenplay is full of questions and a few answers, too. The protagonist, played by Gene Hackman, is a fantasy—an ex-pro football player turned private eye, a sensitive dude who drinks wine, listens to classical music and reads, in addition to being able to have civil face-to-face discourse with his estranged wife's handicapped lover, played by Harris Yulin. Then he gets sucked into an old-school criminal ring, where murders and betrayals occur in a jumble of revenge and theft. The ending, exhilarating and haunting, is one of the best sequences, with the wounded hero stuck in a boat steering itself in an endless circle.

At the heart of the story is the search for Delly, the lost daughter, played by sixteen-year-old Melanie Griffith. It's the old woman-as-victim plot except in this movie the women are stronger than the bewildered men. Can there be a feminist film noir? It's all very much about a mid-Seventies moment. At one point Hackman asks his girlfriend Jennifer Warren if Delly is liberated—there's a famous scene when Griffith removes her shirt—and she answers, "When we all get liberated like Delly, there's going to be fighting in the streets."

When I first saw the movie at the University Theater in Charlottesville, it had a big cardboard promotional sign, with the foreboding image of deep water at night. The film's two central locales are Hollywood and the Florida Keys, exotic backdrops, but also philosophical equals, where certain egos and temperaments go to live and play. With a spectacular supporting cast—Warren most notably—Penn delivers 1940s intrigue dressed up in '70s clothes, talk, and outlook. The film ties to the past without pretense; characters talk like it's either an interrogation or a therapy session. The candor and disclosure is through the roof. Hackman's Harry Moseby's brute strength and fighting skills put him ahead of the curve in this world, but he's behind in the battle of wits and strategy, as his opponents sway, manipulate, and exploit his old-fashioned ethics. All the while, there is an endearing and complicated relationship with his wife, played by Susan Clark. It is one of my favorite screen marriages, the two of them going in circles and sometimes circling back to each other as they intersect other loves.

The cottage at the Cape

13
THE SUMMER oF '82

Half a lifetime ago I took myself to the beach. My marriage had ended; the divorce came through in the spring of 1981. I wanted a break from my life. So I took a sabbatical, with water.

When I look at the cottage I have now inherited, I think: How did my mother end up with this place? Somehow she managed to position herself so that my grandmother Ardelia gave it to her.

Perhaps Ardelia recognized a woman who had, like herself, achieved a hard-won autonomy. And Anita did care for Ardelia in her last years. She changed her soiled clothes and never put her in a nursing home.

The cottage came to my mother in 1968. Her sister Martha inherited *The Barbara,* the place next door, a one-step-above-camping rental. Eventually Martha knocked it down and built a modest three-bedroom Cape. Her son Billy moved into it in the mid-1970s and was firmly ensconced there when I turned up for my restorative summer.

In the summer of 1982, there was peace between Anita and Billy, but things had not always been so tranquil. The Seven Years War between sisters Martha and Anita began in 1974 shortly after my grandmother died, and lasted until late 1981, when my cousin Barbara's first baby, Lily, was born.

It's hard to say what the cause was, perhaps a dispute over a fur coat or a bank book. The Molinari siblings were known scrappers in The Plains and on this occasion, when trouble broke out, Anita and Martha battled with hard blows. Cousin Billy came to Martha's rescue and stopped the fight by hitting Anita in the face with a breadboard. Another version has it that Anita whacked Martha with the breadboard and Billy then hit Anita with his fist.

My mother went to her dentist immediately and for the next seven years she refused to speak to Martha. Cousin Billy, her favorite nephew, she now called a murderer. Anita demanded loyalty for her injury and expected me and my family to avoid the DiVitto clan, but we disobeyed her. She sealed her vendetta with the installation of a six-foot high, ninety-foot long stockade fence between the adjacent beach properties.

Détente was achieved after Barbara became a mother. Anita baked some bread and waited for Barbara to visit the DiVitto beach house. Then she marched around the fence and knocked.

"I came to see the new baby," Anita said. "Can I come in?"

Leaving a speechless Barbara and Billy at the doorway, Anita swept into the cottage, tossed the loaves on the kitchen counter, and that was the end of the family feud. No apology, no explanation. Anita and Billy picked up their relationship where they had left it before he whacked her, resuming evenings of drinking brandy and sharing homemade pizzas.

MY MOTHER DID not always seem completely glued together, and she knew that people sometimes read her as crazy. She did not however tamp down her flamboyancy. Always cackling. She did cartwheels down the beach well into her sixties. Anita and cousin Billy were similar in their theatricality, bonded to each other, and, ultimately, devoted.

Anita made sure I had piano and dancing lessons. She fought my father for those things, as she insisted on driving me to classes with his beloved Ford coupe. Not much confiding, though, because whatever you told her might later on be used against you.

We never talked about what I was reading, though I sometimes dipped into her pot boilers, like *The Carpetbaggers* and *Peyton Place*.

For all of that, what I got from Anita was resilience. When I think of my mother, I see a woman at holidays baking a dozen pies—Hubbard squash and Macintosh apple—and a cloud-like golden sponge cake and then loading it all into the Ford and driving over to Aunties Josephine and Mary Ianzitto, and Donny Palmer's mother Lillian, and Minka Marcus, and Lil Ferrucci. Just giving it all away.

As a child, I saw her doing a hundred things at once and they all came out perfect. When she taught you how to do a thing, you had better pick it up quickly and without errors. In the eighth grade, I took Sewing in Home Economics. Our class was to produce a blouse with a *jabot*—tiny vertical pleats running from the collar to the hem on either side of the front button band. The teacher gave us the option of pleated or not, depending on how confident we felt about our stitching. When my mother heard about the compromise I could barely restrain her from calling out the teacher on her "shoddy practice." As a compromise, my shirt had the pleated *jabot* and therefore became one more example of the many sink or swim skills I learned from my mother.

Another was how to drive a stick-shift car in a snowstorm—but that came with a preliminary injury-free car accident. It was the week before Christmas 1959, and I was fifteen, driving on a Learner's. My mother organized a trip to Milford center with me, my brother Rudy, and my best friend Vicky Voltz. The purpose was a little holiday shopping and a visit to my Assistant Postmaster father's chaotic Santa's workshop—just to say hi. Rudy and I loved to disturb Dad at work, settling into those shiny wooden chairs that spun around, wheeling forward and back. A block square, the Milford Post office was a granite building from the days when the local quarries, and my father's father, a stone cutter, filled every public space with Roman majesty. We thought it was really big, and loved to hang out. The busiest time was Christmas when dozens of regular carriers, plus seasonal college employees—several of my boyfriends got jobs there—sorted mail into countless slots in a vast open room. Moveable canvas bins and sacks in a continuous traffic jam of packages and mail.

My mother decided that I, a high school sophomore, having had my first Driver's Ed lesson, should practice by driving us to Milford.

I looked outside and saw a skim coat of white powder. We piled into the car: Rudy and Vicky in the back seat, Mom in the passenger side, I was the driver. The clutch and I have mostly been good friends—I understand the

Anita and Martha, 1980s

mechanics. On this snowy day I reversed nicely out of our driveway, and first, second, and third-geared my way to the intersection of Mellen Street and Route 140 where, oh shit, there is a STOP sign! I knew enough to do that, but did not know enough about how to brake the car on the hill while carefully easing into on-coming traffic. It seemed for a moment that I needed one more foot. Hah! Like jumping into a skipping rope, I waited until it looked safe and then gunned the engine so as not to slide back down the hill. I lost control of the car and ended up on the wrong side of Route 140. And then out of the snowy fog came another car. I hit it hard, glued as my terrified foot was to the gas pedal. As accidents go, it was slow and quiet. No one was hurt although my father's precious Ford was totally destroyed and he didn't speak to me for weeks. Fifty years later, my friend Vicky remembers that I was so flustered because the occupants of the other car were four handsome seniors from neighboring Mendon. She wondered if that was the reason why, even after we both landed in the same snow bank, I kept hitting their car.

BY THE SUMMER of 1982 I had learned to find the friction point. When I headed north in early July, I was driving my stick-shift 1979 green Saab, purchased almost new in the winter of 1980. It was to become my getaway car.

I had driven Ian and Courtenay to music camp in Maine where they would be installed for a month. Then Voise and I drove to Hopedale to see my mother. We had a few days of family chit-chat wherein I detected that even though Anita and I had agreed months earlier that I could spend four weeks alone at the Cape house, she was having second thoughts.

"What are you doing, exactly? Who's running the theatre this time?"

Her effective interview style since childhood featured both good and bad cop.

"Reid, and the staff. Chief if they have a problem."

Little did I know.

"I might have a rental third week of July."

I sat silent.

"Will you have to go home early?" she asked.

"Nope, I can stay with Billy," I said.

Then I popped the question. "Mom, could you let me have fifty bucks? I can't take any cash out of the theatre for a week, and I need to buy some groceries."

I don't think she was expecting the request; I never asked for money, she usually sent five dollars to the kids for birthdays, more at Christmas. Financially I had been living on the margins since my divorce. Chief gave me a total of $250 in child support each month. My salary at the theatre added $1000 more. And I had the usual—utilities, car payment, home mortgage, plus a loan for substantial house repairs. My plan was to live on $50 a week during my summer away. But already I need a donation.

There was a mighty long pause, and then she said, "I don't think I have that money to give you."

She made a gesture where she showed me her teeth, and then touched them with her fingers to see if they were all still there.

Over her lifetime Anita had given herself excellent dental care to make up for the ravages of wartime malnutrition. Her teeth were mostly her own and a prized possession.

I have never forgotten that moment. It came to make more sense to me years later, however, when my friend Franny Phillips said to me, "Your mother was so proud of you, she used to say 'Oh, you know, Annie's a millionaire.'"

In the morning, Anita and I said our goodbyes; I made myself a mortadella sandwich for lunch, and Voisine and I jumped into the Saab and headed for the Cape. I have taken this trip hundreds of times. I remember my Dad meandering through all these small towns—Mansfield, Bridgewater, Easton—changing it up each year, exploring. Then they built Route 495 and dull driving became the norm.

Until the late 1930s Cape Cod was a peninsula shaped like an arm with a bent elbow that stuck out into the Atlantic Ocean. Commercial vessels wanted a faster route for shipping between New York and Boston, so the peninsula was severed from the mainland when the Army Corps of Engineers built two bridges—Sagamore and Bourne, named for towns at either end of the isthmus—and dug a deep canal between them. Vacation began the minute we drove over the canal. And our first stop was Louis' Variety Store at Sagamore where we would buy mortadella sliced thin and studded with irregular polka dots of pistachio and white fat. We ate it with Sicilian bread, hard crust on the outside, angel-food-cake white inside, not sweet but puffy, and shaped like a big brown horn, *il cornetto*. Never enough of that to go around.

Our family place was always called the cottage, even though Cavi called it *The Miami* after he bought it from Mr. Moro in the late 1930s. A stocky meat cutter who delivered provisions to towns in southeastern Massachusetts and on the Cape, Mr. Moro built the cottage in the days before they built the canal. It had asphalt shingles on the outside that mimicked fake red brick. A big cozy kitchen inside with white-oak floors, charming plywood cabinets stained to look like heart pine. The cottage, including two tiny bedrooms, was heated by a propane gas furnace. There was a poured concrete basement which doubled as the garage for the owner's prized automobile.

The original Moro house, 500 square feet, included a tiny airplane-prototype inside toilet; access to the basement was via a trapdoor, and then you were on your own in finding the underground hot shower spigot over a wooden pallet. As the families grew, Cavi added a sleeping porch, and two more bedrooms. There were often eight of us in this house for a month—four kids, two adult couples. One bathroom.

Mr. Moro had lived in the cottage for a decade and then there was the "incident"—there are so many legends about this occurrence that none carry weight. But the Moro family decided to sell the cottage, and Cavigioli, a good friend of his fellow butcher, asked to buy it. An alternative narrative claims that Cavi won it in a poker game.

Our part of Cape Cod, especially the Dennis beach, was rural and not valued. The Yankee settlers of Dennis resided inland on streets named Whig, Corporation, and Howes. The beach was outlier environs, perhaps even less prized than lobsters were by the native peoples who first inhabited the area.

Today when you head out of the cottage you climb over a fifteen-foot dune. Back in the day, the sand was plowed every year and so you walked out the door and straight onto the beach.

The beauty lay in the expanse. Only twenty feet out from the house you could see the whole curve of the bay. Immediately to the northwest lay Sandy Neck—a peninsula protecting Barnstable Harbor—and beyond that the Sagamore Bridge, then a notch concealing Plymouth, further west the lights of the Irish Riviera, and then Boston. High above planes flew on course to Europe. To the east, tucked in beyond Eastham, were the wetlands of Wellfleet, and, when it was clear, the 250-foot Provincetown tower light blinked on the horizon.

Cape Cod Bay is so wide, and the beaches it borders are so shallow, that it produces a unique tidal sequence. There are two high tides and two low tides every day, and they advance fifty minutes, plus or minus, daily. Say the tide was high at 9:53 am. Then you walked out the kitchen door across fifty feet of white sand and jumped into water that was seven to twelve feet deep, the depth depending on the phase of the moon. At 4:31 pm there would be a low tide where the water had retreated perhaps half a mile, and you walked that distance out to swim. The ocean spent the time between the high and the low tide slowly uncovering the wide beach and its hermit crabs, sand dollars, sea eels, moon snails. Later on that same day, precisely at 10:02 pm, there was another high tide, followed by a low tide at 4:39 am. One day over, Goodnight Moon.

During my summer away I didn't spend a lot of time thinking; it was more about sensation. In my body and out of my mind. Always, go outside and look at the sky, the clouds, the night, the stars. The natural world is more important than your plan, and if you can submit, you stand a good chance of meeting the best expression of yourself.

There were times when the beach was empty, and I often stayed out all day. In the morning I put on my black Gottex swimsuit with the purple orchid up the front and the tiny spaghetti straps that crossed low on my back and I didn't take it off until dinnertime. In the cooler evenings I walked the dog in my sheer cotton, green wrap-dress. Easy on, easy off; no shoes, never socks, occasional underwear.

My superego had been left back at Vinegar Hill; I forgot the "shoulds." I did not think to myself, "I must clean the house," as my mother did when she came to the Cape, only appearing on the beach for her brief daily swim in late afternoon.

At low tide I moved from shallow to shallow and dried myself on the hot sand. Days of swimming and walking, of being too hot and then cooling off. In the early 1980s the beach had not yet flattened out, it had many ups and downs, channels and depressions where the water gathered into pools. And these pools, after standing in the sun for six hours, became as warm as a bathtub.

There was one small interruption. One Monday morning the cottage phone rang.

It was Chief.

"What's up? Why are you calling?" I asked.

"Well, there's been a robbery."

"What are you talking about?"

"At the theatre. Money has been taken."

"How the hell did that happen?"

"It appears that someone hid in the crawl space and stayed there until after the last show. Then they took everything."

"Did you call the police?"

"Eventually."

"How did they get into the safe?"

There was a pregnant pause and then Chief said, "They took the whole safe."

"The whole safe—you're kidding!"

"The safe—yes, the safe. Over three thousand dollars plus payroll checks."

"That's money from three nights. You mean nobody did the night deposit for the entire weekend? I can't believe it."

And then I hung up the phone.

AND I COULDN'T believe it. Here I was, trying to live on $50 a week, and we'd just lost the receipts for one of our biggest weekends of the year. We were showing *Breaker Morant*, first run. The percentage on a first-run movie was high, at least forty, maybe fifty percent. Whatever had happened to us, we still owed New World Pictures at least $1200, and we had lost twice that and more.

When you lose that amount of cash, you just keep going forward, living on the money you make the next day. Chief always thought it was an inside job, a disgruntled former employee. Several days after the theft, the stolen payroll checks were returned to the theatre by mail.

On my long, often solitary days, I suppose I wondered, "Why am I back in Massachusetts"? I had created my silent retreat after an especially exhausting final boyfriend bonanza, but uncannily I had also ended up back in a place I had fled long ago. Cape Cod was not exactly Milford-Hopedale, but it was close enough, and my mental archive was deep. I thought about Bobby Foley, my last high school boyfriend, about how unstable he was and yet about the tolerance he had earned with romantic dinners at Milford's Sorrento Room. In my sophomore year in college, Foley transferred to Marietta and then stalked me until I agreed to resume our relationship. One Sunday afternoon he followed me from the dining hall to my dormitory and pulled a gun out of his coat. Rather than get shot, or watch him shoot himself, I agreed to his demands. But, once Bobby could have me, he got bored and within a few months I got serious about my studies. Bobby joined the fraternity brutes at Delta Upsilon. If I wanted to see him during the summer of 1982, all I had to do was dial 911—he was now a policeman in Milford.

Anita showed up for a few days during my first two weeks at the cottage. She was curious and was also checking on potential dog damage. But three-year old Voise, as in Courvoisier, my mother's favorite cocktail, with a splash of orange juice, was a model guest. And cousin Billy adored her and welcomed us into his home for the third week of my Cape stay.

Billy lived in the basement kitchen, down out of the wind. Upstairs there were three bedrooms and a big living room with views; in the Italian fashion, the windows were shut to keep out dangerous breezes and the blinds were drawn in the same spirit of ethnic paranoia. He lived alone but had a parade of girlfriends. He kept house in piles of organized clutter and lots of books from the Dennis Transfer station where locals recycled generously. Broken musical instruments turned up for repair and then became objects he learned to play. His heroes ranged from Emerson and Thoreau to Scott and Helen Nearing and their back-to-the-land experiment. Billy was perhaps most famous for his imitation of Robert De Niro in *Taxi Driver*: "Hey, you talkin' to me?" I still cannot watch that movie.

At five a.m. I hear Billy tapping on my door. A pink sunrise streaked with blue-grey is just coming up over the marsh. Gulp my coffee, stick a piece of buttered toast in my mouth; my hands gather the tools for our morning adventure. A plastic bucket, a metal rake with a short handle, the clam ring. The outfit is more of a challenge: old sneakers for sure, a bathing suit or shorts but serious warmth for the upper body. I take a small member of the cottage hoodie collection from hooks by the back door. Billy and I jump into the blue Explorer he has been warming up in the driveway—early mornings are cool even in July, lots of dew, and fog.

"Look what I brought," Billy says, pulling a bottle of Martell brandy from the floor of the truck. "We'll need it later."

We drive into Dennis Village and then head south on Old Bass River Road until we arrive at a dead end with a few wooden tract houses on a brackish pond. The tide is starting to go out. This means it will be easier for us to wade in the low water, in our squatting position, while we rake the sand for quahogs. These are hard shell clams and must not be able to pass through the clam ring held around our necks: if it's less than an inch in diameter, you toss it back.

Sweet and salty bivalves, they are eaten cooked in *spaghetti alle vongole,* or raw, opened on their shell.

There are a few other folks in the chilly water. The small settlement nearby is waking up, residents standing on their porches with coffee, waves, and bemused looks at our crawling around in fifty-eight degree water. Slow going, but I get the hang of it: you rake an area of sand under the water and hope to find a clam. When you do, you check with your ring and then put it in your bucket. And we, in the water, submerged to our chests because we are squatting like big crabs, get very wet, and I wish I had brought a change of clothes. When I start to shiver, it's time to quit. There are towels in the truck and that warming Martell brandy.

THAT WAS ONE of the good days. But there were a few when I found myself back in my head and thinking hard about my life.

In the early '70s, as I was imagining running my own theatre, I began writing up notes on the movies I was seeing. Here are some sentences from one of my reviews:

> The importance for us today is that while *La Dolce Vita* described a very elite, rich slice of society in the 1950s, today, these anguished boredoms and calloused infidelities—both sexual and emotional—are suffered by the middle classes, the almost adequately, and overly educated. Like Fellini's people, pleasant sensations evaporate, and we're thrown back into depression.

IS THIS HOW I then felt about my life? It's all a long time ago, but I do think it's clear that I was hungry for something and was trying to find it on screen. The ideology of sexual experiment and abandon many of us had subscribed to during the 1970s was, surely, fueled by the movies, and, while I had tried my best to live it out, by the time I ended my first marriage I had come to see that that path was not for me. Now I wondered, can I grow up, can I grow out of my old skin, into a smarter, kinder snake.

It is therefore disturbing to recall how long I remained enthralled by early Bertolucci, and especially by *The Conformist.*

I see the leaves blowing and hear the mother screaming, "Alberi, Alberi!"

Alberi means "trees," but it's also the name Marcello calls Kiki, the lover of Marcello's mother as well as her morphine supplier.

The blowing leaves linger in the mind. My friend and film scholar Robert Kolker loves the image too. "The great thing in the movie," he says, "is the low angle shot through the blowing autumn leaves." When I ask him why we love it, he says, "It's an image of nostalgia, or of what Bertolucci calls 'nostalgia for the present.' People who have nostalgia for the present feel as if they are missing their lives."

I wonder if such an emotion was what *The Conformist* used to call up in me. I am not so sure that I had a nostalgia for the present, but the main character in Bertolucci's movie does have a big case of it. He tries to overcome the feeling by joining a political movement, but the experience only deepens his sense of alienation.

Marcello grows up to become a little fascist. Jean-Louis Trintignant plays him with a blank face. I see him going to the ballet studio where he takes a tag out of a ballet shoe so he'll know where to find Dominique Sanda. He's stalking her although he really wants to get to her husband and his former teacher, Professor Quadri. The professor is leading an anti-fascist movement and Marcello has come to Paris to kill him. At the end, he will engineer a scene in the woods where both the professor and his wife are killed, again surrounded by fallen leaves.

The movie is an amazing embrace of something despicable that never allows us to forget how despicable it is. You're watching a man who betrays everyone around him. As Bob puts it, "it raises cowardice to the realm of wonder and awe." But you keep watching because it is so beautiful.

In *The Conformist* there is a wonderful scene on a train. Marcello and his wife are traveling from Rome to Paris and at one point there is a process shot of ocean vistas out the train window. A kind of sunset light comes pouring into the train compartment as she sits on his lap, her back turned toward him, her skirt hiked up. Are they in the moment, or merely performing it?

The sex thing in Bertolucci now seems pretty misguided; it's all about the impossibility of finding an intimate partner who is complete. Bertolucci preferred the sexual confusion between men and women to any sense of a happy ending. The sex scene on the train between Giulia and Marcello is the only sanctioned sex in the movie—it's their wedding night, their honeymoon. The many other sex scenes, like a barely clothed Dominique

I GAVE IT AWAY: DAYS AND NIGHTS AT VINEGAR HILL THEATRE

Sanda draped over a marble table, are voyeuristic, soft-porn-ish, violent, and yet mesmerizing.

I remember Bob Kolker introducing Robert Altman's *Short Cuts* at Vinegar Hill one night in the early 1990s when we had invited him down to give a little talk before the film. Bob stood up and said, "This movie is about gender as panic." He could have been talking about Bertolucci. When I was seeing his movies for the first time that sense of dissatisfaction was not something I thought I needed to grow out of. I was interested in *The Conformist* as a piece of my romantic life. But then I went on to produce my own romance and didn't need to have the movie anymore.

At the same time, you don't want to quite outgrow your first loves. Getting older wasn't about rejecting Bertolucci—it was about expanding what I loved while still acknowledging the appeal of my earliest infatuations. Once I began writing about *The Conformist*, I knew I had to watch the movie again.

The Conformist now exists on a Criterion disc with revealing Special Features. In comments made over thirty years after the making of the movie itself, Bertolucci and cinematographer Vittorio Storaro talk about Marcello as a product of his childhood abuse and his belief that he has murdered a man. It all goes back to an early scene in the movie.

One day after school, teenage Marcello takes a ride with his mother's chauffeur, Lino, played by Pierre Clémenti, who has just rescued Marcello from the taunts of his schoolmates. We see a docile Marcello hitched up by his shirt collar and led into an abandoned room. Lino sits against the wall, takes off his cap, and shakes out a head of long blond hair. Mesmerized, Marcello climbs on Lino's lap and touches the hair, his face. The camera moves away, returns, and Lino has pulled out a Lugar. Marcello grabs the gun and fires wildly. There is blood, Lino does not move, and Marcello runs away believing that he has killed the chauffeur.

At the end of Alberto Moravia's novel Marcello and his wife are killed by a strafing airplane as they flee Rome in a car. The war is ending and they are hit by Allied fire. Bertolucci decided to change the ending, in part because he wanted to return to the question of Marcello's early experience. As he wanders through the chaotic streets of the capital—it is the night Mussolini falls—Marcello suddenly runs into Lino. "You had the pistol," he says, "and you're still alive." It turns out that all the guilt Marcello has been carrying has been unnecessary. But he still has his shame. Marcello remains so stirred up by the "homosexual" encounter with Lino that he then yells out to passersby, "He killed the professor and his wife in the woods."

In looking back on the movie Bertolucci and Storaro agree that Marcello chooses to become "*il conformista*" because he believes two things about himself: that he has committed murder and that he has been sexually abused. In the movie proper, neither case is made unambiguously clear. But in their retrospective musings both the director and the cinematographer speak of Marcello as wanting to be "normal" because of perceived early traumas.

Abuse is always about the dynamic between the *then* and the *now*, about how one carries it over time and narrates it looking back. It's like living with the memory of a certain kind of profoundly disturbing movie; sometimes all we can handle are the Special Features. And so it's wonderful that Bertolucci, at the end of his remarks on the Criterion disc, found words to capture the experience of looking back on the making of *The Conformist,* words that also acknowledge the ever-increasing distance between the artist and his art. In looking back on what you have made, or in looking back on a movie you once loved but feel differently about now, or in looking back on abuse you have experienced and continue to re-narrate, you confront, in Bertolucci's words, "somebody else, who was you then."

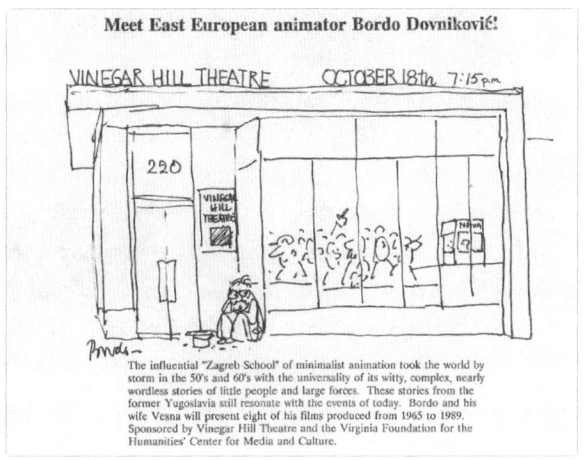

14
SONGS OF THE AUVERGNE

By 1982 VHT was moving away from showing six movies a week and moving toward longer runs. We also booked fewer old foreign films and were able to gain access to more first-runs, both foreign and domestic. The craze for Australian films provides just one example: pairing Judy Davis in *My Brilliant Career* with Peter Weir's *Picnic at Hanging Rock* produced one of the biggest hits of the 1980 schedule. Over six days in July the two films grossed $6540.50.

American art films like *Foxes* and *Breaking Away*, orphaned by their producing studios, also fell into our lap. By the end of the decade we were able to vie successfully for Steven Soderbergh's *Sex, Lies, and Videotape*. Miramax drove the bus on the big change: they shaped the emerging taste for indie first-run films and proved to be as ruthless and deal-driven as any of the major studios.

In looking back, it is also possible to see that as things began to loosen up for us, the great *auteur* decade of American movie making was coming to an end. Arthur Penn opened the blood gates in 1967 with *Bonnie and Clyde* and reflected back to us the violence we were inflicting on bodies halfway around the world. The 1975 *Night Moves* is often considered to be Penn's last great film. It's a movie very disillusioned with cinema; the film crew in the movie is nothing but corrupt, and the boat in which Gene Hackman is trapped at the end is called 'Point of View.' Although *Night Moves* surely marks some kind of farewell for Penn, I see his 1981 *Four Friends* as one of the better movies about Vietnam as a war at home.

Starting with *M.A.S.H.*, Robert Altman enjoyed a decade of bringing us the new look and especially the new sound: his overlapping dialogue and his use of songs by Leonard Cohen in the 1971 *McCabe and Mrs. Miller* was a breakthrough moment. He went on to make *The Long Goodbye* and his 1975 masterpiece, *Nashville*, in which many of the actors perform songs they themselves have written. The moment when Ronee Blakley breaks into "My Idaho Home" still touches my heart. In 1980 Altman directed *Popeye*, which suffered at the hands of American critics. So he went underground, turning plays into movies—*Streamers, Secret Honor, Fool for Love*—only to resurface triumphantly in 1992 with *The Player*, which begins with an extended crane shot, an homage to the dread-inducing border crossing scene at the opening of Orson Welles's *Touch of Evil*.

But what about the problem children: Coppola, Scorsese, Spielberg, and Lucas? Their early movies—*The Rain People, Boxcar Bertha, Duel, THX1138*—still appear to be an inspired response to the French New Wave. But would you have put your money on any of these filmmakers to create future blockbusters?

Look at what happens: Francis Ford Coppola's *The Godfather* comes out in 1972. As an Italian-American, it gave me back the romance of immigration. Like *The Conformist*, it was also luscious filmmaking about a sordid subject. *The Godfather* is literally a dark movie. Cinematographer Gordon Willis and art director Dean Tavoularis deploy reds, ochres, and rich blacks in order to create the velvety feeling of the inside of a coffin. Two years later, Coppola released *another* Godfather movie which, even without Marlon Brando, was better than the first, with Robert De Niro in his finest role.

Martin Scorsese had introduced De Niro a year earlier in *Mean Streets*. Suddenly I was seeing a semi-documentary about Italian American men and their attempts to reconcile a tormenting Catholicism with sexual longing. I identified with actress Amy Robinson, who plays De Niro's cousin Teresa.

Harvey Keitel sleeps with her secretly when it is convenient while Teresa's family tries to hide her epilepsy. It all reminded me of my older cousin Caesar, also an epileptic, who was kept out of school and lived with my grandparents as a kind of pet-servant.

Steven Spielberg's *Jaws* calls up a family legend. When it appeared in the summer of 1975, I was at the Cape with Ian and Courtenay. Ian was seven years old. He desperately wanted to see the film but I said no. The following summer we ran *Jaws* and I held firm.

"But Mom," Ian argued, "everybody else has seen it. And besides, you've let me see *The Godfather*. The knife—Luca Brasi—the strangling—I could handle that."

In protest, Ian made a drawing of a toothy fish which boasts, down in the corner, a big PG. That drawing still hangs in the cottage at the Cape, and once Ian did get to see the film, he later said, "I understood. As soon as the kid gets eaten on the raft I ran up into the projection booth and watched the rest from there. I realized that everybody my age was seeing everything—especially the poor kids—because they're the ones that get babysat by TV."

Of this group George Lucas is the least interesting and the most consequential. When *American Graffiti* was released in 1973, I was on a deep self-education mission and was devoted to difficult films like *Badlands*, *The Last Detail*, *Serpico*, *The Exorcist*, and, for a little relief, *Live and Let Die*. Lucas loves to invoke an unbitter past, but, invested as I was in the overwhelming present, I had little interest in looking back at a warm high school night of cruising around in cars.

Perhaps the entire period deserves the title Swept Away. Because in 1977 *Star Wars* arrived. Pageantry—this is what it offered—an affectless world juiced by special effects. Everything would change, especially the shape of audience desire.

These were all movies made by men and were usually about an isolated and dissatisfied white man. They were our new Westerns. And it is therefore no wonder that my friend Bob Kolker titled his book about the filmmakers of the '70s renaissance *A Cinema of Loneliness*. His title was wonderfully translated into German, *Allein im Licht*—Alone in Light.

Things were ending in Europe as well. François Truffaut died in 1984 at the age of fifty-two. *The 400 Blows* had appeared twenty-five years earlier, to be followed by *Shoot the Piano Player*, *Jules and Jim*, *Fahrenheit 451* and, in

1974, *Day for Night*, my favorite among his movies. The late films, with their unrequited searchings for love, seem to be made by a man who knows he is dying.

Fanny and Alexander surprised us all in 1982. For decades Ingmar Bergman had been engaged in the work of hollowing out the psyche, but here was a Christmas movie, one marking the point in Bergman's career when happiness becomes possible in his character's lives. Earlier, when we attended the 1977 Berlin Film Festival, Chief got wind of the release of *The Serpent's Egg*. An English language film with David Carradine and Liv Ullmann set in 1920s Berlin, it was Bergman's only Hollywood project. We managed to locate a print and ran it for a week. We paid $1000, high terms; we grossed $982.25. Low attendance should not have been a surprise however because all along Bergman was being offered to our audience as good, if strong, medicine.

We never showed much Antonioni; he was even more challenging than Bergman. People came expecting to see a Fellini movie with laughter and tears. But what you feel watching an Antonioni movie is the gap between what you want and what you actually have. In the 1957 *Il Grido—The Cry*—a man wanders aimlessly away from his town and the woman he loves and we never learn why. Three years later, in *L'avventura*, Michelangelo Antonioni rendered neorealism fully existential. He chose blonde Monica Vitti as his Liv Ullmann. Vitti never laughs: her quiet elegance projects a deep sadness and you find yourself trying in vain simply to read her face. In the story an architect goes to an island and loses his fiancée—she just disappears. Gabriele Ferzetti and Anna's friend Vitti become the searchers. They do not find her.

AFTER REID OECHSLIN came over to the theatre from Fellini's he became my transitional object, giving me friendship and support during the period of my divorce, when I most needed it. Having someone on board also allowed me to take a big risk.

"Have you heard that Hitchcock's *Dial M* is finally being released?—in the proper format," I said to him one day at the Riverside.

"You mean in real 3-D? I don't know—it's all about wrangling the machines."

"Look—I really want to do it. Let's talk to Warner Classics."

When people wonder how I chose my movies, the *Dial M* adventure reveals that we went with what we liked, or what deserved to be shown.

IN ORDER TO exhibit *Dial M for Murder* we had to install two Selsyn motors onto our regular projectors. The new motors adjusted the speed of the machines so that they ran in sync. Running a true 3-D film starts with two copies of the same movie—one the green print, the other the red. Both prints of the film are run through two projectors simultaneously and the timing of the passage of each film frame through the projection gates must be exact. When the two images hit the screen they are somewhat superimposed, but the effect only works if the viewer is wearing 3-D glasses. Without the glasses the audience sees the figures on the screen surrounded with a halo of red or green.

Every theatre that showed Warner Brothers' 3-D Natural Vision process had to have an intermission, a time in which the two projectors could be reloaded with the second half of the film. The intermission was announced within the film by a screen card. As an enhanced exhibition technique, screenwriters of 3-D films were encouraged to build an intermission into the drama.

It was like having a pair of horses that had to run in tandem to the second.

The movie opens with Grace Kelly kissing Ray Milland. Then he breaks away and says, "Let me get you another drink." But of course she's kissing the wrong man, who also happens to be her husband. The real kiss comes a few minutes later with her lover, Robert Cummings. And by then she has changed from a grey shirtwaist into a flame red cocktail dress.

Those blonde curls, that plummy voice, those clothes—no wonder Hitchcock loved her. Everything involving Kelly was where his energy was—this was the beginning of his *coup de foudre*. She was the most beautiful woman in the world.

Here's the set-up. Fading tennis pro Ray Milland wants to punish his wife for her infidelity. The jealous husband blackmails a school chum into murdering Kelly while he is conveniently away. The assailant hides in the apartment behind curtains as Kelly, dressed in a sheer peignoir, is lured into the drawing room by the ringing phone. The killer pushes her over a desk and tries to strangle her with a silk stocking but she fights back. The big moment in the film is when her hand reaches out and gropes for the scissors *we and she* know are there. Suddenly Kelly swings her arm backward—toward the audience—and then brings it forward to stab the intruder in the back.

Hitchcock's cinematic interest was to use 3-D within the closed-room situation, although he was not fond, as he later said, of mere "photographs of people talking." All the overhead shots in the movie allow the objects on the screen to pop—including a fully stocked bar seemingly within reach of every audience member.

Otherwise it's mostly people walking around the room with drinks. Hitch got it right, and *Dial M* is considered a masterpiece of in-sync, dual strip 3-D filmmaking. At the time of its original release, however, Warner Brothers more or less orphaned *Dial M*. What they released was a 3-D/2-D format, playable without the fussy mechanicals or the glamour. Its rehabilitation took until 1980 when the York Theatre in San Francisco mounted a successful run of *Dial M* in the original 3-D, and then every art house in America wanted to play it.

In order to promote the movie one of my candy chicks, Moss Dix, cut a four-foot telephone and its endless cord out of construction paper and hung it in our big front window; there is a picture of me in the ticket booth with a huge receiver looming over my head. And I'm actually on the phone, staring down my dog Voisine, wearing 3-D glasses.

We ran *Dial M* for an entire week in the fall of 1981 and it never did less than $500 a night. The biggest night was a $1500 Saturday. For this special event, we were charging $3.00 for adults, so with discounts for kids and cardholders, this meant that at least five hundred people had come and gone on Saturday alone.

REID ALSO WANTED to make movies. He and Chris Farina collaborated on two films—*Route 40* set in Maryland, and *West Main Street* in Charlottesville. The first movie came out of Ellen McWhirter's film class at Virginia when, "willing to do anything to get out of a paper," as his fellow filmmaker Chris Farina put it, "we asked if we could do a film instead."

During a typical work week, Reid and I might have lunch at the Riverside, with its flat burgers and fries, or, as a special treat, soup and bread at the C&O downstairs. What were we going to play and what were we going to fix: these were the two most asked questions. "Let's put carpeting on the walls," Reid would say. "It'll absorb a lot of noise." He retooled the projectors, part by part. Popcorn popper repair was ever-present. By 1985, Reid had brought in a stereo sound system for the premiere of Jonathan Demme's *Stop Making Sense*. Before that we had operated with what looked like a ship-to-shore speaker salvaged from an old naval carrier.

As for programming, during Reid's first year with me we launched three film festivals: the Japanese, the French, and the Russians.

Every Wednesday and Thursday in October and November of 1980 we ran two movies from Japan, titles like *Ballad of Orin* and *Sandakan No. 8*. To help fill seats the University of Virginia East Asian Language and Area Studies Center mobilized their students to make the trip downtown. This was the heyday of Japanese language films, with *Woman in the Dunes* being our strongest recurring hit. When we paired it with *In the Realm of the Senses* the two movies brought in over a thousand dollars on three usually quiet weekday nights.

What I now find hard to believe is that during the very same period we also ran a French Film Series. In one November week we crowded in eight movies no one will probably ever see again—have you ever heard of *Bastien, Bastienne* or *Ma Blonde*? The movies were supplied to us free of charge by the Alliance Française of the Ambassade de France and were promoted by the French Department. And they did pretty well, never grossing less than three hundred dollars a night. In the early days, Roger Shattuck, the great Proust scholar, encouraged Vinegar Hill to join the Alliance Française Film Tour, a venture often accompanied by a star like Marie Christine Barrault or a director like Alain Jessua. Shattuck's love for film, French and beyond, began after World War II when he worked "alone and undisturbed," as he liked to say, at the Henri Langlois Cinémathèque in Paris.

The university proved useful a third time when it granted us $550 to host a Russian Film Series. We led off with *A Slave of Love* and *Potemkin*. When I recently watched Nikita Mikhalkov's *A Slave of Love* again I had an out of body experience, totally dissolving in tears. A chubby and charming silent film director is trying to hold together production of his movie as the Red army moves ever closer. The shallow bourgeois blonde lead suddenly acquires depth as she falls for the equally blond cinematographer, who has been secretly filming the atrocities being committed by the Whites. It's a movie about the love of movies and moviemaking, even in the face of history's big steamroller. Sergei Eisenstein's *Potemkin* is the more obviously political movie, and the much more revered, but I preferred Mikhalkov's film, in which people get to politics through love.

REID, STILL AN undergraduate, often talked about an English course he was taking on the literature of landscape. I had heard about the man teaching the course through Ellen and often saw him around town. His name was David Wyatt, and he was on my radar.

March 1981, Ellen McWhirter and I are in her kitchen on Mulberry Street. She is deep in a cooking project. With a small paring knife she dismantles a large globe artichoke until all that remains is its pale green center, a fussy process that yields volumes of compost and the occasional dinged-up fingers. She performs this task five more times and then floats the hearts in lemon water. She's making *lasagna coi carciofi* from Marcella Hazan's *More Classic Italian Cooking*. I should be helping, I think. I actually know how to do this, but I have another agenda.

> A: I saw the cutest guy at the anti-nuclear Virginia Power demonstration. At the Kmart parking lot. I think he teaches. English faculty. He was wearing a trench coat. And a tie!
> E: Wyatt. David Wyatt. Married.
> A: Still?
> E: He and Libby are separated. Maybe getting divorced.
> A: Let me know when he's up for grabs. (nervous chuckle). I'm kidding … but he's really good looking.

Ellen stands up, towering over me at her kitchen table. She's close to six feet. It makes her seem very adult and mature; I am trying not to make stupid, girl-vixen conversation. She walks to the fridge, takes out two eggs and begins to organize her materials to make homemade noodles for the lasagna.

> E: You don't want him. He's got problems. Many.
> A: You know this? And how?
> E: Libby talks to me.
> A: What kind of problems?
> E: Stuff like your ex. Chief problems.

With that pronouncement, Ellen confidently returned to her pasta board. She broke the eggs into her well of flour and stirred furiously until the wet was absorbed by the dry. Never lost a drop.

Well, that's huge, I think to myself. Another man in the world who likes so many forbidden activities. Many of them combinable. And she knows this for sure. I think I believed her warning—for a few seconds at least—enough to file her information into my precarious future.

It would turn out that he was entirely oversold.

ONE NIGHT, WHEN VHT was showing *Sometimes a Great Notion*, David came to the movie. I was selling tickets; he sat on the maple bench nearby. It was a cold winter night and he was wearing a big blue down jacket. I was standing in the brick ticket booth; we were the only people in the lobby. He remembers a definite tension in the air between us, a sense of something imminent. I do too.

Director-actor Paul Newman's heartbreaking film of Ken Kesey's novel was a revelation to me. Ian explains why I love this movie so:

> *The movie delves right into the issues of middle-minded America, both left and right wings, and sometimes acts as a guide for us navigating the eccentricities of being American. Paul Newman and Richard Jaeckel are brothers who want to keep working thru a union strike in rural Oregon. Henry Fonda is the stubborn patriarch and Lee Remick is the long-suffering wife of Fonda's son; Newman directs against the grain by bringing us a family of more centrist, even right-wing mentality: we end up cheering as much for the bosses as for the workers.*
>
> *Two scenes have always stuck out to me. The first is the pick-up football game where the Stamper family and their antagonists from the timber strike have it out on a makeshift football field near a riverbank. These men are all loggers—they are like pre-beer-commercial characters before the stereotype, more in tune with the outdoors, part of a more physical America that is disappearing. The second film moment is a gut-wrenching scene involving Newman, Jaeckel and a huge log that has trapped the latter on the banks of a river. As a rising tide begins to submerge Jaeckel, Newman attempts to keep his brother alive by diving underwater and breathing into his mouth. Newman surfaces, inhales, dives, exhales, and surfaces again, but he can't keep doing it forever. Finally, there is just not enough air.*

IN MID-OCTOBER I made a phone call. When David picked up—I had called him at his office number—I said, "Hi, this is Ann Porotti." He said "Oh—hi," and then I said, "Are you ever free for dinner?"

I had made him an offer he couldn't refuse. I was feeling a little ruthless: I have the kids, the house, the movie theatre. I'm the Queen, you come to me.

David hesitated, and then said, "Sure."

"Great," I said, "how about Thursday night?"

He agreed to drive and to pick me up at seven.

About a week before the phone call I had gone to a dance party at a big brick house on Northwood Avenue, only few blocks from the theatre. The two people hosting the party were Al Filreis and David Wyatt. David had found the place after the final separation from his wife Libby and had asked Al, a graduate student in English, to share the rent.

I went to the party despite having a terrible head cold and the biggest red nose in America. I came with Ellen, who knew both Al and David. For me, David was a possible someone, in part, because as my children would eventually assert, "Mom, when it comes to guys, you have a serious looks requirement."

On this particular night, I remember thinking, I am really tired. There was the cold plus I had worked an eight-hour cooking shift at Fellini's, that chain gang of endless prep—red sauce, stocks for soup, and deveining a five-pound box of shrimp which covers you in stinky. Not sure if I scrubbed before I went to the party. You know how sometimes you look forward to an encounter, you imagine how it will happen, but then the actual event bears no resemblance to your fantasy. Meeting David Wyatt was like that.

I didn't dance much because my nose was dripping and I smelled like fish. But I hung around the food—chips, guacamole, vegetable cut-ups—and then David walked over to chat. He wore a plaid cowboy shirt. With snaps.

"Nice house," I said, "Ellen says you and Al just moved in. Looks like you're breaking in the dance floor tonight."

"Hopefully not too much breaking, but we did get lucky with this place. The second story porch has great views of the Blue Ridge."

He was a smiley guy when he talked, in spite of his wide dark moustache.

I then broke the cardinal rule of interviewing and asked him a question I already knew the answer to.

"Are you at the University?" I asked, knowing that he had not gotten tenure and now worked elsewhere in town.

"No, I'm with Rob Vaughan at the Virginia Foundation for the Humanities. A new job for me—just started in September. We give out grants. To artists and scholars. We had a filmmaker apply to us that you might know, a guy named Ross Spears."

"Yes, I know him."

I thought to myself: what very odd flirtation skills this Mr. Wyatt has.

But David was still talking.

"Rob and I met Ross for lunch today, he's working on a film about Southern writers and wants the foundation to support the project. He said you played his earlier film *Agee* at Vinegar Hill."

"Yup, I did do that."

And then I thought but did not say: for the last year I have conducted a public and messy affair with Ross Spears, who, all the time, has been in a committed relationship. Perhaps you missed that, and how nice for me that you are a relative innocent to the downtown Charlottesville dating petri dish.

IT WAS THEREFORE with a certain reckless optimism that I made my phone call to Mr. Wyatt.

But on the Monday before I made the phone call there had also been an incident at the theatre: projectionist David Minckler failed to put up the third forty-minute reel of Akira Kurosawa's *Kagemusha*. Minckler had been with me from the beginning and often acted as if he were in charge. When a staff person told me about the unshown reel, I confronted Minckler and he said, "Oh, no, I didn't do that." I decided to fire him.

But there was a problem—Minckler's girlfriend Claudia. When I told her about my plans she said, "Oh, Ann, you cannot do that, I'm going to break up with him."

This exchange happened at five o'clock on Thursday night, the night of my date with David. Claudia insisted that I have a drink with her in order to work out the details.

She and I went to Fellini's and sat at the bar, where we each had a Martell. I agreed that Minckler could work another month but that I was still determined to let him go.

Meanwhile, David had arrived at Rothery Road, to be greeted by my seventh grader, Courtenay. She entertained him with a character analysis of her father for the twenty minutes or so before I showed up.

I've never liked being on time; to this day I'm often in the shower when dinner guests show up. When I did arrive I was wearing a pink and gray silk shirt, croupier vest, jeans, my Frye boots. I explained why I was late and then jumped into David's Valiant.

I didn't go out to dinner often; there wasn't the time or the money. The men I had known did not take me out to dinner. On this evening I had decided to go to Eastern Standard. Eastern Standard was expensive, but I was feeling flush: September of 1982 had been our biggest month ever. And Chief was the reason why.

BY THE EARLY '80s, Mark Johnson, an old friend from Chief's undergraduate days at Virginia, had become a successful producer in Los Angeles, often teaming up with director Barry Levinson. When the time came to cast Levinson's Baltimore-themed movie, *Diner,* Mark called Chief and offered him a small part. Chief appears late in the film as the guy in jail who runs into Daniel Stern after he has been arrested. When Charlottesville learned that one of its favorite sons had been cast in a movie, people really did come out in droves.

The last hurrah of my time with Chief came with the 1982 premiere of *Diner* in Baltimore.

My friend Jean Dunbar and I shopped for a dress. The item had to be sexy because, although Chief and I were recently divorced, I had arranged to drive my Saab up to Baltimore with him and to meet up with Mark as well as with Barry Levinson and cast members Tim Daly and Daniel Stern.

Jean and I went to Levy's, Charlottesville's high-end place for women's wear, where cocktail dresses were on sale. One perfect item was a Flora Keung black and white Japanese print worked up with a layered silk skirt. The top was a bare camisole; no bra. I guess I was in my Lady Godiva phase, wanting to parade through town and be noticed. So I bought the dress, remnants of which are still in my sewing basket.

When we arrived at the premiere the members of the cast and crew were in casual clothes, or perhaps they came as their characters, 1950s high school kids. We rode around the Baltimore harbor in a windowless trolley. Even though it was July it was cold near the water and I was wearing the equivalent of an expensive skimpy nightgown without a jacket. My sartorial statement turned quickly into embarrassment and I sat through the movie wearing Chief's sport coat.

After the movie I sulked even more when I noticed all the guys hanging out with a short, cute blonde who had been in the film. And she wasn't dressed up a bit. I felt a little like Shelley Duvall in *Three Women* when she keeps closing her dress in the car door. Some women aren't smooth enough to be sexy.

I drove us back to Charlottesville. We didn't talk much; it was very late. When I dropped Chief off I asked him if he wanted to come back to the house.

"No," he said, "no, I don't think so. By the way, did you notice Mark's new friend, the blonde?"

"Yes, who's that?" I said.

"Oh, that's Ellen Barkin—she's a babe!"

NOW, FOUR MONTHS later, David was driving. I had chosen Eastern Standard for my date with him because the place was famous for being slow with the food, and I wanted to have plenty of time to talk.

I ordered oysters and caviar; David later said they "looked dangerous." He had scallops. There were delicate little soy-dressed salads with sesame seeds. We drank a bottle of white wine.

David appeared as a celebration in brown: nubby sport coat, tie, the moustache, brown eyes and hair. A funny nose: when you first saw him you expected a conventional Wasp look but on closer inspection it turned out to have many planes, a product of the Czechs of Central Europe.

There was no awkwardness; we just jabbered away. Joan Didion came up; she had somehow become a touchstone. It turned out that David was working on a book about California, and she was his inspiration.

We stayed there a long time. For dessert we split an order of poached pears in caramel sauce. I paid the bill and then we drove around while David played Joan Baez's *Diamonds and Rust*. "Speaking strictly for me," she sang, "We both could have died then and there."

When we got back to Rothery Road the kids were asleep. We started making out on the couch under the three big windows. Then I asked, "Would you like to go upstairs?" There was a double bed in the loft. These were the days when nobody was taking anything slow, and I was in a hurry.

David gave me a long look, and then said, as he stood up to leave, "You'd be disappointed."

The next day at the theatre, Ellen said, "How did it go?"

"Not too well," I answered. "What is he—a war vet?"

David did sometimes walk away, but he always came back in a way that reassured me.

A few days after our first date, David showed up at the ticket window and delivered an envelope addressed to "Anne." Inside was a limerick written on Virginia Foundation for the Humanities stationery:

> There was a young man so uptight
> That when asked with a frankness outright
> If he'd opt for the bed
> Chose his own place instead
> And then slept pretty poorly all night.
>
> That was fun. I'll be out of town
> this weekend. Will be in touch.
> David

It was probably the smartest thing he ever did.

David called the next Sunday and asked me out. On the following Thursday, October 17, 1982, we went to Szechuan Gardens, behind Charlottesville's original steak house, the Aberdeen Barn. I sometimes took my staff and the kids to the Chinese place for big, cheap family style meals, and the one thing we always said was "Pass it the other way," meaning in the opposite direction of my hungry children. Sitting there, in a red, leatherette banquette, I realized I could barely reach the table. We ordered fried dumplings, "Moosh Pork," Chicken with Vegetables. We hurried through the meal and then hurried home. We went straight upstairs, into the loft with the double bed, and nobody was disappointed.

IN THE DAYS after that second evening with David, I hung around the house as much as I could, and played and played again Joseph Canteloube's early twentieth century collection of folk themes, *Songs of the Auvergne*. One song especially, *la delaïssádo*, drew me in with its six lines about the slim life of a young woman's love:

> A shepherdess is waiting over there at the top of the wood
> For the one she loves, but he does not come!
> Alas I am forsaken! I do not see my lover!

As I stood at the window looking out onto my wooded street, Canteloube's humble music spoke over and over about the beauty and the pain in love.

I had stood at that window and listened to music many times, as I would again; it is where I go to gain a prospect on my life. As a girl of twenty, looking out over the Arno, I had seen another prospect and felt disappointed in advance. I knew I wanted something but also knew that I was in no way prepared to make that future happen. "Do something," my therapist often says to me, "the talking is fine, but you also have to *do* something."

It's not that I was unwilling to take a chance. I was in many ways all too willing, too careless with myself. Marrying Chief had been one of those chances. The marriage had been prompted by terrifying things: not having a job, failing at school, being suddenly pregnant. After marrying Chief, I kept taking chances with men, and none of them turned out to have a future. "*I thought he loved me and I loved him so!,*" the shepherdess sings. Perhaps the men I chose did not really like me, or perhaps I could not make myself real to them. While I listened at the window I was crying, and I was crying because I felt that my life was about to change. "People who can be serious together, it goes deep," the poet Anne Carson says, and I was about to discover that.

15
A NEW LIFE

Falling in love with David Wyatt—and it happened really fast—required different groceries, a revised work/play schedule, and a set of power tools. The first encounters were mostly nights. I would come over to his house on Northwood after finishing a cooking stint at Fellini's with stove grease under my nails and fish smells in my hair, my work clothes announcing my arrival. Almost before Hello there needed to be a shower, which usually led to the bedroom.

But when you have kids, a new romance is best kept off site to see if it has legs. I tried but didn't always succeed in doing that. With David, it was clear that preparing food and eating at home was a vital part of his allure. One Saturday midnight, I showed up at Northwood after cooking and there he was, making apricot *kolaches*, a Czech family specialty. The yeast rolls rose, slowly—not as a rule, just these particular ones—and in vain, we waited, baked them around one, and chewed on the little rocks. A man enjoying his cooking project! No judgment from me; baking is its own trial by fire.

During those autumn-moving-into-winter weekends, when we would hike trails on Skyline Drive—which I had never done before—he always brought along avocado sandwiches: in 1982, no one was eating these exotics. Everyone gets half of an avocado smashed into your bread of choice, seasoned with Texas Pete, lemon squeeze, salt, Hellman's mayo underneath. Wrapped in foil so they would survive half a day of climbing. After his Christmas trip to California that year, David brought me twenty perfectly ripe avocados, picked from the trees in his father's Laguna Beach backyard.

By the time David moved into Rothery Road, Ian was in ninth grade and Courtenay was in seventh. Dave, as my children called him, was incorporated into the household at Rothery Road with amazing speed: it was as if there were a space ready and waiting for him. I had been longing for a domestic partner who might actually share the load, and Dave was not only willing but able. Some of the tasks he assumed were of a conventional fatherly sort, as when he drove Ian to an evening basketball game.

Because of his poor marks in the ninth grade, I had forbidden Ian to try out for any of the varsity teams. His work-around was to star for the team fielded by the Spanish Club. "It was an astonishing performance," Dave later told me. "When we got to the gym there might have been twenty people in the stands. Ian played his heart out nevertheless. He kept hitting jump shots from the outside, and by the end of the night he had scored over forty points."

With Courtenay, things revolved around the kitchen. Only a month after Dave and I started seeing each other Thanksgiving was upon us, and we decided to hold a His and Her affair at Fellini's. Chief and his people would have one big table, and the newly-configured Rothery contingent, along with lots of friends, would have another. Dave found a Julia Child recipe for watercress soup and recruited Courtenay as a sous chef.

The blender almost burned out under the stress of whipping up soup for forty people, but, in the end, they managed to produce a creamy, light green masterpiece. I had never thought of the holiday dinner as involving separate courses, but we led off with the soup as if we were serving a semi-formal meal. Courtenay glowed with pride as people licked their bowls.

Dave and I had both gone through so much crash and burn at the end of our first marriages that I think we were looking for something quiet, cozy, and domestic. While I was smitten with his handsome looks and his intellectual ease, it was making dinner at home with our rowdy pets and comedy-stand-up teenagers that put new sparkle in the dream of "raising a family."

When Ian decided to write a term paper on 1930s movies about the French Revolution, including Conway's *A Tale of Two Cities*, Young's *The Scarlet Pimpernel*, and Renoir's *Le Marseillaise*, he and Dave worked out an approach. "It was actually a nice piece of New Historicism, as my colleagues would call it," Dave remembered. "Ian realized that these movies were not simply about the past but were allegories of their present, ways of imagining the coming war."

After the holidays, Dave moved his Sony Trinitron Color TV into my house. Tactically it was a brilliant gesture, but practically—where would we put this gift? Just to recap: television watching for the kids happened on a coal-fueled, black and white Motorola model, a survivor of life at Twin Pumps. One Saturday morning Dave quietly disappeared for an errand. He returned with the Saab stuffed with plywood, two-by-fours, and a big square of medium-pile tan carpet. Then he roared up the circular saw and built the Family Rec Center. The structure consisted of a low-slung lounging platform facing a desk where the new color TV resided. Above were the kids' train-style bunk beds providing balcony viewing for the sleeper on the right side.

My house and its white walls were ten years old and every surface, especially adjacent to the open carpeted staircase, had dirty hand prints from the baseboard, toddler era to the mid-wall, elementary school period. The hardwood flooring had lost its poly-gloss and needed a refinish. Safe to say that I had not noticed my surroundings with any scrutiny, but as Dave and I began a domestic life with the kids, we jumped head-first into a DIY whirlwind of home repair, much of it without prior experience. I was already in a League of My Own in that department, having, back in 1973, painted the entire house without fine sanding the unprimed sheetrock. The walls were left with a bad complexion. The only rescue for my mistake was a lifetime of repainting, and Dave and I did the place four times, twice in Herald Dawn, a color that made the house look like the inside of James's Giant Peach, and then, later, as our taste mellowed, we replaced the effect with a softer version, Western Sand.

The floors needed some love; they had given a few parties in the past decade. First there had been the Sunday brunches for multitudes Chief and I hosted before we even had kitchen cabinets, and then there were the wild dancing, wine-sloshed gigs after the Alliance Française Film Festivals. Dave and I rented floor and edger power sanders to spruce up the living room. We ground away, not always following the grain of the wood, and made some unwelcome grooves. To finish, a Danish oil was the current trend, and, while considered more natural than polyurethane, the oil did not cover our clumsy technique. But we had fun, and, over the years, great pleasure came from doing tasks we eventually got good at.

SATURDAY, CHRISTMAS EVE, 1983. Scaffolding has been rented from Central Virginia Rent-all, and gallons of matte black paint purchased from the experts at Meadowbrook Hardware. Dave and I plan to paint the white ceiling at Vinegar Hill. In the previous weeks, Reid had put up acoustic tile soundproofing with a two-pronged objective: better audio and a darker auditorium. I remember that night as long, messy, and tiring; Ian and Courtenay stayed home with Voise in a countdown to midnight. Before leaving the house, Dave filled the kids' stockings with toiletries—soap, combs, emery boards, the occasional orange—apparently a Wyatt family tradition when he was a kid. They still give him shade for that.

I guess Dave and I hoped Santa might stop by and help us roll the ceiling. Overhead painting, the least fun of all, requires maneuvering the roller on a long wooden extension; you are constantly pressing to disperse the paint evenly from the roller as you try not to notch the adjacent walls with wet color. The pain in your shoulders after hours of this work reminds me of a late-life condition called "birder's neck," something one gets from trying to find endemics in tall trees. But on this night we were both working very hard and giddy with the opportunity to make this space, now ours, much improved.

When we had finished Dave picked up the drop cloths and washed out the rollers and the pans. The theatre had been closed for the holidays since the previous Monday after a weekend double feature of hotties: *Body Heat* with Kathleen Turner and William Hurt, and a *Breathless* remake starring Richard Gere. Our next double feature would not begin until Tuesday and I had it in house; Paul Newman in *The Verdict*, and an underrated conspiracy thriller I barely recognized. I fired up the Xenon bulbs, threaded the projectors, Dave and I found our favorite seats, about four rows from the front, and welcomed in our first Christmas together with a private screening of a film called *Endangered Species*.

I had before invited boyfriends into this room of my own, usually for exclusive afternoon viewings, but never after working side by side together. The feeling of being there in a space I had made and controlled and then of inviting someone in was always deeply satisfying. A guy gets a convertible and all he feels he has to do is drive to the curb and all the girls jump in his car. That was my feeling about having a movie theatre, and my cool modern house—look what I've got—wanna help me paint it?

AROUND EASTER TIME in 1983, Dave and I went to stay with some old friends of mine in New York City. They had an apartment on the eighteenth floor of a building in Yorkville, at 500 East 77th street. The apartment was a small one bedroom and had so much glass you felt you could step right out into space. Our plan was to see lots of movies and to eat some Hungarian food. The subtext of this trip would be my introduction to Dave of what I had come to think of as My New York City.

Even before Chief and I opened VHT, I went to Manhattan at least twice a year. Mostly I stayed with Kathie and Jack, the friends on the Upper East Side, and my purpose was to see as many movies as possible. Conveniently positioned in mid-September and running for two weeks was the New York Film Festival; neither expensive nor exclusive, you just bought tickets in advance and showed up. NYFF included the hits, scandals, and lost classics gathered from London, Berlin, Cannes, Venice, Toronto, and Telluride, plus a focus on filmmakers that festival director Richard Roud believed were underserved, like Krzysztof Kieślowski, Manoel de Oliveira, Hou Hsiao-hsien. I would spend a week in the City, squeezing in at least two movies at first-run houses in the daytime and two features in the evenings at the festival. Four screenings per day, fortified with tart Granny Smith apples, abundant at the corner Asian grocers, and a salami with butter baguette from a French bakery. Seemed like heaven to me.

I loved Dan Talbot's theaters on the Upper West Side, across from Lincoln Center. There were real people working in the lobby—no one wore a vest or a bow tie—people who actually spoke to you. The Cinematheque at Joseph Papp's Public Theater had plush chairs where the sides wrapped around and you felt as safe as being in a confessional. Boudou was saved from drowning there. At the Paris Theater, located just behind the Plaza Hotel, there was a beautiful big screen looming over an auditorium with blue velvet walls. When

Marlene Dietrich cut the ribbon on opening day in 1948, the Paris was the first new movie house to open in New York after the war.

Dave and I had come to the city for the New Directors/New Films spring festival. Committed to debut films, the event had a populist feel: whatever the movie was about, it was not something that had to be confined to a museum. That year featured a student film called *Joe's Bed-Sty Barbershop: We Cut Heads*, a short from newcomer Spike Lee. David Ahearn's *Wild Style*, celebrating graffiti artist Lee Quiñones and musician Fab 5 Freddy (Fred Braithwaite), made it to the Vinegar Hill schedule a year later. Dutch director Marleen Gorris introduced *A Question of Silence*, and we were also treated to Yoichi Takabayashi's *Irezumi— Spirit of Tattoo*.

The first night we arrived, Reid, our Mr. *in loco parentis*, called with an urgent message.

It was late when I picked up the phone.

"Courtie has wrecked Dave's car."

"What?" I answered. "You're kidding!"

"No, I'm afraid she managed to get it started, and then drove it into a cedar tree. Just down the street. She maybe covered fifty yards."

"Is she OK?"

"She's fine. She was going over to see her friend Che and said she didn't want to walk."

"So what's happening? I mean, about the car, the police."

"A neighbor saw the accident and called the cops."

"Is anybody taking care of things?"

"Well, she called Chief, and he said to her, *Go Underground*."

That was my ex-husband's rogue mentality to a T. "Sounds about like what he would say," I answered.

I DIDN'T BOTHER to try to talk to Courtenay that night; I figured I would take care of things when I got home. She was unhurt, and she wasn't in jail. But I did begin to think about whether I had mastered the art of raising teenagers. I never saw the dangers heading for my adolescents mostly because I still saw them as children.

Our little road is an overgrown green in April and May, and, after dinner as the days lengthened, Ian, Courtie, and the dog would play a vigorous tag on the empty asphalt, into the gathering shadows. All three participants had incredible running chops and they looked to be wearing each other out, as kids do. Truth is, Ian was probably itching to sneak over to his girlfriend's house and Courtie, maybe to practice illegal driving. But they kept up the appearance of still being kids—for Mom's sake.

Years after the accident, Ian, the family historian, revealed the backstory behind Courtenay's first car escapade. That spring of 1983, Courtenay had been plotting to drive Dave's car; she felt confident even though she was only fourteen. So it was probably inevitable that, one day when no one was around, Courtenay managed to start the car, even though it was a stick shift. As she lost control, she dove out before the car wrecked up on the cedar. Just like in a Burt Reynolds movie. As Ian said, Dave's car was "on the way out anyway." Nobody was shocked by Courtenay's ambition, just relieved that she was not injured.

WHEN WE ARRIVED at Rothery Road a few days later, there was the car, right up against the tree. It was a Plymouth Valiant, a brown four-door sedan with a slant-6 engine. Dave and Libby bought it in Berkeley in 1973 and drove it across country when they moved to Charlottesville a few years later. It was also the car he had driven on our first date, a car so generic and unprepossessing that the kids had taken to calling it "The State Car."

Dave took one look at it and had it towed to Cosner Brothers. From then on, and for the next four years, he walked to work. But it wasn't a long walk; he strolled to the end of our street, turned right on Ivy Road, crossed Emmet Street and went up the hill to the UVA Grounds. His office was at the end of the West Range, under the space for *The Virginia Quarterly Review*.

His was a nine-to-five job that was actually about being creative. Dave was working for an NEH-funded outfit, the Virginia Foundation for the Humanities, that gave away money to libraries and museums and all kinds of programs all over the state.

There was an irony involved: after Dave was denied tenure at Virginia in the fall of 1980, he was given the usual year and a half of teaching before actually having to leave the department. When the summer of 1982 came, his marriage had ended and he had no job, so he started painting houses. Then, in August, Libby noticed an ad in the *Daily Progress*—she and Dave were having a family outing with three-year-old Luke at Lake Reynovia—that read "Humanities." Dave applied for the advertised position and was hired three weeks later. He had suddenly been restored to faculty status at the very institution that had just fired him and was now lodged in a beautiful brick building designed by Thomas Jefferson. "I feel a little like Emily in *Our Town*," he said. "I've been killed off and then allowed to come back and look around."

Dave was working so close to home that by a few minutes after five he could be in the kitchen cooking dinner. Because he had no need to commute to work we didn't need to buy a second car for ourselves until 1987, when Dave was hired by the University of Maryland.

After Chief and I separated I had begun to think hard about money. My mortgage equaled my car payment and those bills took two of my weekly $200 paychecks. Everything else—insurances, home repairs, taxes, groceries, clothes—came out of the money Chief was paying for both kids as child support and my payroll checks from the second half of the month. Our budget had no lines for travel, eating out, or luxury goods. But I believed in the life I was living.

Dave, it turned out, was making pretty good money; his starting salary at the Foundation was $22k a year, my yearly at VHT was half that. Suddenly there was breathing space, and someone to share the bills with. All those self-help books advise that couples trip themselves in disagreements about sex and money. Perhaps because we both came from families of modest means, our money attitudes were in-sync: we both love to pay bills, although I think I am more the OCD check writer; we both make budgets and then ignore them if reality bends the picture; we don't buy expensive toys; we spend extra—if we have it—on travel and home renovations; and, over the years, we have noticed that we spend more as our income rises and we forgive ourselves for doing so.

Dave and Libby owned a cozy place called the "Honeymoon House," built in 1907 for a railway family. Two lines intersected in Charlottesville, making the city a railroad hub: the Crescent covered the New York to New Orleans distance, and the Cardinal, New York to Chicago.

I loved Dave's house. It was a two-story white clapboard with pine floors and two maple trees out front. And it was close to downtown; someone living there could walk to the theatre in less than ten minutes. But, once Libby decided to take four-year-old Luke and move back to her native New Jersey in the spring of 1983, the house had to be sold. Dave did a For Sale by Owner and split the profits with his ex-wife. He walked away with twenty thousand dollars, some of which went to pay for "the headlight," as Courtenay called it—a diamond solitaire he presented to me on the eve of our first trip to Europe. We now had some travelling money, although most of Dave's haul was set aside for an upcoming transaction.

MY OWN AGE of discovery, after Dave moved into Rothery Road, turned its mind to a quest for the Florence I had left in 1965. Back in 1971, I had dragged Chief to the Duomo and across the Arno, but he, for a man often walking on the wild side, did not enjoy foreign travel.

Now, as part of Dave's first *Viaggio in Italia*, we set out on a two-week car trip from Paris to Florence and back. I imagined us as Albert Finney and Audrey Hepburn in *Two for the Road*, although I had somehow repressed the fact that their repeated trips to the continent led, in the end, to divorce.

We should have taken it slower and had more patience with Italy and with ourselves. After a magical beginning at Bordighera's Hotel Savoy, we slogged the Riviera *corniche* roads, ducking onto the *autostrada* to reach Genoa. Scary business driving in and out of Italian towns, too many *senza unicas*. By evening, Sestri Levante offered us a great meal at Polpo Marina and wading in the warm, quiet Mediterranean off the rocks near our hotel.

Ann and Dave, Yosemite, 1985

Traveling at what now seems like a histrionic pace, Dave and I drove the sleepy, forest and wine roads into Tuscany, stopping for a drive-by in Pisa, city of white marble and vivid green grass. Toward the south, we could see Florence through wheat fields and grape vines when suddenly Dave had to pull off the road as a bicycle race with one hundred riders swept past us. That night we enjoyed an inspirational Florentine meal at La Maremma in the working-class Santa Croce neighborhood. When the waiter brought Dave's grilled fish he slapped it down on the plate and declared, "La trota!" There were fireworks going off over the river as we strolled back to our *pensione*; it was the Fourth of July.

"*Ho bisogno di qualcosa per le zanzare,*" I said to the nice lady in the *dogheria*.

"*Primo o dopo?*" came the reply.

When booking two weeks in Florence in July, I had not counted on the mosquitoes.

But the Arno is their summer resort, and Europe does not screen its windows. I can't remember whether *primo*, the bites, or *dopo*, the itching, drove me more crazy. So in spite of the gelato at Vivoli's, the art everywhere, more great meals at La Maremma, and a day trip to Siena, where there were big signs for an outdoor screening of *La Cosa*—John Carpenter's *The Thing*—we left Florence because of our indoor encounters with *Gli Zanzare*.

Sometimes you can see the origins of your mistakes so clearly in the rear-view mirror.

What we needed was a better hotel, or a different Tuscan city without a buggy river. But, nope, we drove forever to the other side of Italy, through farms growing all imaginable fruits, and brutal cities offering urban despair. Fano, a beach town south of Pesaro, was lined with waterfront *pensiones* offering cabanas and three-square a day for the Italian bourgeoisie. Our need for basic showers and a bed sent us to the old town where they still had all their Christmas lights up. The nameless hostel was run by a young couple; the mean husband yelled constantly, and seemed comfortable cuffing his kids when they didn't jump fast enough. I stayed far away from him. Our twelve-dollars-a-day accommodations were barracks-worthy, and we pined for the cozy double bed and pitchers of *caffè latte* at the Hotel Savoy. Dave and I spent afternoons sunbathing at the blue, too warm Adriatic, and reading to each other from *A Farewell to Arms*.

Even when you are in it, I have come to believe, Italy can be hard to find. There is something deeply stifling about a medium-sized out-of-the-way Italian town, as if all the soporific Sundays of my childhood had there come home to roost. So we eventually fled Fano for a day trip to Urbino, a town that looked to have been invented by Kenneth Clark. In the curving stairways of the Ducal Palace there were little seats embedded in the turns where strolling couples were expected to pause on their way up or down for another round of witty sexual exchange. Nothing pleased us—our own exchanges having more or less ceased at this point—and so we prepared ourselves for a ferocious two-day drive back to Paris, ending up in the dreary town of Dreux, on the Plains of Beauce. Chartres had been fully booked.

Dave remembers our meal at the hotel in Dreux as his best French dinner ever—he had rabbit stew and rum raisin ice cream—but our long detour into Italy had not made us happy, and we hadn't yet learned how to talk about that. In the end we both got very drunk.

DESPITE BEING DIVORCED from Chief Gordon since February 1981, he and I were still very financially entangled. He was a General Partner in the Vinegar Hill Theatre Limited Partnership; we co-owned the house at 115 Rothery; I was still a partner in Fellini's Restaurant; and, after Chief moved out, I had agreed to co-sign his Altamont Street mortgage. When Dave and I decided to merge households, I wanted to own Rothery outright. So we proposed to Chief a trade of his equity in the house for mine in Fellini's. Because those investments were not at all equal—the house being worth considerably more than my share of the restaurant—the three of us agreed that Dave would pay Chief the fifteen thousand remaining to him from the sale of his Lexington Avenue house. Within a year of being together, Dave and I had jumped into mortgage without marriage.

"Do you remember where we made that deal?" Dave said to me the other day.

"How could I not," I muttered. "We were sitting at the *La Dolce Vita* booth, the one near the kitchen. It was four in the afternoon, boxes of produce stacked around the dining room, the staff setting up for the night rush."

"OK—I can see that. But why didn't we meet at the house? Because by then for us Fellini's had become alien territory."

"True—but false. We still went in for a drink now and then."

"Well, maybe so. But the last time I remember being in there with you and with Chief was the previous Thanksgiving when Courtenay and I made that big batch of watercress soup and Chief's people and our people sat at separate tables."

"Yes, and by the time we made the trade Chief virtually lived at Fellini's. I mean, he went to his law office for some of the day, but I often saw him at lunchtime chatting with the Fellini's staff, and then as soon as he could escape from the nine-to-five he was behind the bar dressed as Mr. Rick."

"OK, so that explains why we aren't in a lawyer's office for the closing. But then we were talking to a lawyer, and on his home ground."

When I think back on that day, I remember Chief as being quiet—barely talking—and no sense of struggle or argument, despite the fact that the deal being made was very favorable to us.

"I'm sure the Deed of Trust was done at Lowe and Gordon, as with Chief's and my divorce."

"What I remember above all is the corn."

"Oh, yeah,"—belly laugh—"I remember that too."

"Everything had been agreed to in advance. So, it didn't take long to sign the documents. And then a waitperson showed up with four ears of boiled corn."

"That's right! And suddenly Chief grabs one and begins chewing the kernels like he was Bugs Bunny with a typewriter of teeth. He was having an early dinner—the drinking would start later on."

"I have never seen anyone eat so fast in my life—his moustache got very involved. He just devoured all four ears. It was a little disconcerting, looking across the table at someone becoming totally covered in butter."

"That was how we were being dismissed."

16
THE YEAR OF LIVING DANGEROUSLY

One October night in the fall of 1983, Dave and I were standing in the kitchen when the phone rang. I picked it up, and the voice asked, "Is David there?"

An excited conversation ensued, and when Dave put down the phone he turned to me, surprised and smiling. "That was Lee Mitchell, from Princeton. He just invited me to come up there and teach for a year."

"Let's go," I said.

Why would I have said that? I later wondered, when the shock of what I had agreed to finally wore off. This new romance exhausted me in a good way. My life was good, especially family life: Courtie, having passed through the crucible of early middle school, was in eighth grade at Buford, and Ian was thriving as a sophomore at CHS. Theatre attendance marched solidly along, equal amounts of first-run foreign, over-looked American oddities—*Frances, Missing, Lianna*—and sub-runs like *Mad Max* and *The Fly*.

But, if you counted the VHT design and construction years, the opening and shake down interlude, and the seven-day-a-week schedule that I had maintained since 1976, the idea of not working for a year beckoned. Although I had taken my sabbatical with water during the summer of 1982, I still yearned to spend a year in a city just seeing movies and drinking up art. And Dave, though working with lovely people at the Virginia Foundation, was determined to get back into the academic game and Princeton opened a window onto that. No one I have ever met was more destined for the classroom.

Preparation for our year away zigged and zagged like a hiking path down a mountain. Dave and I drove up to Princeton and realized, "We can't live here, this town is Charlottesville's cultural twin—only more genteel." On our way home we stopped in Philadelphia to visit Ellen and David McWhirter; they had recently moved to the city and were both teaching at the University of Pennsylvania. That evening at a French bistro on South Street, the conversation was all about our renting an apartment in Center City and Dave driving to Princeton to teach as needed. I remember a room of mirrors, bright and bustling, and fantasized about my new urban life.

We began the search for an apartment. One day we were walking down Delancey Street and there was a man carrying furniture. "Are you moving?" Dave yelled. "Sure am," was the response. And that's the charmed story of how we found the Philadelphia apartment: $525 a month, a few blocks west of Rittenhouse Square, walking distance to movie theatres, museums down the Ben Franklin Parkway, eighteenth-century churches on Society Hill, and the stately row houses lining the long, narrow crosstown streets named after trees: Locust, Spruce, Pine. Ours was a rusticated-grey limestone building, a first-floor unit with a huge bay window and one bedroom.

Why only one bedroom? Because, when we proposed to Ian and Courtenay the move to Philadelphia, Ian, a rising high school junior, resisted adamantly. "I'm not going." Courtie stuck with Ian. They suggested that they and our boxer Voisine be allowed to live in the Rothery Road house with their father, who would "look after them." Somehow, I agreed, and the next fall, as we moved north, the man who had moved out of Rothery Road three years earlier moved back in.

There was one obvious choice for who was going to look after the theatre: Leslie Gossage. She had worked at Vinegar Hill since 1977, first as a cleaner, then a candy chick, and finally as a projectionist. Impeccable work habits whether screening a film, popping a batch of corn, or wrestling with the Excel spreadsheet. And she could write—her other job was teaching composition. She was incapable of telling a lie; she would not have known how to do it.

Leslie, like so many of my employees, was a refugee from the English Department:

> When you're in graduate school at that crazy place all your energy is focused on the University of Virginia. I had dropped out of the PhD track but was still teaching some remedial courses. Before that I had been doing a film course for non-majors. I taught it as a "history of film"—we had to rely on Walter Korte's collection of 16 millimeters.
>
> I was teaching film grammar—helping the kids to notice editing and composition. I was so nervous when Wally Kerrigan came to watch me teach. Afterwards he said, "Your kids are very protective of you. But do you realize that you only call on the students on the left side of the room?"
>
> Taking over from Ann was a big responsibility. At the theatre I came in around ten and sometimes didn't get home until midnight. It was Reid and me, and the candy people. I needed all kinds of reassurance; for the first time I was in charge of the money. There was lots of bargaining on the phone and one of the bookers called me "a tough cookie." Usually it was an argument about an unpaid bill—that had been paid. One of the things that made it a great job is that you were on your own. In charge. I was learning about the romance of having your own business. On the other hand, I would continually have to say to people, "No, I don't own the theatre."
>
> Then there was the incident of The Coffee Filter Man. He had a license plate that read HOSTIL. At that time Virginia only allowed six characters on a plate. He would come out of the auditorium during a movie and complain about everything, and he especially liked to pick on the concession person. One night Moss Dix was doing candy—she was an accomplished artist who happened to have decorated our popcorn bags—the big bag had a huge kernel called "Mighty Joe Corn." Well, Mr. Litigious bursts into the lobby and says, "I came out here for coffee and you're sitting on your fat ass." He starts walking back into the movie and Moss—she was really a very shy person—

grabbed the basket holding a used coffee filter full of grinds, pulled her arm back like a sling shot, and let fly. It landed splat right behind his heel. "Next time," I said to her, "just hit him. No, I'm just kidding. Next time, stand up to him and say, 'Don't ever talk to me that way again.'"

I saw Ian and Courtenay all the time. They would stop by after school, do homework. Ian would practice his trumpet in the car. Beautiful music. On one of those weekends—or maybe it was a year or two earlier—Jody and I took them to a Richmond Braves game, and on the way back they asked us what oral sex was. When a kid asks you that, the easiest thing to do is to explain it. They may have known all about it and have just been testing us.

They seemed OK, despite the chaos at Rothery Road. But I do remember writing an article for Iris—*the campus woman's magazine—that year, about* Entre Nous. *It was number one on my Top Ten List for 1984. I think* Berlin Alexanderplatz *was second that year—I remember we named our male dog Meize, the movie's nickname for Barbara Sukowa. We didn't know it meant "pussy." Anyway, in* Entre Nous *Isabelle Huppert and Miou-Miou are so in love with each other that nobody else seems to exist. As a mother, looking back, the scene I now remember is when the two of them get on a bus and leave a child behind.*

Actually there were some earlier examples of the Gordon children having adventures that established a kind of precedent for my leaving them with their father. When Ian was seven and Courtie was five they flew to Mexico to visit Katheryn Gordon and grandpa FG. My mother Anita was delegated the chaperone and traveling companion. The relationship between the two *grandmères* was as cordial as Joan Crawford and Mercedes McCambridge in *Johnny Guitar*, even though everybody enjoyed the sunny beaches and tropical fruits. The comic opera ended when Anita misheard a certain Texas city name for Dulles, and took herself and the children off the airplane at *Dallas*. "I'm going to kill myself," she wailed at the ticket counter. The mix-up was corrected by a then-classy American Airlines, free of charge, and the only inconvenience was to Chief and me as we waited at Dulles until being paged and dispatched to DC's National Airport.

I LEARNED HOW to be a mother before the rules about parenting came to be agreed upon by the culture. My rules were simple: you don't have to do chores but you do have to do art. Art was the chore. And I thought that idea was revolutionary. Chief and I both believed in it.

When Dave came along Ian and Courtie were in junior high and I was still making up their beds for them. "I don't know how you did it," Dave once said, "it looked like there was maybe three feet between the mattress and the ceiling."

Those bunk beds kept me limber.

"You were a major mother," Leslie Gossage once said to me. At the time, I felt that having kids was the best thing that ever happened to me and I said so while I was also raising a business. Work and parenthood were seat-of-the-pants experiences. But in moving to Philadelphia I was leaving both of these behind. I was willing to leave my children because I thought Ian and Courtenay wanted the romance of living with their father; as we argued about whether they would be allowed to stay they had been persuasive, so sure of their decision. But I also wanted to have a break from my work; I wanted the adventure in Philadelphia with Dave.

There was a terrible moment on the day we left. My Saab was all packed; Dave was driving a small U-Haul. It was a beautiful late summer morning, with the sunlight filtering through the leaves of the trees. I went back into the house and downstairs to the kids' room where Courtenay was still in her bed. I touched her lightly, but she refused to speak to me.

I never saw myself as a pioneer in the childrearing department; Spock was the only book read on the subject. Resourcefulness, I thought, was the best skill I could teach. And now, as it turned out, my kids were really going to be on their own.

During his high school summers, Ian was often sent by car, bus, or train into America's heartland, both to polish his trumpet skills and to develop his travel muscles. The most extreme example of my tough love was his summer of 1983 train trip to music camp in Lawrence, Kansas, where he had layovers to navigate in gritty Chicago. All this with his broken right wrist in a cast.

Ian loved to explore on foot the town that was Charlottesville in the 1970s and '80s. It felt like a time not so different from my childhood in Hopedale on Mellen Street, where my brother Rudy and I also freely wandered dirt roads down Bear Hill in a world very similar to the one Steven Spielberg depicts in *E.T.* Maybe there's a grownup at home but the doors are always open.

Because my kids were often un-surveilled they formed a very tight unit. Ian has a strong memory of their being on the town together, just a year after we opened the theatre.

> It was Thanksgiving weekend and one of my Dad's law partners gave me and Courtie tickets to our first college basketball game at University Hall which was walking distance from our house. I was in fourth grade. The UVA basketball team was like a bunch of the coolest superheroes I had ever seen. The game ended at 9:00 pm, and my seven-year old sister and I contemplated staying for the nightcap, a game with VCU. This was long before cellphones, but I thought my Mom would have a stroke if it was eleven and we had not yet come home, so we turned in, but a new obsession had begun for me.

MY PHILADELPHIA FANTASY didn't last long—by Thanksgiving, I would say, I was deeply homesick. I often say "Yes" when I mean "No," and in assenting so quickly to a year away I had gravely miscalculated. Dave had instant status, but no one was interested in me. I missed the society of my work and had no idea of how to invent a lesson plan for each day. After a few weeks of going to every movie in town and shopping for cool clothes at Plage Tahiti or Urban Guerrilla I was simply out of things to do. And above all I missed the energy and chaos of the kids. I was so naïve about living in a city apartment that one morning after Dave headed north to Princeton, I stepped outside to collect the *Philadelphia Inquirer* and oops, there I was locked out on the stoop, wearing only my pink terry cloth bathrobe and a coffee mug.

I did try to salvage the year by typing up a list of every movie we had played up to that moment. With so little to command me in the present my major resource was memory. I typed on Princeton English Department stationery, and I worked on a Selectric in Dave's temporary basement office in McCosh Hall. In the end I produced fifteen pages of two single-spaced columns.

The list begins with *Swing Time* and ends with *Comfort and Joy*. It revealed a number of things: how many times we had played a movie; what we liked versus what made money. It is striking even now to realize how ecumenical we were, how uncommercial and unafraid. From February 14, 1976, to the spring of 1985, Vinegar Hill Theatre screened 1,314 individual titles, many of

Princeton University — Department of English
McCosh 22
= Schedule BREAK
Princeton, New Jersey 08544
Telephone 609-452-4060

Vinegar Hill Theatre   Movie List   1976

SWINGTIME 3
Made For Each Other
High Noon 2
Johnny Guitar
The Lone Ranger
Memories of Underdevelopment 3
Z 2
Angels with Dirty Faces
Footlight Parade 2
Alice's Restaurant 2
Fantastic Voyage
Lavender Hill Mob 4
The Ladykillers 2
The Seventh Seal 2
Smiles of a Summer Night 3   *Feb 15 1976*
On the Waterfront 6
The Hustler
King Kong ('33)
The Most Dangerous Game
The Classic Comedians
Dirty Harry   *MARCH 31*
Bullitt
Day for Night 5
Such a Gorgeous Kid Like Me 2
The Gay Divorcee 3
The Night They Raided Minsky's
8½
Two Women
The Harder They Come 14
Laurel and Hardy
Planet of the Apes
Pat Garrett and Billy the Kid
Ring of Bright Water
The Virgin Spring
The Naked Night 2
Take the Money and Run 3
Traffic
Last Tango in Paris 5
Women in Love 6   *APRIL 1976*
Night in Casablanca
Kind Hearts and Coronets 3
The Man in the White Suit 2
Jules and Jim 4
Rules of the Game
Milestones
Magical Mystery Tour
Elvira Madigan 3
The Garden of the Finzi-Continis 5
Citizen Kane 3
Alexander Nevsky
Easy Rider 2
Trash

(52)

Top Hat 3
King of Hearts 10
Harry and Tonto 4
Bananas 7
Duck Soup 3   *MAY 1976*
Zorba the Greek 2
Harold and Maude 7
Mean Street 3
The Cincinnati Kid
Wild Strawberries
Antonia: Portrait of a Woman
Woman Under the Influence 3
Images 3
Two of Us
Grand Illusion 2
Fillmore
Cocoanuts 3
Sleeper 5   *JUNE 1 — AUGUST 29 1976*
Badlands
Thieves Like Us
Amarcord 4
The Discreet Charm of the Bourgeoisie 2
Cabaret 4
Lacombe, Lucien
Cartoons 2
Slaughterhouse-5 6
The Magus 4
State of Seige
Hiroshima Mon Amour
Bed and Board 2
Chloe in the Afternoon 3
The General 2
Shoot the Piano Player 4
The Long Goodbye 2
Monkey Business '31 4
I'm No Angel
Drums Along the Mohawk
All the King's Men 2
A Man For All Seasons 4
Concert for Bangladesh
The Last Picture Show 2
Sons and Lovers 2
Black Beauty
Love and Anarchy 3
The Seduction of Mimi 4
It Happened One Night 6
The Fortune
Prince Valiant
Black Orpheus 5

48

First page, typed list of all films shown at VHT

them over and over. More astonishing was that I could remember them and their playdates.

In early November I was over at Ellen's house in West Philly, helping to paint some baseboards. Her contractor wandered in and said, "Oh, you're good, you want to come work for me?" A few days later I biked across town and found myself in an old house below South Street that had been gutted and sheet-rocked. My job was to prime it.

For me, doing this kind of work was like going back to zero. No control, and nobody really cared whether you showed up or not.

The house was cool, verging on cold. I painted a few walls, and then I had to pee. But there was no working bathroom. Over in the corner I found something in a pile of trash. Outside I located a safe corner and then peed into my paper cup. When lunchtime came I hopped on my bike and went home. Later, I left a "Sorry, I quit" message on the contractor's answering machine.

What was most humiliating were not the work conditions but the sense that I could not do what was asked of me, even though I had volunteered for it. Another case of Yes-No.

After that I began making longer and more frequent trips back to Charlottesville, where I stayed in Dave's old house on Northwood still occupied by our friend Al Filreis. There was plenty back home to attend to: there were two pregnant females at Rothery Road. After we left her behind my boxer Voisine escaped the yard and was knocked up by the local German Shepherd, Lance. I birthed her babies in our Philadelphia apartment just before Thanksgiving. We kept one of the puppies, and it became our beloved Sylvania.

When Chief moved back into the house, he brought with him his new girlfriend, Trisha Smith, and, by Christmas, it was clear that she too was going to become a mother. I have no idea whether the pregnancy was planned or not; in any case, Chief was about to begin again with a second family, even while living with the two children from his first one.

During that difficult year, Courtenay, newly-minted teen and high school freshman, kept her thoughts close. Dad was back in the house after being gone for three years, and if her sketch books offer any clues, Courtenay's ego ideal had moved from a heavily-crowned princess to a smokey-eyed fashion model. In July 2017, she and Dave shared a conversation about the new regime at Rothery Road:

Courtenay, 1985

Courtie: I woke up in the house to music. Upstairs Chief would be standing on the couch in front of the big mirror, in his boxer shorts, conducting The London Philharmonic Orchestra, Wagner's "Ride of the Valkyrie." Either he got up early or he never went to sleep.
Dave: When was this?
Courtie: Sunday morning. After you and Mom moved to Philadelphia.
Dave: Was this a regular Sunday event?
Courtie: Often. Then we would go to The Virginian for brunch.
Dave: Ian also?
Courtie: Maybe … but Ian was often elsewhere. I would have the French Toast and Dad did the Bluefish on Toast.
Dave: Why did he have that?
Courtie: That's what they served. He would be drinking Bloody Marys before we went, and during. Someone thought I was his girlfriend, once. Just part of Sundays with Dad. Here at the house, I can hear him saying to Ian, "Hey 'Big I', how about you make me another gin and tonic?" Ian hated being his bartender. So he got involved with Beth and I got involved with Che.
Dave: You and Che visited us that fall in Philly.
Courtie: She was a year older, a little wild, and she could drive. We used to go up to the Blue Ridge Parkway. Spent the night until the sun came up. Once we stole Dad's '66 Mustang and went to the *Rocky Horror Picture Show*.
Dave: You stole my Valiant, too, as I recall.
Courtie: Yup, stealing cars in those days—that was my thing.
Dave: How did you guys get to school?
Courtie: There was a daily routine. Ian and I slept in the same room downstairs, our upper bunks facing each other. We had this white Zenith alarm clock that got us up. Everyday. Sometimes Chief was passed out in the bathroom but no bother. Ian would wake up and find wine bottles and cigarettes everywhere. Initially he was very aggressive about removing trash left in the house, he hated the booze, the marijuana and the smoking. He wasn't a drinker or a smoker. Over months, Ian became increasingly angry at

Trisha—because she smoked and she was pregnant. They had some enormous fights.

I was the hellcat, Ian was the prude. Maybe even the parent.

Ian drove us to school in the reliable but unglamorous Dodge Diplomat Uncle Rudy bought at a Massachusetts car auction. There were some funny scenes at CHS:

School Administrator to Ian: Why are you late?
Ian: I had to drive her.
School Administrator to Courtie: Why are you late?
Courtie: He had to drive me.
We both got detention. But it was fun. All in all, I don't think the year of living dangerously was all that bad a year.

WHEN, YEARS LATER, Dave asked Ian, "Do you regret not going to Philadelphia?" he said, "I'll answer that with a 50-50. Yes and No. What I should have done was to go to St. Anne's-Belfield—in the ninth grade. It would have been a much more focused classroom environment than Charlottesville High and I would have had the sports attention there too. I could have played basketball, maybe even been a starter. Where I was, it was too easy to be distracted and a blow-off."

"What about the girl friend issue?" Dave said.

"Well, we got all the friggin' sex we wanted out of the way. When kids hear NoNoNo they say YesYesYes."

At this point I chimed in. "But we never said No. And I'm sure your father never did either, when he moved back in."

"Well, after some attempts by Chief to lay down the law, Trisha did say, 'Who the hell is your father to set any parameters for you? He's a joke.' By late September she was lying in the bedroom surrounded by pizza boxes and bottles of Coke. He wasn't there. She even rented *Zardoz*—that's a movie that believes that killing is good and procreation is bad.

"We would come upstairs for breakfast and there was lipstick on all the glasses. Trisha's cleanliness was based on her mood. There were lots of TV dinners. Chief and Trisha were hotboxing us by nine in the morning. I just recently charted out a potential connection for Chief but it never would have

Ian on stage

worked out because Granny would never have allowed it. He was involved with a fellow restaurant owner."

"Really, the one who owned that Cuban place? No wonder I was so mean to her."

"I liked her. She seemed like a normal person. She was hard-working. Conservatively dressed. This was happening the year Dave showed up. But she would have wanted Chief to go to church."

"She had a serious restaurant commitment."

"Well, it never worked out." Ian shook his head. "As you get older, it's slim pickings. If someone is loyal to you, you stay in there. But now everything is so transient and people don't expect things to last. We are very afraid to be vulnerable. You guys took the chances and were willing to experience something grander."

WHATEVER DAVE AND I were seeking to experience, it had been imperiled by our year away. The sudden proximity to his son Luke, who was growing up in New Jersey, made for more frequent visits, but reentry for Dave after seeing his son was difficult, and led to prolonged withdrawals. I was already too much in my own head to be of much help, and our overlapping miseries resulted in a serious decline in our ability to have—let alone enjoy—a sex life. When Princeton dangled another year of teaching, Dave did not even allow himself to be tempted, so clear it was that our life was centered in Charlottesville. Having to go back into his office job at the Foundation was so painful for him that in the fall after our return Dave embarked on a two-year course of three-times-a-week psychotherapy.

There is therefore something disarming about the warmth expressed in the letters we wrote each other once I moved back to Charlottesville. Dave started the correspondence:

April 15, 1985
Dear Ann,
Hi! Thought I'd write you a letter. I realize that it's my first and that seems strange. Shows how little we've been apart.

Dave went on to describe his day of wandering down to see *Paris, Texas* at the Ritz Cinema, watching haircuts at Julius Scissors, and counting trash bags as he walked back to our apartment.

It seems as if one could stay here a long time without much happening ... my last little bit of Philadelphia karma seems to be to live out the life you had here.

I try to imagine you, you are moving around, bending to pick up a sock, dancing in and out of the kitchen, opening the door for a dog. You never sat still much before this year. You used to burst into the house, full of some story, a bag in your hands and joy or indignation in your heart!

My reply to Dave jumps straight into Rothery Road's *You Can't Take It With You* vibe:

At 8:00 am, school day. The dogs are barking and the house is filled with so much light that you couldn't sleep if you wanted. But my life without you is very quiet and adventureless—except bursts of activity when Ian and Courtenay are coming or going.

Ian ran in a track meet Saturday at Western and I finally got to see him run. His time in the two-mile was 10:30 ... Courtie looks divine and is going to the prom in the blue dress. She and some senior girls had a leisurely day at Chris Green Lake, discussing how to give and receive hickeys.

Clearly I had been missing the adrenalined lives of teenagers. My letter continues:

The most disturbing news was Courtie telling me how undermined she had been by her father and Trisha. Weird stuff. Last fall Chief and Trisha used to tell the kids that I was not coming back, and that I had chosen you over them, and that now Chief and Trisha were the adults that were going to take care of them. This explains the cold reception I got when I came back in September after our Nova Scotia trip. Courtie remembers calling me up and asking me to go out to dinner as a way to break the ice. She said that Chief and Trisha fought with each other, and that Trisha yelled at them. Constantly. And that she would break down at school with Ann Hudson and Kara about how much she hated her life and how being at home was hell!

"Ann will never find out" became Chief and Trisha's chant of conspiracy. "Ann's not here so we can do what we want" was said during the final clearing out of records and books. And when I came home in the middle of their packing Courtie heard the alarm, "Oh, no, Ann's back."

Can you stand all this family melodrama? Hope so, miss you terribly, can't wait to fuck. I feel like I lived in a stranger's life this year—my memory of feelings and fears I had, places I couldn't go to, insecurities at every turn and now I wonder why I felt that. My head is free of that pain now, but I wish I understood how that cloud of fear came over me.

Dave replied with news of friends we had made at Princeton and with plans for a summer trip to California. My final letter of our exchange that spring found me dealing with two children who had more than learned to fend for themselves and with my lingering regrets about the missed opportunities in our year away:

> *On Tuesday—which was the nicest day of the century—Reid-O and I were just getting settled into our jobs when into the lobby come Ian and Beth. "We just walked away from school," they said. They hung around playing tag in the auditorium with the dogs and whiled away the afternoon looking through the VHT poster collection. Beth walked away with a gift—the* American Gigolo *poster. Richard Gere and his venetian blinds looks, she thinks, like Ian in a certain light.*
>
> *At home—before going to* Paris, Texas—*Courtie. No practice, got a cramp, and came home. A glimpse of a foreign bathing suit under her shorts.*
>
> *Later, at dinner, I tell Courtie I think she skipped school. She gleefully tells me how she planned out the whole event, tracing my signature off the box office reports and re-forging it on an excuse note. Clever girl—but she forgot the incriminating borrowed bathing suit. A strange combo: one skips by walking into my office at 10 a.m. with his girlfriend and the other plans a James Bond caper with pre-arranged pick-ups in the out-of-the-way high school parking lot. Everyone else got "in trouble"—lots of disappointed parents who see the first glimmer of rebellion in these little birds leaving the 'burb' nest.*
>
> *I love your letters—I read them all the time. I'll be true to you, I love you, and I wish I'd loved you better this year. I'm sorry I was not a better person, or nicer—all of those things. It's hard for me to remember those feelings now, but I do remember what you looked like this winter and in the past few weeks and I get some sense of what a drag I was to be with. But I'm thrilled to be back here, with all the nature, and the sunlight, and the noise.*

17
THE BREAK-UP

In the summer of 1987, Dave and I were apart for a month. He and his college roommate Barney O'Meara drove their three boys—Barney's Patrick and Timothy and Dave's Luke—across the country in an aging Subaru, finally landing in James Wyatt's apartment in Costa Mesa. In a letter penned at a campsite in Zion National Park, where Barney was waxing the car and the boys were spilling the stew, Dave wrote, "When I am with you I sometimes miss other people, but when I am with other people I always miss you." Another postcard simply read, "I am looking desperately for a liquor store."

Dave and I reunited in Seattle in late August. Seeing him was something of a shock, since he had shaved off the moustache he'd worn ever since he was nineteen.

I brought along Ian and Courtenay; we were all invited to Dave's sister's wedding. Thirty-year-old Meleesa Wyatt was, after living with him for six years, marrying Larry Knappert. Our friends Tim Coffin and Katie Van Wie also came along and brought Katie's daughter Andi and son Jeremy. The two sets of kids were just about the same age and hit it off nicely—Ian and Andi even started a little romance.

While Dave was on the road I wrote him a letter about my time at Cape Cod:

> *August 5, 1987*
> *Dear Dave:*
>
> It's a perfect beach day, 90 degrees with slight breeze, green water but no green head flies. The girls and I walked to the channel as far as we could, nude swimming at the low tide.
>
> Yesterday, you were in my thoughts. Rain took back the day, I retreated to a noon TV movie with Dale Robertson and Ann Francis in Hollywood's Haiti, director Jean Negulesco's 1952 historical romance set during the Toussaint L'Ouverture revolution against France. The heroine and the movie's name was Lydia Bailey; Thomas Jefferson claimed to be her father's friend.
>
> Finished up the afternoon with a sewing project; made a set of napkins out of chair-covering fabric.
>
> Unspoken thought: I am basking in the quiet of my mother's recent departure back to Hopedale. But there were storms abrewing next door with auntie Martha, Billy, Barbara and the two toddlers in close quarters. Lots of yelling. I offered to keep the kids at my cottage until Barb was ready to leave.
>
> Melodrama is often my co-pilot, when I'm here.
>
> Gotta run, and pick up Ian who arrives by train into this whirlwind. I miss you, don't really want to go back to Charlottesville—extraordinary beach days are like nothing else in my life. But I can't wait to see your furry little body.
>
> Xxx I love you. A

"What do we think of this letter?" I wrote to myself later that fall. "Seems like a woman in love. To me. I do."

The fall had a lot of bounce to it: Dave was starting his new job at the University of Maryland; Ian was launched into his sophomore year at Carnegie Mellon, and Courtenay was hammering away on a dozen college applications.

I believe that in the letters we wrote each other during our August apart we each meant what we said, about missing each other. But there had been lots of danger signs when we were together—a bad trip to Mexico where we kept changing locations until we found ourselves kicking coconuts on trash-littered Progreso Beach. Dave falling into sudden silences, sometimes at a dinner party we were hosting. And there were his repeated attempts to again secure a teaching job, some of which had resulted in offers he had to turn down: a partner with a movie theatre was not portable. Maryland, however, was within driving distance of Charlottesville.

"It was against all odds—my getting back in," Dave said later. "People who are out of the profession for five years like I was just cease to exist. What happened with Maryland is a kind of a fairy tale."

There was the donor figure, Richard Cross. Richard had been hired out of UCLA to chair the Maryland English Department. As a result of his years in Los Angeles he was, unlike most Eastern academics, prepared to give a serious look at a book called *The Fall into Eden: Landscape and Imagination in California*. Dave brought out his second book in 1986, so he was able to hand it to the Maryland interviewers at the MLA convention in New York.

But Richard wasn't at the interview—I think he fell ill. The person he sent in his place, Leo Damrosch, had been at Virginia with Dave before moving on to Maryland, and he had no love lost for their former department. So he may have been an ally. Wally Kerrigan was another refugee from Virginia teaching at Maryland at the time, although it turned out that he favored another candidate that year, an old friend who however made some sort of off-base remark to a graduate student during his on-campus visit. When the friend was eliminated from the search, Dave moved closer to the top of the list.

During his New York interview Dave talked a lot about Bruce Springsteen, the subject of a chapter in a book-in-progress. Later Dave discovered that one of his interviewers had a huge poster of Bruce taped to the back of her office door.

So lots of things came together to make the improbable come true. The formal offer of a job involved a final snafu, however, because, when we returned home after our trip to Quintana Roo, Dave had no notion that Richard Cross had been in touch until someone at the theatre made casual mention of a phone call. Back home I asked the kids about it and one of them said, "Oh, yeah, somebody called. There's a note in one of your cookbooks."

Once Dave located the note he called Richard and immediately accepted the job.

We rented a little apartment in Takoma Park; the plan was for Dave to spend three nights there, do his teaching, and then to drive back to Charlottesville for long weekends. He had what he wanted and had worked so hard for, but our ambitions were clearly moving us apart.

Dave also wanted something from me that I was not going to be able to give, a re-centering of my life in Maryland. A letter written during his summer road trip lays out the script:

August 4, 1987, Page, Arizona

> *The little apartment in Takoma Park has been pleasantly on my mind. For some reason I've built a fantasy out of it already, as our special place, like the bedroom was at Northwood. Maybe I have been feeling a little invaded lately. Anyway, I see you getting on the early train, catching the Metro, and walking in my door just in time to shove down the coffee pot and climb back into the futon with me. Or perhaps, we'd walk to a little coffee shop nearby and have them make it for us. I like the idea of your coming to me, of my being asleep the whole time, and then of being awakened by your usual noisy hello.*

I therefore was shocked but not entirely surprised when Dave came home in mid-November and told me he had fallen in love with a colleague at Maryland.

What happened after that is a blur. Of course there was lots of yelling and crying—even some hitting—I flailed away as best I could. I do recall that Dave did not leave the house immediately, that he spent that awful night and part of the next day in our bedroom, that I visited him there to cry and make love, that Ruth Drexler went downstairs to greet him and said to him, "No, you won't, " after he said, "See you later," and that when he talked to Courtenay just before driving away, she said, "Well, even if you came back now, it wouldn't make any difference."

Then he was gone. I went to Ginn's Stationery store and bought a journal in which I wrote my thoughts from November 23 to December 29, 1987. Here is an excerpt:

11/23 Reid gives me the Bryan Ferry Bête Noir *CD to change my mood and I co-operate. Rock n roll always helps my broken heart. Today, since Tuesday, at four pm, when Ellen's phone call from Philly woke me from a nap—I haven't fallen apart.*

The danger of feeling numb to all this pain—I don't want to feel numb. I am smiling as I dance around the living room to Bryan Ferry. Reminds me of last fall when I bought Dave the Bruce Springsteen album—we drank martinis, smoked dope and made love in the loft.

At one point I wrote, "What makes me cry is the demonstrated love from my friends, I am overwhelmed, and sometimes embarrassed by their kindnesses."

Someone once said when you are in love you don't need friends, and I worked so hard in pursuit of love that I often neglected them. We all have our preferred grindstone, the wheel we like to work at, if we are lucky enough to like our work. I loved the theatre but I had few friends except my employees. Then Chief and I started a restaurant, and there were more employees who might become friends. But it is exhausting to pretend that just because you work alongside of people you also have to like them. Most of these "friends" came and went. Even when people stayed and I became truly fond of them, there was never enough time to enjoy them. Mine was an unintegrated life, separated into fragments which I barely polished. Now I was discovering how much I could depend on people around me that I had taken for granted.

11/25 I've stopped the helpless crying. I believe that you are gone, and as Courtenay says, "He's not coming back." Crying is replaced by thinking, scrutiny, as if I could figure out the puzzle of your disappearance. Writing is my comfort. I used to think that your ease with words and paper got in my way, like anything I wrote couldn't compare.

There is a copy of the novel you left behind in your closet—are there clues buried in those pages that would unravel the riddle of you, David Wyatt, a man on his second name, his third life and career, a man who can't look too closely at himself because the pain is so great?

Saying miserable things about you is only half of my feelings. I still love you very deeply—not because I have to make my own fires

Courtenay and Ian in Seattle

and food, but because you were my best friend and lover for five years.

Your sister just asked me to print pictures of the wedding—with such trepidation, but I like facing my life with you, the more I look at it the stronger my disbelief that you were miserable.

I see that you were contemplating an exit since our fight in June (even though you said you were staying: obviously you wanted the Cape, Meleesa's wedding, and friends to settle you in your new life.)

Dave and I were very fond of Meleesa and Larry so had been happy to agree to attend their August wedding in Seattle. And there was another reason to go: because she and her father were not speaking at the time, Meleesa had asked Dave to give her away. We decided to make it a family vacation and to bring the kids along.

It turns out that our family likes backyard weddings. We all gathered in the foothills of the Cascades at a motel owned by Larry's sister. Larry had purchased a huge salmon and wanted to cook it whole. The only heating device large enough to accommodate it was the dishwasher, so we cooked it on the "Pots and Pans" cycle, although I had first recommended using "Rinse and Hold."

It was a beautiful, cool day, and there are nice pictures of Katie's kids and mine standing around a big fir bonfire. Dave walked his sister down the aisle and then toasted her as having now taken her "second big leap in Seattle"—the first one, he explained, involving a trip to the World's Fair at the age of six, when she had run full speed toward the railing at the top of the Space Needle.

> More 11/25 Bryan Ferry sings "The Name of the Game." Repeatedly. I remember the Boys and Girls tape that we played to death, on that beach trip to Avon to stay with Leslie and Jody. We were fighting on the ride down. That business over the Subaru looms as the culprit, and the malfunctioning tape deck stood in as the object of disorder. You were really bothered by that car mess—my temper, anger, persistence, aggression terrified you. That was a critical time for us—I think you learned to hate me, and then suppress it.
>
> Face it: You would never have gone after the Subaru dealership with the tenacity that I did. I forced you to be part of something you found personally embarrassing. You had already decided that in your second-chance academic career you were going to be perfect, no chinks in the armor to cause worry or rejection.

That Subaru really did lead to a mess.

We decided to buy a car when we were on the way north for a day of double features in DC. We stopped at Stohlman Subaru and, because we had a movie deadline, quickly went with a demo. There was a lot of back and forth—the saleswoman conferring with people in the main office—and later, when I looked at the documents, a thousand dollars had been added for things like "rust proofing." So I stopped the check.

Subaru sued. We hired a lawyer and some weeks later I found myself on the stand in Fairfax County. Our lawyer accused Stohlman of "sharp practice," but a contract is a contract, and I swore audibly in the courtroom when we lost.

And more from 11/25:

But we had a good time with Jody and Leslie, passing Sue Miller's The Good Mother *around, sunning ourselves, and leaving in high spirits.*

A week later we were fighting about getting married. Your charm and facility to create romance exceeds your ability to maintain the fiction. Just below the romance are all the scary control tricks that you can't efface—I realize you want to possess me so as not to be odd, unmarried, alone. You didn't need to hold on so tight.

In our files there is a letter written by Dave to our friend Bob Schultz that I now find somewhat astonishing. The letter is dated May 7, 1987, so it was mailed some six months before the break-up:

Dear Bob,

I am writing with big news—Ann and I have decided to get married. We decided last night—we went to dinner at the C&O (downstairs!) and talked around the subject and then I asked Ann if she would and she said "YES." It stunned me that she had been waiting to be asked. But she was right to wait. I had slipped so far into myself for so long that the move had to come from me, I guess—there had to be some "me" to offer somebody else. It's been four years or more since I gave her the ring, which she calls the "headlight."

Vaguely, I do remember saying "Yes" to the C&O proposal; it was one of the several made to me over the years. But then anxiety took over, I told no one, and any agreement made did not hold.

11/27 Tuesday night, Reid started sobbing, crying very hard, saying how difficult this month has been on everyone. I thought—Dave never did this, he never wept in my arms with this kind of emotion. Crying means you trust someone enough to be vulnerable, and you aren't worried they will judge you for it.

David left because he had everything he wanted—the job, tenure, a family, friends in two places and he knew he still wasn't happy. How would he explain this?

11/29 Lots of rain as I drive to Lexington to see Jean. The hour-long trip gives me too much time to brood on what Courtie said at breakfast, "Why do I chase after guys so I can reject them?"

Jean isn't home when I get there, so I fall asleep in the car, the rain is too raw to wait on her porch. When Jean and I talk it's apparent that I've felt this break-up coming on since the summer, maybe since last spring when he got the job. The marriage fight is an easy landmark, but we have had five years of regular "dust-ups," as Jean calls them. His rules, his repressed irritation, his possessiveness: did these make me afraid to marry him?

ONE OF THE strange things that happened during this time were our telephone conversations. I picked up the phone whenever I felt like it and gave Dave a call. "Hi, how are you?" I'd say, as if nothing was off. Then we talked about ordinary things. And there was also the event of his first visit back.

A week or so into the separation Dave called and asked if I wanted to go for a drive. His love of driving around in cars was a California thing, I guess, but, in any case, I said, "Sure, pick me up at noon." We drove down Preston Avenue, up past the theatre on Market Street, and then over to the Woolen Mills.

I decided to wear a sweater he had bought for me. It was a cream-colored cashmere, an off-the-shoulder cut with a big bow below the neck.

We chatted away about this and that—there seemed to be no agenda. Finally I said, "So why are you here?" When he answered, "I don't know," I said, "Take me home."

Unbeknownst to me that turned out to be a pivotal moment. "You acted with such class that day," he later said, "and I acted like a complete fool."

12/1 Well, he did walk through the door, sort of. On days when he's in town to see his therapist, Sy, I can't work or think straight. Polly from the Darden School comes by to pick up the questionnaires, and then the phone rings:

I'm in the lobby of the Omni Hotel ... can you meet me?"

I just walk out the door and come back six hours later.

It's all very surreal. The $100 room that he pays for with cash *because he has $800 in his pocket. The hunger and ease with which we make love for hours before we can talk to each other. Nothing is difficult, or awkward, and no one cries about what we've done to each other. Dusk, then dark. I phone home and work, just to let people know. Know what? I don't know.*

We talk and drink a lot of water; at one point Dave goes to McDonalds, returns with three Big Macs, Cokes, and two orders of fries, which we devour. Everyone looks like they took a trip around the world in the last two weeks.

When I come home, Courtie tells me it's OK to try again. She'd take Alexis back if he ever did this. Sometimes I worry about what I'm showing this kid of adult life. Dave has promised to call and talk to her tonight; she is innocent, and she has been hurt by our split.

I play Sting not Bryan Ferry before bed.

Dave returned to Maryland for the next week of teaching but said he would be back—that he was going to tell K. it is all over.

12/2 Dave said last night on the phone that it was painful telling K. he was re-involved with me. She thought he and I would not see each other, but be alone. My deep fear is getting caught in his romantic ricochet as he tries to decide.

12/5 Yesterday I walked into the nicest party. Reid and Leslie had arranged to take me to lunch, a belated birthday, since I turned forty-three on December 2. The three of us walked to the C&O, and bumped into Caroline Dix, Ruth and Milton, Elaine. A surprise party. Jody showed up, released from his successful dissertation defense on Tom Jones *and other eighteenth century things, Courtie slipped in from school, Sibley, & Catherine. Carnations mysteriously sent by Dave Simpson, a spectacular cake—the world's largest Napoleon— baked by Caroline, and an excellent young wine, Clos de Gilroy, that Elaine opened. Delicious food. I felt loved and happy.*

VINEGAR HILL HAD many casts of characters that worked there over the thirty years. This '87 crew was cream of the crop, and they all gathered for my party. Leslie Gossage came on in 1976, a graduate student in English. When she and her husband Jody DeRitter, a tireless candy dude, graduated and moved to the University of Scranton in 1990, collectively they had performed every job possible at VHT short of laying carpet or cinder block. They lived in an old-style farmhouse on King Street, planted with peonies, iris, and shade trees that encouraged Sunday morning brunches; a dedicated hostess and pioneer locavore, Leslie cooked expertly from *Gourmet* magazine and fed invited staff on cheese strata, strong coffee, and splendid cookies. Sibley Johns and Elaine Futhey were candy "chicks" but Elaine also worked as a sommelier at the C&O, and Sibley was getting her Graduate MSW. Ruth and Milton were the elders. My old pal from the Fellini's kitchen, Caroline Dix, was now a partner at C'ville's baking destination, Sweet Inspirations. It was Caroline Dave and I had stayed with on our trip to Paris together. She was working as an *au pair* near the Arc de Triomphe, and our first night in the city the three of us shared a big mattress in her fifth-floor garret room. Dave likes to say that he'd spent his first night in France with two women in his bed.

Reid, I think, was the glue that held VHT together—we collaborated on the film booking, the layout of the printed schedules, and endless fix-up repairs and improvements for the future. It seemed that we had lunch out every day, where we talked business but in a relaxed way that made work seem like play.

During this terrible time Caroline, a devoted friend who rarely gave advice, sensed my despair and said, "Honey, you continue to have the same heartbreak with all your men since and including Chief. I listen but I don't believe I can help you—it might be time to find a professional."

THE BREAK-UP WITH Dave was the second great crisis of my life. Losing my father had been the first. When I was twenty-six years old and my father died so swiftly from pancreatic cancer, I saw my life system dissolve. Every notion I had about the possible arc of things—myself, barely an adult but now with two children, my dead father no longer holding his place in our family—even, perhaps especially, the trickster ideologies of Catholicism— well, none of the offered explanations had saved Eugene Porotti. I battled my first grief epidemic with weeks of depression and sleep. After that, I searched for a template to fix future loss or contain a crisis, but my ideas were never wise, or expansive. What was in my head was immature, and regional; it was as if I were back in Milford, in the immigrant ghetto, protecting my shame. Ever since high school I had used my girlfriends as unpaid listeners for my man troubles, but I had not changed. Now, listening to Caroline, I did not think about changing—I simply wanted to get help.

I asked around and was given the name of a therapist. His name was Philip Halapin.

> *12/10 A second visit to Dr. Phil. I give him the highlights of the week, my inability to say no to men, to David, and my need to mother, my fear of being a wife. Phil suggests that when couples have difficulties sometime a trial separation is in order.*
>
> *Phil doesn't talk much about Dave but rather reflects on how I feel. I suspect he thinks I'm burying my grief too fast in too many projects—sewing, bathroom painting, romantic rendezvous. He could be right. I don't want to feel the pain because then I miss him and our life so much and I can't imagine staying away from him.*

During all this time I had not begun to worry about supporting myself; I had long since learned how to do that. But a look back at annual ticket receipts for the mid-eighties reveals the somewhat alarming shape of a bell curve. In 1983, we made $188,000 on ticket sales; in 1987, the year of the break-up, we took in $4,000 less than that. In the middle year—1985—sales topped out at $204,000. In those twelve banner months two movies made the difference, Jonathan Demme's *Stop Making Sense* and Jamie Uys's *The Gods Must Be Crazy*. *Sense* grossed $11,311, and *Crazy* brought in $9,432. The only pattern to be discerned in the upswing is that in 1985 I was enjoying the end of my *wanderjahre* in Philadelphia and that people were drawn to titles about not being sane.

During the rendezvous period with Dave there was a strange trip north to Chevy Chase to a farewell party for a Maryland colleague. I tried on a dress that he vetoed—the leggings were inappropriate. Later I discovered that I could have worn a lampshade and no one would have noticed. The party was actually fun, a terrific bunch of people, smart, funny, although a little too quick to say, "You should move up here." Dave seemed surprised that I was not behaving like a wallflower, not miserable, but having a good time.

12/17 Dave left yesterday and I think I feel better. Things were impossible in the house with him & Ian not speaking. Dave thought he could put up with it because he's lived in houses where people didn't talk but I can't.

I had picked up Ian at the train station on Thursday in D. C. It was so foggy and raw. I tell him Dave's at the house and he says "I don't plan to speak to him." I realize he has a right to be angry—he's been ignored by this man—not even a phone call.

So when we sit down to lunch and we all huddle around bowls of soup, and Dave makes "How was the semester small talk," Ian stares at him and says, "I have nothing to say to you."

"Suit yourself—but I think we should talk—there are things to say."

"I don't want to talk to you."

"Have it your way."

"I will—you obviously had it yours."

We have a terrific fight standing, walking in the rain. People drive by, friends come to visit the kids, and we continue to fight. Dave cries but won't apologize—talks about discovering power and cruelty and feeling better about himself and trying to learn how not to misuse it. I feel like a laboratory rat. Finally we agree that he has to leave until Ian goes back to school.

AFTER TALKING TO Halapin it was clear that Dave and I needed more time apart before any moving back in. I had the kids alone, for Christmas, while Dave drove north to see Luke. He stayed with Larry and Meleesa in Cobble Hill, where they were spending the last of their five years in Brooklyn before returning to settle in Seattle.

12/20 It's a Monday, Elaine and I are going to Chincoteague on the Eastern Shore to stay at Donna and Sandy McAdams's beach house. Rain squalls welcomed us but we went for a long walk on the beach anyway, forgetting about the time until the horizon melted into the blue grey waterline. We knew it was five pm, going on night. The winter solstice.

The house is old and being fixed-up. Some parts are like grandma's kitchen but the upstairs bedroom is soothing whites and greys. Champagne and snacks for dinner, then sleep in the double bed so we can continue to talk after lights out.

Tuesday the sky's blue, blue like it was in the San Juan Islands, after Meleesa's wedding, when she and Larry took Dave and me and the kids along on their honeymoon.

Christmas may be just around the corner, but you would never know that here—I love the isolation of this place. Elaine and I drive around looking for houses to buy, and fantasize a small shop that could occupy our life on this island.

We look for oysters in an unappetizing grocery named Meatland, then someone gives us directions to the shacks out by the ocean, where we buy a just shucked quart and wonder if we can eat them all.

Back at the beach house, I boil spaghetti, fry up garlic and parsley in olive oil, and throw in the quart of oysters. We eat it all with Sibley's great red wine; finish the evening with a split of Billecarte-Salmon and chocolate. I am coming back to life.

12/22 Home. I call David and relate my good time with Elaine. "Is this separation some kind of revenge?" he says.

12/29 Today I split wood for the stove until I completely exhaust myself. No hike or fuck ever shut me down like this exercise. Pain is mostly gone.

A few days later, Dave moved back into Rothery Road.

The Sheltering Sky

18
HALAPIN

When I was in the fourth grade I asked my parents to buy a piano. For years I had been playing on my grandparents' Mason & Hamlin and I felt I had to have a piano of my own. There was deep inside emotion I needed to get to and playing was the way I could access and express it.

My mother bought an old upright and put it in the corner of our tiny living room. She was adamant that I practice every day but I didn't really need the pressure or care about the rules because, for me, playing was a pleasure, and a little obsessive. Some girls had dolls, but I mutilated mine—I cut off their hair. When I played the piano I was making something beautiful.

I was given lessons by Alex DiGiantonnio, my mother's piano teacher, a fussy, once aspiring concert pianist who lived in a big house on Congress Street. His wife Elsie was a hairdresser, so her half of the house smelled like permanent processor. His half was filled with antiques and a Steinway grand. On the weeks Alex was not available his tiny sister Ada—she was shorter than

I am—taught me on an upright. Cousin Billy—all four of the Porotti and DiVitto kids were forced to have lessons—called her 'Ada Mouse.'

I have small hands. I can barely reach seven notes cleanly. Because a lot of music has chords of ten notes, when I play I sometimes have to leave out the middle notes. At the beginning of my piano study, I liked lots of pedal, bombastic pieces by Grieg and Chopin. Years later when I saw Holly Hunter in *The Piano*, lost in a swoony romanticism, it took me back to my grandparents' parlor, and the baby grand I pounded as an imagined gateway to my escape—if only from Sunday dinner. My cousin Billy and I shared a rivalry for the most airtime: he was much more serious than I was and suffered tremendously when his father denied his career choice to study piano.

As the years went by, it became clear that Alex did not want any of his students to perform in public. None of us ever participated in student recitals. Our music, however good, was something we kept to ourselves. To this day I have difficulty getting up in front of people; it is no wonder I am happiest working in a kitchen or in a projection booth.

WHEN I STARTED playing I was devoted and therefore always prepared. Once I became a teenager, I was distracted, and there were scenes with Alex. When I went to college, I assumed the end of my piano career. By my sophomore year, however, I began studying with Genevieve Greene, one of Leonard Bernstein's classmates, became serious again, and even managed a few recitals. I got comfy by practicing in the student lounge while couples made out. For my Junior Recital I performed a Bach Invention, one of Debussy's *Nuages*, Dvořák's *Slavonic Dance No. 1,* and finished up with a fellow student on Debussy's four-handed *Fetes*. In my last fall at Marietta College, after my trip to Europe, I blew off the Senior Recital.

In looking back, I can see now that the piano was a safe place. It gave me a way of dealing with the abuse I had begun to experience. Someone had his hands all over my body, and I played my piano as fast and as loud as I could.

When I began telling Philip Halapin stories about my childhood, and about how my parents had looked away, he said, "You were dropped on your trust." That was why I loved therapy with him—because he could say things like that.

In Jane Campion's movie, the piano is Holly Hunter's dowry. She comes with it and her daughter to New Zealand, where she has been sold into marriage with Sam Neill. She is mute, and the piano is her voice.

When she plays she is playing composer Michael Nyman. Campion had full control of her movie, which she wrote and directed, and when it came to choosing a score she knew what it needed, Nyman's lush minimalism.

The new husband is not sexually available. But Harvey Keitel, a nearby landowner, is. He retrieves the piano Neill has abandoned on the beach, trades some land for it, and invites Hunter to teach him to play.

What he really wants is her. Or maybe he wants to free her from her black, entrapping hoop skirts. When she begins visiting him in his cabin, Hunter gives nothing away; she makes Keitel pay for any access to her, key by key. A look up the skirt is one key—she is buying her piano back. Ten keys gets them naked in bed. Slowly but surely, she falls in love, and then she gives it all away.

When it threatens to drown her, Hunter finally gives up her piano. "My will has chosen life," she says, as she untangles her shoe from the rope bearing her overboard with the sinking piano.

After abandoning the piano when I was twenty-one, I really didn't begin playing again with a will until my early seventies. In the meantime, my whole life had become my piano: my theatre, my restaurants, my gardens, my cooking, my homes. I put my hands on my life.

IN THE FALL of 1990, about three years into my therapy, I flew to London for a film festival with Ruth and Milton Drexler. One night down by the Victoria Embankment, I found myself crying uncontrollably. Again the journal:

> *Sunset over gates to Whitehall. Everywhere in sky was vibrant pink softened by cloudy white puffs. Walked, crying, repeating the dream of my dead Voise, kissing me goodbye, felt the kiss like a bite on my lips. Sobbed, staying in the shadows of the riverbank until eventually seated in St. Paul's for Evensong. It was exactly where I wanted to be; in the largest church imaginable, listening to a choir, thinking about everything all at once. Psychological jumble, psychological peace. Could have stayed there forever.*

I thought I was missing my departed Boxer but I was clearly missing much more. One evening I found a phone booth in Russell Square, went into it. I called home and Dave answered. We had been living together for almost eight years, and we had worked hard to create a new life together after the break-up. From three thousand miles away, I asked him to marry me.

We were married on May 4, 1991, under the big trees on Barney and Mary O'Meara's Rappahannock County farm. But before all that there was a glitch—and it had to do with a movie.

I OFTEN SPENT my evenings looking at couples walking out of my theatre and wondering what they might say to each other about the movie they had just seen. Phil Halapin often came to the movies, sometimes alone, sometimes with his wife, and it could be complicated to see my therapist outside of his cozy room. On the other hand, one of the things that made me trust him was that he was a devoted moviegoer.

I am standing in the ticket booth in the corner of our big glass lobby. Phil walks up to the window and says, "Two, please." Often he has a VHT discount card, so all I have to do is punch it. I say "Hi," or nothing. He usually asks, "Is it good?" My answer comes with a "Yes" and a smile; I do not launch into an instant précis of what the critics have to say. After the film has ended, and Phil walks out with his wife, I wonder how they have liked it.

Nowadays, in the second decade of the twenty-first century, when TV series have taken the place film once occupied in our lives, we no longer argue about what's on the screen. "Oh, I loved *Friday Night Lights*," we say, and then leave it at that. But in 1991, when I saw and loved a movie and Dave didn't, I still cared enough about what was happening on the big screen to think to myself, "I can't marry this guy—he's a philistine."

Going out to a movie with someone meant talking about it afterwards. If you were on a date, there was a definite erotic component to the outing. You watched, you talked, you may even have argued, and then, well, seeing movies could be a kind of foreplay.

Our post-movie "argument" went something like this:

"So what did you think?" I say, as I push open the heavy double glass front door of the lobby. Dave is often quiet, thoughtful after a movie. Like his son Luke, he lets it sink in.

"I felt anxious the whole time—most of the time—especially during that scene on the cliff."

Now, I am surprised. "Hmm. Why is that?"

He has stopped walking. "Because it was interrupted. The sex was interrupted—I don't get that."

We have just seen *The Sheltering Sky*. Americans Kit and Port Moresby are traveling in 1930s North Africa; having arrived at a godforsaken outpost, they ride bicycles out of town to a summit. She is wearing a red and white sundress.

"Make it to the pass?" he says. He gets there first. They start to walk, hand in hand, and they come to what looks like the edge of the world. Just red desert. The score by Ryuichi Sakamoto swells up. They sit down and look out. He takes off her sunglasses, and she his. There's an awkward embrace, and she lies down. Soon they're making love, while still in their clothes.

"I was anxious earlier, because they were not getting along and I couldn't figure out why."

I open the door to my old green Saab, parked in the VHT lot. "They were sharp with each other. That doesn't mean they were not getting along."

"Isn't that not getting along?"

"They were not in their own country, they were sleeping with other people." My voice is shrill. "I don't know—there wasn't a lot of background given."

Why had I liked this movie so much? Here we were, it was February 9, 1991—two days earlier my son had turned twenty-three, and Dave and I were set to get married just a week before Ian was to finish his junior year at CMU. Back in the fall, I had gone up to DC and had seen *The Sheltering Sky* at the MPAA exhibitor screenings. I liked those prerelease events with their perfect projection and no talking, but the downside was that there was no audience buzz, just the bean-counting of other exhibitors and bookers calculating box office revenues. In booking Bertolucci's movie I expect I behaved as if VHT had a built-in audience for what the business school analysts had called "The Prestige Factor." At the time I was also quite swept away by all things desert.

Our silent ride home allows me to rewind the gorgeous cinematography of Tangier, Morocco, Niger, and Algeria. Was the movie just a beautiful travelogue for me?

But for us the evening is not over. "Can we imagine," I say, "what do you think—why were they not getting along?"

Dave answers immediately. "It could have something to do with Port's preferring men. I mean, we know about Paul Bowles. But in any case, let's get back to the scene on the cliff. He gets on top of her and he stops—"

"—No," I interrupt, "they talk. It's not that they stop making love—they stop being silent. Before, they are silent and just move their heads around each other like they are mute. And then they start talking as if they have forgotten what they are doing, but they keep doing it."

"*You*," Dave says, drawing out the sound—"*you* never say anything during sex."

"Nope—I'm your silent partner. But this is not about us—this is about them."

"So finally they figure out what they need to say to each other."

"They do," I answer, as I walk towards the freezer to make a celebratory martini, believing this argument has ended. "And for you the movie is clearly over."

"Well it wasn't over. There was a long denouement, and he dies—"

"No he doesn't just die." There's a quaver in my voice for Port and his final situation. "He gets sick, and she takes care of him, and in spite of that, then he dies."

Dave is silent, still not sure he believes this reading.

"Then she goes off and joins the caravan, and has sex locked in a room with a man who in real life is actually a ballet dancer."

It's clear I've added this to piss him off.

"I don't buy that resolution. Her being carried off by a sexy Arab. "

"He's a Berber."

"Berber—whatever. Do you buy that?"

"I do. All signs have pointed to it. Earlier she sleeps with Tunner, the Campbell Scott character, but he's a less daring, moneyed imitation of her husband. The Berber is tailor-made."

"Let's get back to the scene on the cliff. Because that's the heart of the movie. When they start talking the title comes in. The sheltering sky. He's not afraid of what's behind it but she is."

"No, she's not afraid." I am beginning to feel very warm—almost hot. "She's not afraid—she's full of knowledge. She says 'nothing' is behind it."

"I thought that makes her feel afraid."

"Yes and no. Doesn't it go—he talks about the sky as something that's going to protect them from what's behind it. And she says, I know what's behind the sky, 'Nothing.' And he says—"

I can't remember what I'm talking about; the urgency I feel for this martini puts me to work—combine, stir, pour. I take a sip and am back on track.

"Doesn't she say, 'But you are not afraid of being alone.' So that's the equation: 'nothing'—to her—equals being afraid of being alone, so therefore their marriage has not been enough. Is that a Yes? Do we agree on any fucking thing? Martini?" I wave a filled glass in his direction.

Dave puts his hand around the glass. "OK—but what's going on when you are in the middle of sex, and suddenly you stop and start talking? That disturbed me."

"Never happened to you before?"

Dave pauses and then says, "I can't say that it has. That moment is pretty strong: her cry-like gasp, or is it a groan?"

"She makes an animal sound—from an unmapped place."

"Which is where she ends up."

"She ends up in the café. Or the car. But she runs away from both."

"What is it about the scene that you really liked? Obviously you liked it. I was upset by it."

"I guess I recognize that I have been in her shoes. Where I am having sex and I cry because it reminds me of what's missing in my life."

BY 1991, BERTOLUCCI had become my Snake in the Garden, nibbling at my heels with that lurid pat of butter.

What was it about the film that made me take it so hard? I liked the pushing each other in the marriage; only later did I see that the two characters were pushing to destroy the marriage. Did I want Dave to be someone like John Malkovich, and did I fancy myself a sort of Debra Winger, people who set out to wreck a marriage because it is so Western and normal?

Stopping the sex in order to talk felt to me and still feels to me like a brave act of filmmaking. Then, in 1991, I think I was responding mostly to style, to the look of the thing. But there was an emotional digging at something too, at what I used to call "intimacy."

This word once acted for many of us as a god-term, although I'm not sure we even knew what we meant by it. All I knew was that something had been missing in my life with Chief, something that did not happen after my father's funeral. Not once did he ask me how I felt. *Asking a person how she feels*—that is what it comes down to.

People often confuse sex with intimacy because you feel so much while it is happening and so will say anything. As in the scene between the husband

and wife on the cliff, I often cried *after* sex and I was not crying about the sex but about some other longing the sex had tapped into. But Dave accepted my behavior: he let me cry, and he didn't pull away when I did. All this had gone on without our being married—so what was the point of changing things?

The fact that in my mid-forties it all felt like such an important thing makes me think I wasn't fully formed. I no longer believe that we should build our philosophies on film directors. On the other hand, a movie was then and is now something to be moved by, and then to talk about, intensely. But there is danger in arguing about a film. And, despite the vehemence of my opinions, over the years I have also found myself changing my mind about an initial response to a work of art. Life demands that you change your mind, about movies and about people, although not everyone is able to respond to the demand.

The hesitation I let myself feel on the brink of my second marriage was not another case of "Yes-No." I had been saying "Yes" to David for years, and I meant it. I loved him in many ways, and for many reasons. For one thing, Dave and I were often talking about each other when we talked about movies—we were not afraid to get personal. And I trusted him, even though he had dinged me up a bit; I knew he would never talk about me behind my back. We were, finally, intimate, and we were able to become so because I knew he would stand and deliver. He didn't walk away when the argument heated up.

David had a way of talking that was the opposite of the academic husbands I knew who always turned the conversation towards themselves. He was serious, but never pompous. None of his ideas came out of other people's articles; he was, as one of his best students one said, "such an independent thinker." His template for talking about movies came from the Westerns he loved, with their deeply elegiac sadness, but somehow his affection for a very limited genre never determined what he might say about any other kind of movie.

The outcome of our strenuous encounter about Bertolucci was never really in doubt. I suppose I hesitated in the way I did because I wanted my "I do" to carry with it none of the ambivalence I had often felt but never before allowed myself to admit, and the argument about *The Sheltering Sky* simply offered me one last occasion to play devil's advocate with my undivided heart.

ON MY WEDDING day I found myself worrying about other people's needs. I don't like being the center of anything although I did love my dress, a reaction to the disaster of trying to sew something out of pink taffeta that made me look like the doll on the top of the cake. Dave and I went to Nordstrom and picked out a vivid blue Nicole Miller short sleeveless sheath with an open scissored back.

I worried about Luke, Dave's son, who had at first said he would not come. Then twelve years old, Luke had become a devoted gardener with a strong preference for perennials. "I like things that last," he once said to Dave. "Divorce is like an annual."

When Luke did relent we sent Barney's son Patrick, newly equipped with a driver's license, to collect him from Dulles Airport. Two hours later they called to say that they were lost. Barney talked them back to the farm, and they pulled in an hour later after having eaten to the bottom of two bags of Cool Ranch Doritos.

I worried about whether my mother would have a good time. My cousin Barbara and her husband Chris agreed to fly south from Boston with her and, after their plane was delayed, Chris got a speeding ticket on one of Northern Virginia's back roads. Anita blended right in and eventually found her accustomed niche in the kitchen, washing dishes.

Dave and Luke at the Cape

I should have worried more about the food and drink than I did because, disastrously, we ran out of wine some two hours after the ceremony. When it came to the meal, Marcella Hazan was our co-pilot: an appetizer of gorgonzola and pine nut toasts followed by cauliflower in béchamel, savory carrot sticks, green beans and almonds, grilled chicken and lamb speidinis. I baked eight loaves of Como bread and we served it with the cheese my sommelier friend Elaine ordered from the Market Street Wine Shop—Bucheron, Black Diamond Cheddar, and a big wheel of Stilton. Until it disappeared, we poured Alexander Valley Champagne and a rosé from Provence.

Ian was running the music and had assembled a five-piece combo, musicians he had grown up with including two members of the Dave Matthews band. They played mellow jazz all afternoon, although no one danced. It more than made up for the fact that Ian arrived late for the ceremony and missed his cue to usher us out of the farm house with a trumpet fanfare.

I did not worry about Courtie who looked great in her little black Anna Sui sheath and who had agreed to be the kitchen admiral. Her note to the sleepers in the Rothery Road house was playful but firm:

Boys—
  1. *chicken wings in the kitchen*
  2. *mo' beer in the fridge*
  3. *sleeping arrangements:*
      a. *me & Andi in A & D's room*
      b. *Jeremy in loft (he has strep)*
      c. *2 people can sleep in our old room (one on couch, one on bed)*
      d. *1 person on living room couch*
      e. *last person can either sleep in the chair or take the front door rug, throw it on the bench and grab some blankets from downstairs (beneath the bathroom sink).*
  4. *Tomorrow:*
      Gotta be out there by noon, so we gotta leave BEFORE 11 am, O. K?

Sorry for being so anal.
Courtenay

In return for her efforts, Courtie was given a trip to Europe: on the day after the wedding, she and I flew to Nice. It's fair to say that I honeymooned with my daughter.

The highlight of the ceremony came when we were exchanging our vows. I was on Milton Drexler's arm; he was my surrogate Dad and I was delighted when he agreed to give me away. As I turned to Dave to begin saying my "I do's," our beloved German Shepherd Sylvania trotted up in front of us and began writhing on the ground. She managed to balance herself on her back with her legs in the air and held the position while we plighted our troth. I could only catch a glimpse of her antics out of the corner of my eye, but there was too much stifled laughter to be able to ignore her.

I had asked Reid to give some remarks, and he wrote something lovely:

> *I looked for a long time for a quote that would tie movies into what was happening today. I kept looking for stories about 'the first time I saw such-and-such a movie,' but didn't find any, probably because I was looking in the wrong places. Then I came across a quote by François Truffaut from 1957. At this point he had directed a few short films, but was two years away from his first feature* The

Courtenay reading at the wedding, May 1991

400 Blows. *He was writing about how great the French New Wave was going to be:*

"The film of tomorrow appears to me even more personal than an individual and autobiographical novel, like a confession, or a diary. The young filmmakers will express themselves in the first person and will relate what has happened to them: it may be the story of their first love or their most recent; of their political awakening; the story of a trip, a sickness, their military service, their marriage, their last vacation … and it will be enjoyable because it will be true and new.… The film of tomorrow will be an act of love."

When Truffaut wrote this, he had been through a lot: he had dropped out of school at fifteen, lived on the street, worked, enlisted in the military, gone AWOL, gone to military prison, and been married. But he had so much more in store for him.

If we can imagine lives as movies, I feel that Ann and Dave are poised at the same point as Truffaut was when he wrote this: They know enough about life to appreciate what's interesting about it, and they know enough about each other to be able to live together. Now they are about to put a frame around it and make it a work of art.

Years later, when Dave and I were reminiscing about the break-up, he revealed to me that after coming back he had gone to one person to make amends.

"I went to see Reid, in that tiny apartment on Altamont Circle. He was kind; he let me in. And eventually I said, 'I really messed up.' And he said, 'Yes, you did.' That was about the size of it. Maybe I went to see Reid because I knew he'd be nice to me."

MY IMMEDIATE REASON for beginning therapy with Philip Halapin in 1987 was that David and I had broken up, but I returned weekly, and stayed for many years, for something much different.

Does abuse tenderize? It is a strange resource—the ability to tolerate mistreatment. I did not make any calculations about whether my prime time was over or not, but I took Dave back because I loved him.

In the abuse narrative, the notions of an adult are a philosophy developed from the injuries of the child. In "Italian Girlhood", Richie Speroni tries to finger my crotch. But there was someone else who had already done what Richie Speroni could not do.

He used to sit me on his lap, on his penis, and put his finger up my vagina. This started when I was eight years old, about the time I asked for a piano.

My earliest memory of the abuse is during a party in a relative's living room. He and a laughing sidekick are drinking, smoking, and one of them starts bouncing me on his leg. Wearing a dress, facing them, I bounce, bounce, harder and rougher on my groin, until I slip off and slide all the way down his pant leg. My knee lands hard on the leather toe of a man's shoe. A two-inch slice across my kneecap. Blood everywhere. Patched up in the kitchen by the women, no questions asked. I have the scar to this day.

After that, the abuse became more or less habitual. Whenever he saw me, he pulled me onto his knee. And in spite of the broad daylight, and other adults and children in the room, he would put his hands under my clothes and into the crevices of my body. Boldly done, I would say now—then I just felt frozen, paralyzed, feverish. As I got older, I struggled to wish the shame of it away, but then I came to the outrage: how could the adults not see that he was sexually abusing a young child. In the sixth grade, about the time I scissored off my eyebrows and eyelashes, I also began wearing to school what were for me my mother's very outsized clothes. My misery was obvious, and they were looking away.

IN REMEMBERING MY analysis with Phil, I have found myself brooding on the limitations of the narrative offered in this book. In looking back over my pages, I see how often I have described how I once looked. And yet I give few physical descriptions of anyone else. Was I—am I—narcissistic without even knowing it? Perhaps. There are many mirrors in my house. But another way to think about it is that I was conditioned from early on to regard my own body as *unclosed*. There was a path to the inside over which I had little control. Someone was messing with my "parts," but I did not feel whole. Eventually I reacted to this feeling not by shutting down but by treating my body as a lure.

During the period of my abuse I was a chubby little girl. In the summer before the eighth grade, I got my period and began to redistribute my weight. I became, in a word, beautiful, and the consequence was that he finally left me alone. Once I looked sexual his interest waned. I didn't have to give a lot away in order to get rid of him: growing into a woman's body set me free to become, and now on my own terms, alluring. Because of the way I was hastened into becoming a woman, I never renounced my belief in the value and the power of female beauty.

The movies showed me how to become beautiful; in them, women always looked good. But a movie also tends to zoom in on a woman as a collection of legs, arms, breasts, hands, and this way of responding to the body spoke to me.

MOMENTS OF RECOGNITION: after so many years in Charlottesville, I was used to having people walk up to me and say, "Oh, don't I know you?" And I would reply, "Maybe—I'm the Vinegar Hill lady." The only downside of saying so was if my interrogator had had a bad experience at the movies. In the early years of my therapy with Phil, he never complained about, or even mentioned, the movies he had seen at my theatre. Now, over thirty years after I first began driving up Hydraulic Road to the little house under the oak trees, the relationship with Phil has shifted to a place where we talk easily about books and movies.

Halapin suddenly grabs a book, Hanya Yanagihara's *A Little Life* and says, "I am not getting very far. Page 225."

He's in "The Postman chapter", I think, realizing that I loaned him this book a month ago. "Don't you like it?"

"I know what happens," he counters, "Jude dies. I have treated so many self-mutilators. It too often ends that way—there is no way out."

"OK. Give it back. I don't want to make you read something you hate, that hurts you."

"No, no. I want to talk to you about it."

"I know the point you are at. The book doesn't take hold until the "After Vanities" section. It is about Jude but it's about all of them." As I speak, trying to recommend the book, the memory of it explodes in a thunder of sobs. I am gasping my way to the end of a sentence, amazed and embarrassed that I cannot control my crying. What I get out in words is this: "The simple life—

the little life—is to find someone who loves you and who you can love back. But it's not that simple, or that easy."

He breaks in. "But you have to love yourself to get someone to love you."

"Yes," I say, "but even more essential than loving yourself, you must be willing to recalibrate. That's Hanya's word for what we have to do."

Halapin gives a puzzled look but I plow on with my mini-lecture.

"Recalibration comes out of a regard for the other. The one you love whether it is your child, your partner, your parent, maybe even yourself. You can't have ego-driven expectations for the people you love. But, of course, we expect anyway—we want the movie to end happily—and then, if it doesn't, we have to recalibrate. And that's what I have been trying to learn how to do ever since I came in your front door."

"Sounds like recalibration is the Jiminy Cricket on your shoulder."

Halapin may have said other wise words, but I was only half listening. In the past I would have controlled my crying, vain as I am about the unattractiveness of full-throttle sobbing. But not this time. I sputtered on:

"In my life I know so many people who don't have love, and it kills me, because whatever is amiss or imperfect with Dave and me, I feel his love, and I feel my love for him. But *A Little Life* stands up to every obstacle in life about love, about how to get it, how to keep it, and how to lose it. I feel the whole current of that book just crying and talking about it with you."

Wrung out as I am, I think: how did this happen? I feel so comfortable falling apart here.

Have I been ambushed? Thank God!

19
TOWNWATCH

I wasn't a visionary. There were many things I did not see coming: the advent of the VCR, which began to keep people at home in the evenings; the rise of the multiplex, and its power to corner the available product; and, perhaps most sadly, the slow decline in the quality of movies themselves, as the century approached its end. But I did install Charlottesville's first authentic espresso machine, a reliable Italian Faema in 1991. That was the extent of my visioning.

It was eighteen years in to the running of Vinegar Hill when they came for me. They came in the form such changes so often come, by way of a development scheme. And the city fathers were behind them; politicians, I have found, like to build things. At the time they came for me I was behaving as if my little operation on Market Street might go on forever, so happy was I in simply going through the days. When I realized that they had come I fought them as best I could and fell back on some long lost skills; it turned out to be important, for instance, that I could still sew a dress.

Two brown dresses: that could be a title of this memoir. I was wearing a homemade brown and white gingham on the night we opened in 1976. In preparing for this later showdown, I decided to make myself something really nice. At our local Les Fabriques I found a beautiful muted white, grey, and brown fabric, a piece of striped Swiss cotton, and cut out a sleeveless scooped neck A-line with the small, sexy detail of a low ruffle at the on-the-knee hemline. That was pretty much my battle plan. And I wrote a speech.

When I stood up before the City Council on the night of August 9, 1994, and made my plea, I was wearing the dress and a pair of gold sandals. I suppose the dress did the trick or at least sent a shiver though the lawyer for the opposing side, because Dave, sitting next to him, heard the lawyer, himself decked out in a thousand-dollar suit, whisper to a colleague, "Oh shit, look at that."

It all began with a man named Lee Danielson, identified in one newspaper article as the "Scion of Cyrus McCormick." A California developer—he had been involved in building something on Wilshire Boulevard—Danielson had moved to Keswick in Albemarle County two years earlier and was looking to tinker with the Downtown Mall. In the spring of 1993 he shared his idea for a project with a fellow developer in Los Angeles. Then, that winter, he contacted the City of Charlottesville about locating a sixplex movie theater in the soon-to-be-empty Grand Piano Building, three hundred feet from Vinegar Hill. The plan was to have the complex run by my old nemesis, Neighborhood Entertainment Inc.

Long after our battle with Danielson was fought and lost, he left another mess behind. When you come to the middle of the Downtown Mall you confront a nine-story concrete structure without walls and a boarded-up first floor. In 2008, Danielson and his partners began erecting on the site of the old Central Fidelity Bank Building a project they called the Landmark Boutique Hotel. Cost overruns, bankruptcies, and court battles left the building unfinished, a place for pigeons to breed. The skeleton high-rise was eventually sold at auction to another developer who as of this writing has resisted all calls to clean up what the town has called a "spot blight."

At the height of the 1994 controversy Danielson described opponents to his development scheme as "self-serving, lefto-socialist garbage from a counter culture group." He also went on to say that "It doesn't matter how many signatures you get—this project is going to happen."

Much of the resistance to Danielson's plan had to do with his insistence on allowing vehicular traffic on the all-pedestrian Downtown Mall: he wanted easy drop off for the new movie customers. On June 2, 1994, Danielson made a formal request before the City Council for a car crossing at Second Street West. "No street? No project," he later said. "It's not really meant to be a gun to the head, but that's unfortunately where we are."

I wasn't happy about the thought of cars on the Mall, but my real concern was with having six new screens only a short walk from my front door. And with the fact that the City was being asked to grant an unprecedented right of way for the benefit of a direct competitor. The stakes for Vinegar Hill Theatre on this uneven playing field seemed ripped from the narrative of familiar movies—*A Flash of Green, Norma Rae, Mr. Smith Goes to Washington, Erin Brockovich*—that last one still waiting to be written.

We quickly rallied our troops. Twelve of us formed a group called Citizens for an Open Mall, later renamed Save the Mall, and finally Townwatch: several theatre concession people, a mother and son from insider local politics, owners of a jewelry store and a hardware store, a member of the Department of Anthropology, a rusty-haired motorcyclist who yearned for local office, Reid, and Dave, and me. Temperate summer days of Xeroxing, canvassing, cobbling signs for impromptu marches: "Avoid six-plexation without representation," "Don't Californicate the Mall," and my personal favorite, "Reid Stays, Lee Goes."

The Summer of '94 was my crucible, and my resistance was not shy. With our unlikely assortment of fierce activists, we flooded the local papers with letters of complaint and gathered almost three thousand signatures for a petition to stop what appeared to be an unfair advantage for this big, rich, corporate outsider. But I knew ultimately that members of the City Council, persons known to me all my adult life as acquaintances, realtors, planners, customers, would be deciding whether Vinegar Hill Theatre would live or die.

One of the arguments in favor of Danielson's project was that the Mall was somehow failing. In a letter to the press, he wrote that "This project will be a small and reasonable step to reversing the mall's slow but steady decline." But Lee Richards, the Commissioner of Revenue, was also quoted as saying, "It's an open secret that the Downtown Mall is thriving."

Early meetings about Danielson's fourteen-million-dollar project had happened off-stage and involved members of the Planning Commission, the

Office of Community Development, and the City Council. When confronted with the town's own planning standards, standards that seemed to mandate a car-free Mall, Director of Community Development, Satyendra Huja said, "not every action that you take has to be consistent with the Comprehensive Plan." I had worked for Huja in the early seventies on a survey of every sidewalk and curb in Charlottesville and had found him to be devoted to bringing the city into the twentieth century, but the variance he was now supporting seemed like municipal swag for a developer.

Four members of the Planning Commission eventually voted against the proposed crossing. Commission Chair Sue Lewis saw "no compelling reason to destroy the neighborhood aspect" of the Mall. Another Commission member noted that "we have wrested this much from the automobile and I am loath to relinquish it."

Danielson's project eventually expanded to include a skating rink as well as a multiplex. Original drawings show an open-air rink, but, when built, it was a covered brick structure. Some twenty years after it went up, the rink was failing; one afternoon in the winter of 2019, I was meeting a friend for lunch on the Mall and, quite out of the blue, witnessed the demolition of the skating venue.

Looking at my yearly movie grosses, I knew it was a huge gamble to go to a public City Council meeting and make the focus of my presentation a candid financial statement of what Vinegar Hill required to exist. But there were no secrets about the ups and downs of our movie attendance: truth be told, movie exhibitors are required to report their receipts, and these grosses are published within the industry for anyone to read. Perhaps, to the big theatre chains, Vinegar Hill looked like easy prey; twenty years after opening, we were after all still in business, showing a mix of edgy, arty, foreign, indie. All the "ie"s. And though we had changed with the times, our customers were loyalists, trying our wares even when we didn't score one-hundred percent.

And this is how I found myself standing up before the City Council in my little brown dress. I was the first to speak that evening, and, when I stepped to the microphone, the auditorium was full.

> *My name is Ann Porotti.*
> *Tonight I want to speak about three words: conspiracy, competition, and survival.*

The developer has twice characterized the Save Our Mall movement as a conspiracy sponsored by VHT. As if half a town had risen up solely in defense of a small movie theatre near the Mall. I wish it were true, I wish the issue were that simple. Since 1976 I have owned and operated Vinegar Hill Theatre, and I know that my customers are very loyal. But nearly 3000 names just to save Vinegar Hill? If this is conspiracy, give me more of it.

Second is competition. Mr. Danielson has suggested that our opposition is trying to stifle competition. I don't really want six more movie screens two blocks from my theatre. I would be a fool if I did. What I do object to is the city government subsidizing this project with taxpayer money and a questionable variance to the comprehensive plan. The developer publicly says "No street, no project"—meaning the city should pay for car crossing modifications to the road. Danielson's demands from the city look to me more like special treatment than competition.

Finally, survival. Many of my friends have said, wishfully, "Oh surely, a sixplex won't hurt Vinegar Hill." Nope, not true. I am in the movie exhibition business and all the city experts who have spoken about the possible effect on VHT are not well informed. I am quoting the Community Development & Planning memo, from August 3, 1994, page 9, section N:

"In our discussions with the developer and other theatre owners, it is clear that the type of first run movies that would be offered at the new multiplex would be unlike what is currently offered at Vinegar Hill."

Just to be clear here, no one from the Community Development office ever asked me or contacted anyone at Vinegar Hill Theatre about the overall economic implications of this project. And we're very locatable, hard to miss in that showroom window, on Market Street as you enter downtown Charlottesville.

Standing there, facing the City Council and facing away from a room stuffed to the gills with friends and enemies, I felt that there was a target on my back. My heart was pounding, and the over-efficient air conditioning system was failing in any way to cool me off. But I continued:

> And what would I have said if I had gotten an invitation to one of those "discussions"? Bold news, possibly surprising to the town leaders and developers, that Neighborhood Theaters and Vinegar Hill compete for the same films; we both operate within the same highly competitive industry. In the previous year, 1993, Neighborhood took The Piano and Four Weddings and a Funeral which were for them, both blockbusters and art films; Vinegar Hill played Much Ado About Nothing, Like Water for Chocolate, Strictly Ballroom. For us that same year, a mere eight very successful films out of a roster of seventy-five titles would gross over $100,000—or about half of the VHT yearly film receipts.
>
> Can you see the strategies of art house booking where the big hits pay for the riskier fare?
>
> But the projected volume of screens, with Neighborhood having six art-house friendly screens to fill week after week, translates into Vinegar Hill missing out on any, and all, bread and butter hits. Next stop: out-of-business.
>
> Nothing about this project seems careful or adequately planned. If the City Council votes to go with the developer, and pay for his crossing, they are voting for one set of business interests against another. And while this may mean big bucks for the developer, and for Neighborhood, it certainly will not have been achieved as a result of what we normally mean by "competition."

That's what I said and then I sat down.

ALL SUMMER LONG Danielson and the Mall Crossing dominated the news in the *Daily Progress*, the student-run *Cavalier Daily,* and the two weeklies, the *Observer* and the *C-ville*. In pawing through my archive, two letters really grabbed my attention. The first is from my late friend Ruth Drexler (a feisty seventy-three in 1994) to Frank Novak, CEO of NEI, in which she thanks him for all the fine movies she has seen on NEI's Charlottesville and Richmond screens. She then warns him about Danielson, who has been harassing citizens if they do not agree with his project—especially Sue Lewis, to whom he said, "You are risking your political career by siding with people against the crossing." Like the stern but tender Jewish lady she was, Ruth wrote to CEO Novak: "A bad side-effect of this situation is that people are considering Danielson and NEI to be one in the same ... your company has an excellent reputation in Charlottesville, and Danielson is now tarnishing it." It felt like an old-fashioned letter about the company we keep.

Another letter to Frank Novak came from VHT customer Reg Marshall: "If NEI goes ahead with its six-plex, I feel you have a moral obligation to do two things: come to an agreement with Vinegar Hill that enables you both to prosper and share the hits, and commit to screening the same marginal films that Vinegar Hill now does, so that Charlottesville filmgoers will not lose the film selection they currently have. Perhaps you scoff that a business has any moral obligation to its competitors. Let me remind you that you call yourselves Neighborhood Entertainment. You are about to expand into someone else's neighborhood now. Good neighbors don't drive out residents of twenty years who have given as much to the community as Vinegar Hill Theatre."

After we decided to hold a rally to "Save the Mall," Townwatch and friends gathered at the house on Rothery Road for a poster painting party. One of the best slogans emerging that day was "Huja Planner?" On August 9 we took our signs and our indignation downtown. There were not as many of us gathered there as I had hoped—only about 150 souls. But we gave our speeches and then marched down the mall to confront the mayor. Dave and I knew David Toscano from the old days, when he was a candidate for the left-leaning Citizens Party. By 1994, he had become an establishment figure. "It is really great to see all my friends here today," he said, to the assembled crowd. Before that, however, he had turned to Dave and said, in an aside, "I don't like to see my friends marching on City Hall." A few days after voting in favor of the proposed crossing the mayor sent me a consoling letter featuring a choice piece of boilerplate: "It is change to be sure, and change is difficult and sometimes threatening."

So, in the end, none of it made any difference. Despite all the signatures we gathered and all the noise we made, on August 15 the City Council voted to allow traffic across Second Street West, a move that eventually made it possible to drive right up to the sixplex's very front door. As Planning Commission member Stan Tatum had so prophetically said, "This has felt like a done deal from the beginning."

Within a year of our uprising, NEI sold all its screens to Regal Cinemas, the largest movie exhibition corporation in the US, and that's when my staff began referring to Vinegar Hill as "The Regal 7."

Two years later the *Daily Progress* carried a front-page article on the aftereffects. The article was illustrated by a beautiful nighttime color photograph taken by Stephanie Gross. In it the high glass windows of the lobby give off a warm, cozy light, and we see customers approaching the front door out of the shadows, with one man standing patiently at the ticket window. The chalkboard reads *Lone Star*, so we were showing John Sayles. The article is entitled, "Are art house theaters seeing closing credits?"

"Vinegar Hill was expecting a hit later this month," the article begins. We had booked *Trainspotting* from Miramax and were looking forward to a good run. "But in mid-July," the article continues, "the owner of the small art house on Market Street in Charlottesville learned that the film had been steered down another track; to Regal Cinemas' spanking new six-screen movie theater."

It really is a lovely and a long article, and, in its way, a kind of elegy.

"The 4,000 calendars printed last month," it reads, "listing Vinegar Hill's late-summer movie schedule—including the now-incorrect 'Trainspotting'—symbolize the transient times independent movie theaters are living in." There is a detailed account of our having been promised the movie and then its having been pulled. "The picture was committed to her and we would always live up to that," the regional sales manager for Miramax is quoted as saying. "We just decided we would like to help Regal if the film buyer was willing to go along with the request."

As I told the *Progress* reporter, "that wasn't the way it was explained to me. I felt much more pressure when it was explained to me that I really didn't have a choice in the matter." We were offered *Emma* as a consolation prize.

I got pretty worked up. "Before we had this thing under our nose, showing the same kind of stuff that we do, it was just competition," I told the reporter, referring to Regal exhibiting foreign films at other places in town like the Seminole and Greenbrier theaters. "Now it feels much more like 'I wipe the floor with you.' It doesn't feel like competition anymore. It feels like eradication."

In the article the last word is given to Richard Herskowitz, then director of the Virginia Film Festival. "It's a question of how much people really want their cities to have unique venues," he said. "The 'Trainspotting' example, though, sets a discouraging precedent about which films will end up in which Charlottesville art theater.... It's pretty obvious from the lineup that Regal is going to do the same sort of films as Vinegar Hill.... It's definitely what Ann Porotti predicted and I'm amazed it's happened right away."

Anita at clothesline, Cape Cod

20
A DEATH IN PORTUGAL

I wish I had been kinder to my mother. If there ever was a person for whom I don't have a pat answer, it is Anita Porotti, and the more I think about her the more I find myself coming out the door of generosity. In the year after Dave and I were married, she really came through for me.

In 1992 Chief finally agreed to sell me his share of Vinegar Hill Theatre. The settlement with Chief cost me $80,000—a scant 50% of the $170,000 assessed value of the property in 1991. Ten thousand of that amount was given to me by my mother, the same woman who, in the summer of 1982, was unwilling to give me fifty dollars. The remainder I borrowed against my life insurance.

TWO YEARS BEFORE my mother gave me the money I needed to complete the buy-out, Ian graduated from Carnegie Mellon with a degree in music performance. Now he was well on his way to a career of playing his trumpet, with a sidebar of public school teaching. Dave, Courtie, Anita, and I attended his graduation ceremony in Pittsburgh. One evening we found ourselves drinking brandy with my mother in the lobby of the William Penn Hotel:

"You know, Annie, your father always wondered why you didn't finish your degree."

"But Ma, I did graduate. From Marietta College. You were there."

"No, no. The Master's Degree. In Drama from UVA. He was so disappointed that you didn't finish."

"But I did other stuff … guess he missed that." My voice trailed off.

"That's my biggest regret."

"You? Too?"

"No, no, my biggest regret is that *I* didn't go to college." And with that my mother polished off her Martell.

Dave and I were shocked by this sudden window onto my mother's life. Was she yearning for more, or just being a noisy gal? Anita's intellectual aspirations sometimes appeared as status marker air balloons. "Be a teacher, not a nurse like me," was a popular refrain. And yet her letters, usually small town and gossipy, could include surprising reflections, as in the one mailed to me thirty years before our conversation in the William Penn:

October 20, 1969 Thursday
Dear ann, chief and ian:
   Did you ever come across Susan Sontag—the author-director just made a movie in Sweedan. Can't think of the name which I think I would like to see. She appears to be a smart young woman. The movie is not a 'nudie' from what I gather. I almost think it's something like the picture you and I saw of Richard Burton-E. Taylor about the professor. Who is afraid of Virginia Wolf. Anyway, in spite of the sex liberties in Sweedan, she claims as far as justice is concerned, they surpass the U.S. That's something to be considered.

In the spring of 1994 Dave and I took my mother and Ian to Italy for two weeks. Ian was brought along as Anita's valet, and they often shared a hotel room.

"There was a funny story about how that trip took shape," I told Dave the other day. "Anita was well over eighty, and I used to promise to take her to places like Nova Scotia. I remember saying to her that you and I had plans to visit Rome and Naples. Then she went to see Angelo Roberti, her lawyer. 'They want me to go to Naples,' she said, and he said to her, 'I go to Naples all the time. I love it.' That seemed to decide it. Only after the trip was over was it made clear to me that *l'avvocato* Roberti did travel to Naples—Naples, Florida."

Anita arrived at Fiumicino with Ian and her stash of homemade bread in her checked luggage. She never traveled without a few slices, just in case there was no food. We joked that she had brought along her own communion wafers, but clearly she needed a piece of home.

Our quarters were at the Hotel del Sole, on the Campo de' Fiori. At Café de Paris, showing off her Italian, Anita flirted with the older waiters as they deboned her roasted *branzino*. After dark every night we made our way across town for gelato at Giolitti. Anita loved Rome, and the mistake was to leave it.

The problem was the cuttlefish. "They're trying to poison me, the fish is *stinco*," she shrieked at our *pensione* in Sorrento, when presented with a dish of *seppie* that did resemble a spare tire. There was more screaming on the drive to Amalfi. But there was one good day, on Capri.

Anita had not been back to Italy since leaving on the boat in 1920. When we arrived at Capri, Dave and Ian and I decided to walk to the Belvedere. Anita stayed behind on a bench in the piazza. When we returned, she was chatting with a nice lady.

"Annie—I met someone from my village!"

The village was San Felice sul Panaro, home, when she left it, to a few hundred souls. The odds of meeting a fellow villager were not high.

We had not planned a trip down memory lane and had made no attempt to schedule visits to the old spots. And yet the past had come to meet the girl who had left Italy seventy-four years earlier.

Another moment: after arriving at the Hotel Panda, on the plain below Assisi, my mother immediately began inspecting the drains. "Smells—there are smells here!" We quickly decamped to a hotel within the city walls. Anita trooped around in the pointy Joan & David black boots I had purchased for her in Bethesda. "I know why the Italians have so many churches," she said to Dave one day as she stared at her sore feet. "They have lots of faith and lots of rocks."

In the journal Anita kept during the trip, she wrote, more than once, "I don't know why Annie is so mad at me." It's a question any mother might ask of any daughter. If I had then given an answer, I would have said that she had failed to protect me. But that seems too easy, or too harsh, because protection is the thing most parents struggle and fail to provide. I had myself so often left my own children wide open to the world to be able to claim any superiority in the matter. And I also have come to believe that no one person can stand in the way of the all too much that comes at us every day.

Near the end of our time in Europe together we returned to Rome and everyone seemed happy. Then, during an afternoon stop at a café on the Campo de' Fiori, my mother and I fell into an argument. When I got mad at her, I got mad at a thing, in this case the temperature of a *caffè latte*.

"This is just not hot enough," I said, as we began sipping our coffees. "No way."

"Honey, it's fine," Anita responded.

I jumped up and went back inside. When I complained to the barman, he shrugged. Back outside, I fled. The first door I came to was the entrance to Sant'Andrea della Valle, otherwise known as the *Tosca* church; the opera is set there.

The sun was setting, and the church was filled with a deep yellow light. I sat and thought about how long I had been living with my hair-trigger temper. My brooding time did not last long, however. Before I knew it, my mother and Dave and Ian appeared at the doorway.

"We weren't even looking for you," Dave later told me. "We just got up and started to walk and decided to take a turn through the church."

PERHAPS THE DRAMA in Italy was about the unsaid thing. The summer before the trip to Europe, there had been an evening when it tried to surface.

In the early fall of 1993, I drove to the cottage with my dog Sylvania to see my mother; Anita had just turned eighty-five, and I had recently bought a Toyota truck which revived my road warrior spirit. I brought my camera, and not much else.

Of all the shots I may have taken, there is one that stays with me.

In the photograph my mother is at her beloved clothesline. She is dressed for deepest winter in an oversized, broken zippered, "boys" down jacket, jeans rehabilitated from my brother's discards, knock-off Frye boots, and her signature red and blue wool tam. She struggles to secure one of the many colorful cottage bedspreads to the line—in this case, a lime green, orange, and blue plaid. In the picture, a dog, our beloved Sylvania, sits watching her.

What did she and I do for a week when all the summer pastimes were unavailable?

We cleaned and prepared to close the cottage for the season. More vacuuming, more putting away, and finally we boarded up the windows to protect them from the pitting sands of winter. Later a plumber would come in and drain all the pipes. As a respite from our labors, my mother suggested that we invite her friends Angela and Ronnie Hague and my cousin Billy over for dinner.

Anita made meatballs, her specialty, and I made the sauce and the spaghetti. I am sure she triple-washed the lettuce for the salad, even the iceberg. Angela brought biscotti, Billy came over with jugs of his favorite plonk. I had my own drinkable wine, and my mother had the E&J Brandy which she mixed with orange juice, so as to get her Vitamin C.

The five of us sat at the kitchen table of my youth, a handmade item from my grandparents' sausage-making salesroom. My mother had replaced the distressed wooden top with an inlay of smooth yellow Formica.

That night was a sea of conversation in which no one was truly listening. Billy was honking on about local politics, and Anita, who loved hanging out with the boys, indulged in various vulgar malapropisms, something about women who cheated on their men. A man who had been cuckolded—a *cornuto*—she called a *cornetto*, the name of the horn-shaped Italian pastry. As Anita put it, the world was full of *cornettos*.

Angela Hague worked as a social worker and had recently counseled clients with a history of sexual abuse. The topic rounded the table, from person to person. Anita, like the men in her circle, had an opinion even when there was no knowledge. Sometime during this drunken squawking, my mother, sitting at my side, said quietly, "Were you ever abused?"

I nodded yes.

And then she said, "Was it your father?"

"No," I answered.

"Was it Cavigioli?"

A second time, I answered, no.

And she turned away from me and never mentioned it again. It was then I knew that she had loved the man who had abused me.

IN THE FALL after we took Anita to Europe, an envelope arrived at Rothery Road. I preserve the spellings intact:

Sept 10–94
Dear ann:
Inclosed you will find the deed to the house at the Beach. take care of it—you and David and the children are now the keepers of the flame. Rudy has one regret that he was never aloud to bild on his lot—so do I—oh well. Life has to go on—I do hope that you will enjoy it and love it has much as I did—and share it, which I confess I also did.
Love, Anita

The cottage—just like the theatre—was finally mine.

It was now possible to imagine a future in which I could keep the Cape life going.

Many of the good times I remember involved a community of chaos—often at the Cape. There was the day Barbara and I made a very complicated eggplant dish out of *Marcella's Italian Kitchen*, aka Book Three.

"Why does it have to be so hard?" Barbara kept saying. First we made a tomato and herb risotto, then we fried slices of eggplant. For assembly, you layered the cooled risotto, the eggplant, the grated pecorino, parmesan, and shredded mozzarella mixture. Repeat. Butter and more cheese on the top; bake to light brown crust. The thing ended up a savory rustic *torta*. Serves a crowd—which is what we had.

During this day of abundance, a neighbor had dropped off a bag of littlenecks. I whipped up a humble *sformato*—an Italian baked pudding—using the cooked clams mixed with riced potatoes and a sauté of garlic and parsley. Barb and I were in the kitchen forever. And all this time our two dogs, Voisine and her daughter Sylvania, were underfoot.

Meanwhile, Dave and cousin Billy were setting up a slide show outside. They moved the big picnic table under the kitchen windows and placed the screen at its far end. When the casseroles were served there must have been at least a dozen of us at the table. There was lots of wine, Billy's favorite, a coppery Pollo Brindisi, and his good crusty bread. Somebody threw together a salad. Barb loved to make desserts, so we probably finished with her blueberry pies.

After it had fallen dark, we showed the slides. There were bugs all over the screen but I didn't care; I had always loved drive-in movies and their various discomforts. Courtenay and her boy friend, Alexis, were spending the evening, along with his brothers, Marco and Michael. And Ian was there, and Luke, who must have been about eight. And my mother whose eyes widened at the number of guests.

When it came time to go to sleep that night, everyone found a spot and bedded down. And I thought to myself, this is everything I've ever wanted.

DESPITE HER GENEROUS decision to give me the cottage, my mother was tired and grouchy after her trip to Italy. One day on the phone she said, "That trip destroyed me. I'm never coming to see you again." I thought she might be crying but I also thought she might be cranking for a dust-up.

In the days before hypervigilance of the elderly, I let these conversations slide even when Anita began to say things like, "I fell down the other day at the Big D Shopping Center, but the checker helped me to my feet." Or, "The police man picked me up when I slipped in front of the Milford Post Office."

"Did you go to the doctor?" was my response.

"I called Dr. Stearns." He was her loyal doctor of osteopathy until he died in the early nineties. After that, she had Plan B: lots of prayer to Blessed Virgin Mary and the Baby Jesus, plus two Dristan, as needed.

Anita died in November 1995 while David and I were in Portugal. She collapsed on a Wednesday, and passed away forty-eight hours later. During that time, no one could find us. It fell to Courtenay in her first year of medical school at Emory to attempt contact. She conferred with Ian in Pittsburgh about the how-to and he responded, "Try Interpol."

Meanwhile my mother, having suffered an aortic aneurysm at home and been revived by EMT personnel, lay at Milford Hospital, where she had worked as a nurse fifty years earlier, receiving her friends and family. The news caught up with me in Lisbon. I still have the ominous yellow post-it from the York House staff.

Mr. David & Mrs. Porotti Please call U.S.A. To your brother.
Tel: 508 478 2071
"Your Mother is not well, very ill. Teresa Tavares 18-11-95, 20-10

My brother still has that phone number.

I WASN'T EXACTLY fleeing my life, by going to Portugal, but, with the imminent arrival of the sixplex on the Downtown Mall, things were shifting for me at Vinegar Hill. In 1995, we began to include advertisements in our schedules; there are little boxes in the margins touting nomadic textiles at the Sunbow Trading Company and "cool women's shoes" at a place called Scarpa. The ads, we told our customers, "will allow us to distribute our schedules more widely." We also began to promote the deep archive of our poster list. All of this in an effort to bring in a little more cash.

But the biggest challenge was in the kind of movies we were able to show. In January we did a reprise of *The Conformist*, an offering the schedule described as "our favorite movie of all time." The other movies on the list were 1994 releases, films like *The Browning Version*, with Albert Finney, or *To Live*, by Chinese director Zhang Yimou. These were fine enough, but there was now simply not enough product to go around, so we had to fill one weekend with the Bertolucci.

The biggest challenge was in the fixity of the schedules themselves. While we kept printing them and sending them out in the mail, we did so with the proviso that our subscribers ought to call ahead in order "to avoid disappointments caused by schedule changes." Good new movies were becoming harder and harder to find, and we had to be willing to run a film that might suddenly drop into our lap. The era of the fixed calendar had come and gone.

DAVE AND I left DC for Portugal on November 6, 1995, with a return scheduled for Wednesday, November 22, the day before Thanksgiving. This trip was the first time in my life that I paid great attention to premonitions.

Lisbon to Coimbra with a stop at the massive Gothic cathedral in Batalha exposed us to driving in a country with the highest accident rate in Europe. My worry gene climbed on board. At the university Dave gave a lecture arranged by his former Maryland graduate student John Mock and his Portuguese partner Teresa Tavares. A home stay, when you travel, can be magic; you get tips on where to go next, perhaps cook communal meals, enjoy a peek into domestic lives. My photographs of Coimbra show a very ancient city, struggling with the pains of modernity—a foot bridge stalled mid-repair—even as food vendors ignore the chaos, and make kale and potato soup for hungry pedestrians.

John and Teresa took us to Buçaco for port and to Pedro dos Leitões for a Sunday lunch of roast suckling pig, champagne, and potato chips. One evening we drove into a village where the migrant workers from Cape Verde were celebrating the grape harvest with bonfires and dancing to *forró* in the square. Portuguese *Streets of Fire*.

It was only on the road between Fatima and Tomar that I started to feel like my mother was taking the trip with us. We stopped for directions from a woman peeling cork from a tree, and I was reminded of my mother's mother: the woolen stockings, black skirt, grey sweater, head scarf. Somber, elderly women working in the fields.

A couple of days later, we drove west to a thirteenth-century mountain town nearly at the Spanish border, Castelo de Vide. It was a stern ancient place, filled with ghosts when the wind blew hard. Here was Portugal's oldest synagogue, plus a Jewish ghetto, *Judiaria*, that had remained intact. Touting Castelo de Vide, John, back in Coimbra, had also spoken of hold-out communists who still dressed all in black. I nosed around with my camera, as a cure for boredom with the food and lodgings; every house a white cottage surrounded by robust olive trees. No one made eye contact. Of all the omen-laden towns we'd passed through in Portugal, Castelo de Vide was the place where people seemed to be living out their superstitions with passion and little regard for the interruptions of tourism. It scared and dazzled me, such an unwelcoming welcome.

In Lisbon, on Monday, after the news got to us, I was finally able to reach my brother.

"In the hospital, at one point," Rudy told me, "Ma was reaching out with her arms, calling *Annie*. She died on Saturday."

My mother came for me, at the end, even though I was too far away, and too lost in my travels, to be able to come for her. It is more than a little humbling to carry this image with me, and years later, when I really needed her help, she came for me again.

WE MANAGED TO book a night flight on TAP to Gatwick and the plane was all over the sky. The storm was so bad that the man sitting next to us went up to visit the cockpit. When he came back, he said to Dave, "It's OK. They're a young crew, but they have it under control." It turned out he was a pilot being ferried back to London.

Anita's funeral: Ian, Dave, Steve Miller, Rudy, Courtenay

Back in Hopedale the clan gathered. The photographs make it look like a Thanksgiving party, and it really was a funeral folded inside of a holiday. In the line-up there is Dave and Rudy and Ian and Courtenay and her boyfriend Steve Miller and they are smiling. Maybe that was the evening we had found some of Anita's famous meatballs in the freezer and made a meal of them.

The funeral mass was held at the Sacred Heart Church. There was a moment when my brother handed me a small plastic bag marked "Haz-Mat." Inside were two earrings, rubies circled with rhinestones. "These fell out," Rudy said, "when the EMT were trying to resuscitate her at the house."

Only one family member rose to give a eulogy, and it was Ian. I was surprised to see him stand up. But I also knew he was deeply fond of Anita and looked on her as the closest the family came to possessing a Jedi master. I can't recall everything Ian had to say that day, but I do hear him reading a Bible passage about humility, perhaps the Parable of the Talents. He spoke about the gift of mental strength and about not looking for people to acknowledge what you are doing but just, simply, doing it.

I did not need to speak because at some level I knew that I had already made my farewell, and I had done so without realizing it during one of my last days in Portugal.

On the Saturday my mother lay dying Dave and I drove to a little hilltop village called Marvão. Fog rolled in and never left us. We found a pastry shop and ordered a couple of *pastéis de nata*. As we left the shop and headed for the square a brown dog, the same color and size as my beloved and long-gone Voisine, came out of the mist and began walking with us. We moved along low houses with white-washed courtyards and borders of unmuted calendulas.

Dave and I were passing the camera back and forth in the intensifying fog. The dog followed closely at my knee. Then I looked up and there, behind one of the houses, there was a clothesline with towels blowing in the mist. I stopped and stood still for a long minute. I have no memory of what I might have been thinking, but something held me to the spot. The dog came and stood next to me sharing the view, and Dave, who was walking behind, took the picture.

L'avventura façade

21
A NEW LOBBY

When people ask me about the most fun I've ever had, I say, "Designing and building my second restaurant. With my little band of helper elves. And a husband who really liked to cook."

When things got rough I also tried not to crumble, like a *sbrisolona*.

On a warm June morning in 1996, Russell Skinner walked into the lobby of Vinegar Hill Theatre with the preliminary drawings for a space that didn't yet even have a name.

Russell liked the word "vocabulary," as in "Here, for the cornice, we borrow the vocabulary of a Palladian style." He happened by during the week the *Daily Progress* carried an article about Lee Danielson's progress on his new sixplex entitled "City Wants Delay in Theater Work." It turned out Danielson had torn the brick off of an "historic" building. "What will Joe Blow carpenter think?" our irate mayor had fumed. A week later, while attending a Planning Commission meeting, Reid heard that Danielson was out of money, and that architects from Regal Cinemas had taken over his mall project.

Russell's design showed a triangle pushing out toward the city sidewalk and also deep into the VHT lobby space. When Russell submitted his plans to the city they came back with "The new lobby isn't big enough." Apparently a theater lobby is required to have 1.5 square feet for each seat in the auditorium. With 220 seats, Vinegar Hill needed a lobby of 330 square feet, but Russell's plans—he was trying to buy as much space as he could for our dream of a restaurant—showed a space only a little more than half that size.

And so it began: almost a year of negotiations with the city, the bank, the contractor and his many good men—even with the Department of Health. "You've decided to become a developer," Reid said one day, deep into the project. "This is your mini-mall."

In an attempt to solve our space problem, Dave and I found ourselves laying out a dining room design on our front deck. We outlined the walls in purple chalk and cut table tops out of pieces of cardboard. At one point Vine, our cat, walked over to a square of cardboard and threw up on it. "Our first meal served," Dave said.

"Everyone's a critic," I answered. "Take it back to the kitchen, it's undercooked."

From the beginning we never stopped worrying about money. A week after seeing Russell's drawings, Dave and I dropped in on Spencer Birdsong at Central Fidelity Bank. Grey hair, a rep tie, photos of his kids on the credenza. The piped in muzak was playing "Everything's Coming Up Roses."

"We need $150,000," I said. "The collateral is the theatre; it's debt-free."

"Well, you'll need an appraisal, and a survey. When your contractor wants to make a draw I'll have to walk down and make sure what he's asking for lines up with what is being built."

"I'm having a hot flash," I whispered, as we left the bank building.

"Take off your sweater."

"No—then my tattoo will show."

I had gotten a tattoo two years earlier, to mark my fiftieth birthday. It may have been a sign of my feeling restless. There were in any case many such signs, as on the day when, while Dave and I were making love on the living room rug, and I was having a good time, I suddenly sat up—as if I were channeling Debra Winger—and said, "I know what's wrong with me—I need a new job."

I had clearly come to the end of something.

Our contractor was a man named Dale Abrahamse. "He's the most competitive of the big guys," Russell told us, and I was glad to hear it, although I already knew a lot about Dale. "He was, in fact, an old boyfriend," I told Russell, "someone I dated briefly after Chief and I separated. I know his work well. He even shingled my house."

"Sounds like *my* life," Russell answered.

We agreed on a design-build approach. The idea was to keep adapting to problems as they arose, to let the shape of the thing emerge. "I've been working on the numbers," Dale said to Dave on the phone, after looking over the initial plans. "It looks like we're bumping $200,000. But don't tell anybody until we're sure."

"You mean—like my wife?'

"Yeah."

"There's always creep," Russell liked to say, raising his eyebrows, "and it's never down."

The first time I really solved problems as they came along was when we built the restaurant. Before that I didn't know enough; I had a desire to succeed but no real sense of how to do it. At the theatre I learned day by day, often too little, and too late. But with L'avventura, it felt as if someone had given me a fresh piece of paper.

The biggest problem facing us was the limited space; there simply wasn't much room between the glass wall of the lobby and the city-owned sidewalk.

One day Dale said to me, "Buy yourself some more space—you're already spending a lot of money." We decided to move the exterior wall of the restaurant out to where our property line met the angling sidewalk along Market Street, a move that yielded a beautiful diagonal wall paralleling the street. After repositioning the exterior wall the interior space became a trapezoid with two parts. Along the wall facing the street we decided to hang high, wooden casement windows with a booth at each one. Six windows, six booths, twenty-four seats. When customers walked in the front door, they were going to be looking down a straight aisle that ran along the outside of the booths. To the left would be a curving cherry-wood bar with a soapstone counter and, beyond that, a rectangular space we called the Manhattan Room. It featured a long banquette fronted by square oak-topped tables—another sixteen seats. It was all very tight, and pretty tiny, with a floor plan totaling only 770 square feet.

Edith MacArthur worked for Russell on the restaurant project from the beginning. She had finished up her Masters of Architecture at UVA after taking a degree at Williams College, where she had rowed crew. Now she was getting practical work experience in Charlottesville and rowing on the Rivanna Masters team. We hit it off right away. Taller even than my friend Ellen, Edith always wore skirts and little Italian flats. She was a pleasure to look at. Plus, having a woman on the team gave me a pal to involve in my menu experiments. Our favorite sauce was a vegetarian leek and lemon item Dave pronounced inedible.

Russell was compelling too, in his affability, with a big beard, rosy cheeks, and a twinkle in his eye.

"He reminds me of Santa Claus," Edith said one day.

"I know," I answered. "Is this just his day job?"

As Edith remembered, part of the design challenge was a site that angled away from the lobby at a pretty steep slope: "Russell was struggling with how to fit in as many four tops as you needed, and with the grade change. The entrance sequence was equally tough. The big square arch that peeled off the lobby and sheltered the door to the restaurant was another breakthrough that allowed us to deal with the grade change there. I remember a struggle with the blue whale: a giant HVAC duct that just had to go through the space—ugh—so why not paint it bright blue for UVA."

Once we found room for a little kitchen and for a dining area of forty-one seats we were up against one remaining problem: where to locate two handicapped bathrooms. But nobody could find a place to put them, not without losing at least four two-tops.

After that I even started listening to dreams—not to mine, but what we came to call "Edith's Dream."

As you looked down the main aisle, there was a long wall on the left and the booths to the right. The wall had an opening to the Manhattan Room, then a door to the kitchen, and beyond that more wall until you came to the end of the aisle and to the end of the building. But, in this procession of walls and openings, as Edith dreamed it, there were two unused trapezoidal spaces. If you simply added doors to them, they became bathrooms. And the beauty of it all was that these doors, as you looked down the main aisle, were hidden from sight.

"Don't tell them," Russell said to Edith, when she came to him with her dream. "It'll slow the project down." But Edith sneaked out and spilled the

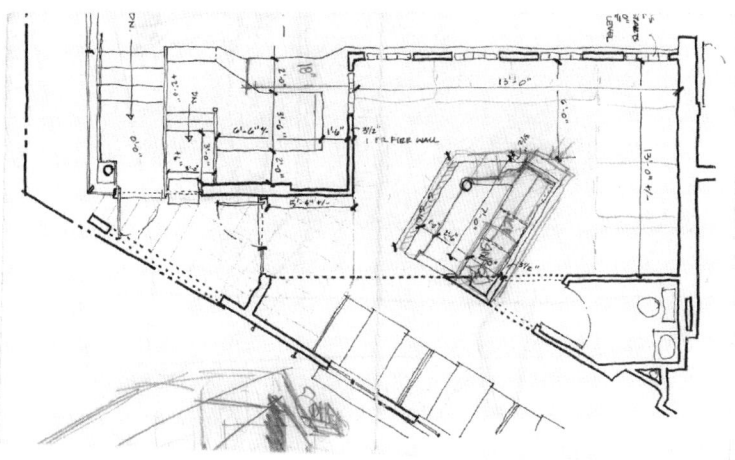

Edith's Dream

beans to me. The next day, Dale, Russell, and Reid met with me in the lobby. We went over the new plan and decided to go with it. Meanwhile, all the men had their retractable tapes out, measuring things. Russell was poking his tape measure into a hole in the ceiling. "Feels like concrete," he muttered. At that point Edith and I dissolved in laughter. "I could make a comment, but I won't," I said. Then everybody laughed. Later, Reid said, "Ann turned *red*."

The interface between the restaurant space and the theatre was very intimate; the one thing was designed to be *nestled* into the other. The interior wall of the dining room pushed so far into the existing lobby space as to reduce it to a long hallway—hence the problem with it not being seen by the city as large enough. This new hallway-lobby was to be elevated; customers would now climb up three steps to enter into the lobby. From there a new, much compressed concession stand would hand out its goodies. It was even agreed that the restaurant and theatre would work off of the same electrical service. "They can share bodily fluids," Reid remarked.

Another design breakthrough came when we decided to open the wall between the two new spaces. We "opened" it, that is, with three tall windows of glass bricks. Diners sitting at tables in the Manhattan Room could look up at people walking toward the auditorium, and movie-goers could look down at people eating their baked rigatoni or their grilled pizza.

But many of these changes had to be *approved*. Because the theatre was located in an historic district, permissions had to be sought for everything from window treatments to exterior paint colors. One day we found ourselves standing in our parking lot with Reid, Russell, Edith, the mayor, city planner Satyendra Huja, our contractor, and a few other officials. "We approved *that*?" one of the men exclaimed. I had painted six swaths of color on the old cinder block, and he was looking at an overripe red called "Tomato Bisque." Eventually we settled on a lovely shade of cantaloupe, like the Western Sand in our living room.

First, we had to go through the City Planning commission. "So you're finally going to do it," Chair Ron Higgins said. "If we can," Dave answered. "Well, it's not a very big restaurant, but then you have no room for a big restaurant. And on the exterior, use real stucco, not dryvit; you can put a nail through dryvit."

This was the same man whose office had called me a few weeks earlier to announce that the flat roof on the theatre had a corner that hung out over the city sidewalk by about a foot. "That corner of the roof will have to be removed," a voice said, "Or you need to get an easement, or write the city agreeing that it can remove the corner, if we ever widen the street." I dutifully wrote the letter, ceding to the city a portion of the roof that had shaded the sidewalk for at least fifty years.

When the commissioners went on about our needing to carve out a handicapped parking space, I said something about there being "an outlaw mentality" when it came to parking downtown. "Ann was a bulldog," Russell said afterwards, "and I just slipped the proposal in."

The next step was the dreaded Board of Architectural Review. Anyone driving around Charlottesville could see that it was a red brick town; once Jefferson had established the convention few builders seemed to want to vary from it. But we were proposing an addition to an ex-motorcycle showroom made of cinderblock. We were also building an Italian restaurant, and in Italy these are often buildings surfaced in stucco. This hadn't been a problem for the Planning Commission, but we knew that the BAR often preferred the look of "Ye Olde Charlottesville."

Meanwhile, Dave and I had gone to the Cape, so it was up to Russell and Edith to make the pitch.

I called Russell on the morning of August 20. "Have you been to the firing squad yet?"

"No, we're sitting around trying to imagine every question they could ask and we're sorry you're not here to attack. Then I could take the middle ground and sound really responsible."

At five I called back and Edith answered. "How did it go?"

"Really well. No complaints about not using brick. There was an older woman sitting in who said, 'I am so tired of seeing brick smeared across Charlottesville.' Then they talked about not wanting us to have a messy roof."

That week the *Daily Progress* carried an article with the banner, "Board of Architectural Review granted a certificate of appropriateness for the design of the 1,000-square-foot restaurant." The article went on to say that "The plans were approved less than a month after Regal Cinemas opened a six-screen theater at the Downtown Mall, which is already drawing the kind of films that Vinegar Hill used to have all to itself in the Charlottesville area."

I CALLED RUSSELL a few days later to compliment him on his performance. "Well, Edith was the hero," he said, "although I didn't get vapor lock too badly. So, let's pay homage to the worry gods. But hey, what we're doing is really important for Charlottesville. Originally I took the path of least resistance. Now I think we should do something wonderful."

For Edith, the payoff came a few winters later: "After the restaurant opened, I came to Charlottesville in a snow storm with balding tires. Watching people slide off the road into the ditch, near head-on collisions, white-out conditions, unplowed roads—the trip was harrowing. I'd navigated New England winters and wasn't freaked out by snow, but this was different. I got to L'avventura and you or David handed me a hard drink. I'm sure we exchanged hello's first, but in my mind the drink was instantly in hand, allowing the color to return to my white knuckles. I don't have a taste for whiskey or bourbon, but man did I that night. So soothing, not just the drink but the familiarity of space, friends, conversation. It was like being hugged by a nice, cozy, village restaurant."

BY THE MID-'90S we were showing mostly first-run movies at Vinegar Hill and, in order to compete with the big guys, I had hired a New York booker named Jeffrey Jacobs.

Because Jeffrey booked a lot of independent movie theaters, he had leverage with film distributors. Once I hired him we were in touch every

Monday morning about how much I had grossed during the previous week and about what to run next. I avoided the phone if we'd had a bad weekend.

As my booker, Jeffrey also had to deal with what came to be called "The Miramax Apology." After Regal Cinemas opened its six screens in August, and, after they peeled off *Trainspotting*, I made my "I wipe the floor with you" comment to the press. Customers began walking up to me and saying, "I love this place so much, how can I help?" But Jeffrey had another problem: how to calm down a corporation—Miramax had recently been purchased by Disney—renowned for being litigious.

Jeffrey convinced me that we needed to send a letter of apology about what I had said. I'm sure he wrote the letter; I have no memory of writing it. The point, I guess, was to avoid being sued.

But the news wasn't all bad. In September Jeffrey called. "It looks like *Emma* might be a record for you," he said. "It made $8,000 in the first four days."

"No, I said, "*Emma* was great, but the record so far is *Much Ado*. It made even more than that—it turns out Charlottesville loves book-movies."

DEMOLITION OF THE lobby began on December 10, 1996. Dale had assembled a top-notch crew: Project manager Mark Mandell and the two men who would actually do the construction, tall, skinny dreadlocked Kevin Kinnehan and his boisterous and big partner, Marvin Chambers.

Marvin never stopped talking. "Don't call me Melvin," he said, after introducing himself to David. "Kevin's sometimes callin' me Melvin. So I call him Kenny. He hates that."

"Well, I'm Dave."

"What kind of restaurant you openin'?"

"Italian."

"Yeah, what kind of food?"

"Pasta, grilled stuff, chicken."

"*Fried* chicken?"

"No—grilled."

"Ah—you need fried chicken. You need a taster, you give me a call."

For the rest of the project, Marvin will call Dave "Dan."

Two days later Dave pulled up in front of the theatre and the lobby was gone. The brick ticket booth and concession stand were a pile of rubble, and,

before Kevin began cutting a hole in some cinder block with a chain-saw like blade, he grabbed a T-shirt and tucked his dreadlocks up into it. "Man, look at that dew rag," Marvin said. "Wouldn't want to get none of that caught, no way."

The space was filling up with dust. Marvin moved outside, white on his ears. "You've aged," Dave said.

"Man, I want to look forty-five when I'm sixty-five."

"You married, Marvin?"

"Who—me? You kiddin? No sir—not by a long shot."

Mark Mandell pulled up on his Harley-Davidson, and Dave asked him about his average day. "Start at six, end at six. I took the job with Abrahamse because I wanted to learn discipline. How to handle the paper work. But I'd rather be out in the field, with the men. Seems like the more you succeed, the further away you get from what you liked doing in the first place."

When Ruth and Milton Drexler drove up, and she saw the gone lobby, she had only one thing to say: "I hate it!"

One of the most suspenseful moments involved the poring of the slab. It was a cold day in January, and Mark was concerned about what might happen later that night. A big concrete pour has trouble setting up if the temperature drops below freezing.

At 6:15 that morning we were all there, along with an order of nine yards of concrete. Once they began the pour Mark quickly saw that it was not going to be enough. "We've used it all," he said, "the whole nine yards." It turns out that's where the phrase comes from. Mark ordered five more yards.

The slab man was there until after dark, crawling across and smoothing the surface. "They've had to add some calcium to make it set up," Mark told us. "Concrete generates its own heat, and calcium helps it heat up and dry faster."

The next morning Kevin was up at four to check on the slab. It rained a little in the night, but the surface didn't lose its nice, shiny finish.

The now elongated but skinny lobby had its carpet put down about a week later. We chose a sort of mottled Pepsi stain-resistant brown. Three carpet layers arrived, with baseball caps and scruffy beards. "Looks like a jigsaw puzzle," one said. "My knees hurt already."

"Are you Ed?" Marvin asked the older man.

"No, I'm his son. Daddy was the first carpet layer in Charlottesville. He started in 1955. Used to *sew* his carpets together."

The next day we opened—or tried to open—our new lobby. Somehow the issue with the city had gone away; they had to oversee too many regulations to be able to keep track of us. All we needed was a new front door. I stayed home test cooking a chocolate angel food cake while Dave went in to supervise.

"When I got there the plumber was working on a square hole in the middle of the slab," Dave later told me, "I guess for pipes in the kitchen. Marvin and Kevin were framing out walls, and the locksmith stopped by. But there was no sign of the door guy. I touched up some paint and Reid began focusing the new spotlights in the lobby.

"Around two the door guy showed up, cursing. It had also started to rain. At first he couldn't get those big old glass doors out, and, when he did, he discovered a hole in the ground where the new swivel had to go and so he mixed up some Sakrete to fill the hole. The door arrived around four, along with a continual string of curses out of the door man. An hour later he came over to me, with a frantic look in his eye and said, 'We can't get the door in.' I yelled back at him—'That's your problem. And I don't like the way this job is going.' 'Neither do I,' he said, as he went back to work, cursing.

"Reid and I moved the popcorn machine back into place and began heating it up. We also started bringing out Milk Duds and Raisinets.

"The door finally went in, but there was no handle on the outside. Once it closed, it locked, so we had to prop it open for each show."

The next day, when I went in to open the theatre, Joannie, the cleaning lady, had thrown the dead bolts on all the exit doors, and, with a non-functioning front door, I had no way to get in. While I was waiting for the locksmith, Edith strolled by. I found a tool kit in my truck, and Edith unscrewed the temporary plywood panel covering over the as yet non-existent ticket window and climbed right in.

WITH DALE ABRAHAMSE we finally agreed to proceed on a cost-plus basis. This led to constant negotiation over all the "puts" and "takes." Can we eliminate one exit door? Do we really need an industrial size grease trap? Dale finally said, "I feel we've massaged this almost to death. And with cost-plus the benefit comes to you if my estimate is higher than reality." Dave's notebooks began filling up with a continually shifting list of budget items. By early February I found myself saying, "I came as close as I have in a long time to running away from my life this morning. There's just not enough money."

Dave agreed to go to the Credit Union and to take out an equity loan. So now our house was going to be up on the block too.

Then there was the day I drove up and saw Mark hurriedly leaving. "Kevin can tell you the bad news." Kevin gulped, and then said: "The long and short of it is, we've got Lake Vinegar Hill. There's a permanent body of standing water on top of the theatre—the roof has failed." He told me that there were holes in the rubber, that the insulation was soaked, and that the brackets holding the insulation in place had been installed upside down and were now pushing up through the rubber. "The roofer doesn't see how he can guarantee his new roof if he ties into the old one." All I could think to myself was that *Sling Blade* had done so well in the previous week—almost $4,000—that maybe I could skim something out of the theatre.

It was this sort of moment that led Dale to say, "Some of the things that have been miscues have really helped this a lot."

"We've got it goin' our way," Mark and Kevin liked to say, whenever the boss came by, but it wasn't something that applied to their personal lives. Marvin might claim not to have been married—I never quite figured that out—but both Kevin and Mark were pretty open with us about the fact that their marriages were ending.

"I love women," Mark once said to me. "I just can't get enough of them."

"I hope you're talking about your wife."

"No, I just love women. My best friends are women. Men are assholes."

You get to know people when you work on a building with them for six months.

"Wives, man," Mark said to Dave one day.

"Yeah?"

"We're having some domestic difficulties. Been married seventeen years and find ourselves going in different directions."

"When did you get married?"

"At twenty. Way too early."

"I got married at twenty-one. It lasted about ten years."

"You have a son—and Ann's kids. But we don't have any. Now she may want some. I can go either way. I mean, I like kids, and I know I'd be a good father."

"However it goes, it's a good thing."

One day, as we watched Kevin and Mark ride off together in a huge Dodge truck, Dave said, "Forget the motorcycles and the new girlfriends. This building has become the transitional object. Everybody involved seems to be changing lives."

DAVE AND I fought less about money than about the pace of things. By April, Russell had become an astute observer of our marital dynamic. One night, at a party at Edith's, Russell said that the secret to his success as an architect was "not being a control freak."

Then Dave asked Russell, "Who do you think—between Ann and me—who wins the fights?"

"You do."

"Really?"

"Sure. I see you as walking along strewing flowers and Ann coming behind, wringing her hands."

I may have sometimes wrung my hands, but I also remembered something Phil Halapin once said to me. "Fear is what you have to work with. Women are phobic, and men are counterphobic, but—whichever—it's all about dealing with fear."

Over the months we had become so fond of the Abrahamse crew that we began talking about giving them all a farewell dinner. Dave came home one day while I was trying out a risotto and said he had set it up for May 24.

"Really? Isn't that a little preemptive. I mean I'm not sure we can be finished by then. Besides all I have is rags. It's the winter of junk clothing. And my waist is going—it's gone. The button of my jeans leaves a scar."

"We'll be fine—the kitchen staff is rarin' to go."

"I know you think I'm afraid to open," I said, "But that's not it. I just want to be really ready, to do the mature thing. And the health department lady is driving me crazy."

"I know you think I just blow past people. And I guess sometimes I do. But I'm tired of being criticized for what I *do*. It's the not done that you should be worrying about."

"You're just so damn controlling—always have to get there first. So you decided just to 'announce' that we were having the Abrahamse dinner. What about the electricians—they're not nearly finished."

"OK—OK—you name the date."

"Fine—I will. I know what it's like to open things before you are actually ready."

A few days later, on Main Street in Lexington, where we had driven to pick up some paintings for the dining room, I turned to Dave and said, "I'm sorry."

"So am I," he said, as he hugged me.

"Let's try to open on June 6."

"I don't want to do this if you're philosophically opposed to it," he said.

"No, that's not it. It's purely practical, and you're probably right. But it feels worse than getting married. Much scarier. Because everybody's looking at you—the expectations are so high. And lots of people in Charlottesville have nothing to do except to expect."

When Dave told Ian about the new opening date he said, "Interesting choice."

"How's that?"

"D-Day."

Meanwhile, Phil Halapin was talking to both of us—Dave had been seeing him as well since 1994—about "the relationship as spiritual path."

The hug on Main Street was not the end of it. As the days came crashing by, I felt a rising tide of panic. When Catherine Cummins of the health department showed up it all came to a head.

Dave and I had just finished having lunch with our two cooks, Terry and Jonathan. As we were cleaning up Catherine walked through the back door and straight into the kitchen. She moved over to the hand sink, saw a calendar, and tore it down.

"I'm getting very disturbed," she said. Then she made us recalibrate our thermometers. "Where are you washing your hands?" she asked. The mandatory hand sink in the kitchen hadn't yet been plumbed in.

"In the bathrooms," Jonathan answered. By now, Terry was grinning madly. I saw him looking down at her feet; she was wearing the whitest tennis shoes I had ever seen.

Catherine started making a list. "Look, there's sawdust here. You're cooking and you haven't even cleaned up from construction."

Dave tried to intercede. "We're just trying out some things."

"Well, your freezer needs a rolling base. Put some wheels on some plywood. And the reason I'm coming down so hard on you is that you should know better."

"It's as much my fault as it is theirs," Dave said. "I've never worked in a commercial kitchen before."

Catherine began handing out stickers for the three-part sink: Wash-Rinse-Sanitize. She told us she'd be back on Tuesday at eleven for a final inspection.

"Before I leave," she said, looking over at a bar of Ivory, "you should know—and I wouldn't have believed it except science has shown it—that hand soap can carry bacteria."

Afterwards Terry said, "It must have been me that ticked her off. At Rising Sun Bakery she was always on my case. She knows that I hate her. Once she made me throw out three dozen knishes."

On the day of the threatened final inspection I got up and typed a letter. I put it in an envelope marked "Dave" and left it in one of the booths at the restaurant:

> *I'm leaving, tired of fighting, of being the odd person out, the one without any allies. This is not the way I want to start our restaurant.*
>
> *Have you noticed that there are no glasses in this building. And we're having a practice run tonight. We've talked this one out. If you want to do it this way, you have supporters, I will sit this show out.*
>
> *The toll of our recent fights is severe—I am exhausted, frustrated by your folly of opening when we are not ready.*
>
> *I capitulate. Have it your way. But I don't have to have it*
> *your way.*
> *A.*

I had planned to get away early, before Dave could find me. But once he discovered the letter he rushed back to the house. I was sitting at the table, looking out into the yard.

"You're breaking my heart," he said.

"You've already broken mine." I didn't want to talk—I thought my letter had said it all.

By now Dave was on his knees. "I don't care about anything but being with you. I did this whole thing to bring us closer. We'll do what you want."

"I don't know what I want. On my way home from my radio show I wondered how I could get into a car accident. But I don't want to die, I just want to leave."

"What do you want to do?"

"Slow down. Did you see all those vegetables from Standard Produce? I can't cook with those. And I have a hard time with all these *men*."

"They're sweet guys. They cleaned up all day after Catherine came in. They'll do what's asked."

"First of all we call off tonight." We had planned a staff dinner with lots of trying out of dishes. "We all need to cook together, to give ourselves a real chance."

AFTER ALL THE dust had settled, and after we had been open for a few weeks, with the food getting better and better, and a sense that we were already establishing a devoted group of regulars, I remembered something Dave Simpson had said to us, at some point along the way. Simpson had purchased the C&O from Sandy McAdams about eight years into Sandy's run, and eight years in the restaurant business, it turned out, was what we were facing as well. "Muster all the forgiveness you can," he said. "There are so many things that can go wrong."

L'avventura staff

22
L'AVVENTURA

My somewhat rambunctious adoption of a new business was a way of finding my first one a pal. The two businesses were also vitally linked and not only through shared utility services. The restaurant helped to feed the theatre, bringing people in for a quick meal before or after a show. And, with the help of my film booker, the movie business held steady into the new century, cresting with the arrival in 2000 of Ang Lee's *Crouching Tiger, Hidden Dragon*. Once again we had lines out the door and I found myself directing traffic as I had in the old days, trying to herd the crowds through our skinny new lobby so we could start the show on time.

Fellini's had created a scene. At L'avventura, Dave and I never aspired to anything like that.

What we wanted was to make Italian food that was casual, relaxed, and yet scrupulous. If there was one dish that brought our vision of food to life, one we never took off the menu, it was *bucatini all'Amatriciana*. It's very simple to make: you sauté a handful of chopped pancetta and onions in a mixture of butter and vegetable oil. Then throw in a few cups of canned tomatoes, salt and black pepper, plus hot pepper flakes to tolerance. The sauce cooks for twenty minutes, is tossed with al dente pasta, and finished with a generous grating of Pecorino Romano.

At L'avventura we started out from the conviction that no cuisine was more misrepresented in our country than Italian food. We wanted to give authentic cooking to our customers; I suppose we wanted to educate them, although of course not everyone was up for the lesson. As business people we also followed the rules, paid bills on time. We were idealists about the work and believed that the fundamentals of Italian cuisine have the same rigor as the French. A friend likes to say that French food is about the glory of man, but Italian food is about the glory of God—and maybe he's right.

But we were dreamers. The salesman from International Gourmet once talked me into buying a shipment of *spigola*, a kind of sea bass. I thought it would be a nice fish to grill. When the order came in, two dozen fish had to be cleaned; I spent hours gutting and scaling. The fish didn't sell and I had to feed seventy dollars of product to the staff. However, my fish butchering skills got very good, such that, years later, when a Cape Cod neighbor caught a forty-one-inch striped bass and did not know how to clean it, there I was all helpful with my knife.

As for the L'avventura wine list, our collection grew, embracing the regional and the affordable. There are over two hundred red wine varietals grown in Italy; it was no wonder that we carried seventy reds and thirty whites, plus Italian sparklers like Franciacorta from Lombardy and dessert classics Picolit and Recioto. The wine, when it was ordered, spoke for itself, so we avoided adjectives like "floral" or "flinty." If pressed to describe a bottle, we talked about the grape and its geography. This obsession led me to the esteemed wines of Friuli, especially their Super Whites, grown along the Isonzo River and its eastern hills, as well as the coastal flats of Latisana and the inland plain of Udine, the regional capital. I loved the producers Ronchi di Manzano, Venica—women winemakers—and Volpe Pasini, Hermann, from the Colli Orientali. To my taste, Friulian varieties, many based on the Tokai grape, are the most perfectly balanced Italian whites.

AFTER READING HALF of this book, Philip Halapin said to me, "I hope you can find a way to incorporate the traveling you have done and how it has changed you."

Dave and I began our travels to Italy together in 1983, but for me the search had begun much earlier, in the moment of discovery at the train station in Florence. The magical potato *gnocchi*. And it turned out that even during the restaurant years the search was more about finding a dish than about presenting it to a customer. My own private Idaho. Out of the many trips taken with Dave, my fellow searcher, three stand out.

1983. THE FIRST trip together, the one in which we fled Florence for the coast, had made it clear to me that the Italy I was looking for was going to be hard to find. But there was one night in an otherwise exhausting two weeks when things came together and gave us a foretaste of the kind of food we later tried to make come true at L'avventura.

We had left Bordighera early that morning and, after slaloming down the Italian Riviera along the autostrada, by eight that evening we were hungry and tired. We found a cheap hotel on the outskirts of Sestri Levante and then strolled into town looking for dinner. We were cashless, it was a holiday weekend, and long before an ATM would have solved our problem. We found a sign-less place with an Amex decal on the door; it was almost nine pm, they appeared to be closing, but we talked our way in. It was their opening night, and just chaos—a modern space with blond wood, lots of glass and a barking noisy crowd. We pointed at something on the chalk board, smiled, and said "*uno per due.*"

What arrived at our table was a wonder: a *fritto misto* of fried baby shrimp, fried baby octopus, and fried baby sardines. A composition in pink, white, and silver with little bits of seaweed tossed in, hinting of green. But the genius of the dish was that every piece was the same dainty size. This meant that you could get each element into your mouth with any bite; a little bit of crisp, and then it all dissolved like the essence of the sea. And after every mouthful there was the promise of another sip of mineral-y Vermentino. For dessert the waiter came by with a *budino*, a carmelized vanilla pudding, in a big porcelain baking dish. We sealed the evening with two espressos, and walked back to the hotel in a state of *illuminismo* that brightened our one-light-bulb room.

I don't know if I have ever made a meal as good as that. Still, at L'avventura, we tried.

2000. IN PUTTING TOGETHER our wine list I became fascinated with a Nebbiolo-based red called Inferno, grown on slopes nearly in Switzerland, and in our third year in business Dave and I set out to find it.

We endured two boring weeks of driving through the industrial endlessness of Lombardy, the Piedmont, and the lesser Italian Lakes. In the D.O.C of Valtellina Superiore we never saw another tourist as we drove for a week through this valley of stunning wines, one boasting four different varietals of the famous Piedmontese vine—Grumello, Inferno, Sassella, Valgella—and each vineyard facing the sun at a customized angle as the road marched to Sondrio.

We drank wine at lunch, and therefore needed to eat food too. On offer was the local *pizzoccheri*, made differently in each provincial town. Very stick to the ribs aprés-ski fare, this baked buckwheat pasta was one I knew from Marcella Hazan's second book, *More Classic Italian Cooking*. Marcella does a little PR for the uninitiated about the virtues of *pizzoccheri*, a dish combining homemade buckwheat noodles, Swiss Chard leaves, Savoy Cabbage, waxy potatoes, browned butter—years before it was trendy—plus cheeses Parmigiano and Fontina from the Valle d'Aosta. And garlic. Never one of my culinary successes, Ellen and I often discussed our mutual and failed attempts. And here I was at the source.

One night in Chiavenna we went to a restaurant called Al Cenacolo. The Last Supper. The place was run by a woman, and it turned out that her take on *pizzoccheri* was revolutionary.

She started us out with some Cured Meats of the Valley. After our tiny salamis, she brought out transparent, ruby-red slices of *bresaola*, air-cured filet of beef. As we feasted on these dangerous delicacies, we noticed a nearby table being served potatoes mashed with green beans, a humble and succulent *contorno*.

Then our pastas arrived. Dave had ordered tagliatelle with tomato, but I, of course, went for the *pizzoccheri*.

What arrived were not the usual heavy, flat buckwheat noodles but little light-brown gnocchi. They floated; they did not sink to the bottom of your stomach like a stone. These airy, speckled dumplings were made with half white flour and half buckwheat flour and were combined with Savoy cabbage, leeks, garlic, and bits of potato. "No chard," the owner told us, "not in Valchiavenna." The lovely and local melting cheese, along with a grating of Parm, pulled it all together.

I saw that this dish had magnificence, and now I understood its legend. And I was already known as the gnocchi queen; there was going to be no trouble reproducing what I had found. So I stole another dish. The trick—besides the mixed flours in the *gnocchi*—was all about the prep. Every blanched vegetable had its solo ride in the garlic-flavored browned butter. They were then combined with the boiled *gnocchi* and the cheeses and baked with additional butter to get that golden burnish.

2011. *PRIMO O DOPO*? That was the question the pharmacist in Florence had asked me when I went looking in 1983 for something to deal with the mosquitoes. Before or After. My most satisfying trip of discovery was definitely a *dopo,* occurring six years after we had closed the restaurant. What it gave me was found too late for L'avventura but not too late for me, and I try to bring it to life every summer at the Cape, on my Five Star stove.

We found what we were looking for in a two-hundred-year-old restored farmhouse near the town of Udine. The place was owned by Toni and Paola Costalunga, a couple about the same age as my son Ian.

Dave and I had driven from the Trieste Airport through the vineyards of eastern Friuli, wound through tiny Faedis, crossed the canal, parked our car in front of a low stone wall, and begun walking across the front lawn of Casa del Grivò. There, under the largest cascade of white roses we had ever seen, were strangers having dinner. They smiled at us, we sat down, and soon were talking like old friends. Meanwhile Toni brought us a plate of fried sage leaves. Gunter and Marion had already finished their meal, but they lingered with us as we moved through the courses: fresh ricotta with house-made marmalade, asparagus risotto, roasted pork wrapped in prosciutto, strawberries from the garden. We had come to Friuli for its famous white wine, and that night we drank the first of many of Toni's self-bottled whites and rosés. The white tasted like honey. Later that night, Gunter and Dave sat with Toni around the fire in the fogolar and drank refresco, the local red.

In the backyard there were donkeys, and I breakfasted with them every morning. Three of them, a mom and her two babies; lovely grey coats, in their rose-trellised pen, extremely well-behaved family pets. Breakfast was served at the back of the house, in the sun, where we looked out on a garden of Sweet William, antique roses, all the summer vegetables, lettuces under shade. It was as if I had finally come upon the Italian girlhood I had never known.

THE BACKYARD AT Toni's reminded me of my own lost garden, the one I turned my attention to in the early '90s at Vinegar Hill.

It all started with ripping out the foundation plantings under the marquee. Those killer junipers. Then I discovered two things: that the VHT property caught eight hours of sun and that its hard red clay was easily amended. My Greene County pal Milton Drexler found me good dirt, and I discovered the world of "Garden Porn"—catalogs of delirious hope from places like White Flower Farm, Seed Savers, Thompson & Morgan, John Scheepers, Heronswood.

In the early '80s, VHT's master gardener Leslie Gossage had begun terracing the area below our parking lot with peonies and spring bulbs, framing the flowers with a rustic staircase to the street below. She encouraged the inter-planting of shrubs with flowers; we built a few raised beds for edibles. If I was just selling tickets on an evening, I loved weeding and getting sweaty in the garden between shows.

Daylilies from Gilbert Wild were, I think, the first things to go in, along with more peonies, old fragrant pink ones. Later I got fancy, growing my own plants from seed; Zulu daisies, penstemon, and sunflowers of every height and colorway. I became an aficionado of flowering shrubs, the hard-to-grow daphne and the delicate tree peony. (The yellow one from Vinegar Hill still grows in my backyard). Hollyhocks at the back wall of the theatre eventually marched all along the walkway to the auditorium's right exit. I introduced white nicotiana as an after-theatre feature. When people exited the back door and walked through its tobacco-y smell, maybe that would extend their movie-going experience. After all, a garden moves through time too, though more slowly than a film, and no two days are ever the same.

After L'avventura opened, I threw down more perennials: lavender bushes, baptisia, and German Iris followed the hill ridge. Later, when we built a restaurant patio attached to the garden, we made two key additions: hop vines, and Dublin Bays. The hops twined around the rambling rose canes as they climbed up the trellis Dave built. The roses bloomed like something out of Sleeping Beauty, a wall of true red.

I gave it away, transforming this minor urban banality into a leafy, flowering first window onto Downtown Charlottesville. We were squatting on the land I had developed—the city owned the parking lot and the hillside—although it never mowed the grass. We gardened for twenty years as if the land were ours.

Why did I hurl myself into this obsessive, expensive world of planting and maintenance? I think that after fifteen years of working in the dark, I wanted to be outside. And gardening was in my blood. As kids, my brother Rudy and I would pull weeds at the Mellen Street property where the garden was twice the size of the tiny house, tending zucchini, later Hubbards, green beans and tomatoes throughout the season. Summer evenings in the garden, I remember the best selves of my parents, Anita and Eugene, enjoying the harvest of what they had grown. Now I was also paying tribute to their planting hands.

IN FRIULI, EVEN when we got up as late as eleven, Toni greeted us in his Italian-inflected "Incray-dee-bull"—meaning he didn't know adults could sleep so late—and then he served us eggs scrambled in olive oil. These were accompanied by thick toast, Paola's homemade preserves, and, from a friend's nearby farm, the most intensely flavored honey we had ever tasted.

Normally we are suspicious of instant intimacy, as is supposed to happen on cruise ships, but what happened with Toni and Paola was quite different and very unusual: we became part of a working home. We argued about movies, shared music, used their washing machine, sought out tips on where to go and how to get there, and came home happy every night, looking forward to dinner, conversation, and falling asleep in the big, soft, farmhouse beds.

After five days at Casa del Grivò we drove away into the Julian Alps of Slovenia, on to Trieste, and then to a Roman ruin on the plains called Aquileia. The approach ran past two-hundred-year-old cedars and into a basilica where the floor was covered with mosaics of domestic life. *Serenissima*. It was all beautiful, but as we left the church I said to Dave, "Why don't we go back to Faedis—why did we ever leave?"

At the farmhouse, the doors were open. Toni was planting roses, Paola making pizza dough. The German guests chilled the beer they had bought from Munich. Kids ran through the garden paths and circled the donkey pen, the source of Toni's healthy fertilizer. The stone pizza oven got fired up and it was a parade of stracciatella and arugula, speck and olive. Eating into the night—conversation in three languages. A guitar arrived from someone's car and everyone knew the words to the lullaby of the evening. I hate to leave this beautiful place.

ONE NIGHT WHEN Dave and I were both working the front of the house at L'avventura, my old friend Ellen and her new husband Ted came in and stood at the bar. They were thinking of leaving Seattle and were looking to buy nearby. For Ellen, it meant a coming back to the Virginia she had left two decades earlier. Sitting right there on the soapstone was one of my lemon tarts with the twenty tablespoons of butter, the fifteen egg yolks, the seven lemons and their zest. I poured them some red wine, probably a Barbera d'Asti or a Chianti colli Fiorentini. We had no bar stools so Ted and Ellen had to stand. Like Sandy McAdams at the C&O, we poured big drinks. Our wine pours came to within an inch of the top of the glass, not like the mincing three ounces so fashionable today, so we sold only four glasses of wine out of a bottle. At six or seven dollars a glass, we were almost giving it away.

"No," Dave said, as we thought back on the evening, "we never figured out what it took to create a bar scene. I finally was able to seat them at the round table, in the corner of the Manhattan Room. So we could visit with each other."

"I called that the drive-by table. A place where we could rectify our mistakes, if we had overbooked. Our space really was so small; we just didn't have that much room to work with. And that night we were both behind the bar, so we could see the front door. Being in that bar space was like sharing an airplane bathroom."

"Yes, although by the night Ellen and Ted came in we had learned how to maneuver. Not without a lot of bumping into each other."

"I even remember what was playing on the stereo—*Caballo Viejo* from Ry Cooder's *Mambo Sinuendo*. I used to love it when people walked in and there was good sound on the floor. The whole place felt elegant, and hip, and tight. And it wasn't thematic."

"What does that mean?"

"It had a unique taste and a style but it wasn't a themed restaurant. I mean, you could barely tell what we were offering from the name of the place. It was hard to nick it."

As Ellen and Ted were settling into their table, she said to me, "Oh, by the way, when we called Information, they couldn't pull up your number. I even spelled L'avventura, but no dice."

"I know," I said. "We made a mistake. But I so loved that movie."

Ah, the name. It haunted me for years even after we closed the place.

Toni Costalunga frying sage at Casa del Grivò

AUGUST 28, 2018. It's 8:30 in the morning and three of us are swimming in a hazy blue low tide, a half a mile from the cottage.

"What do you think—did they find her?" my cousin Barbara asks, backstroking through the dead calm water.

I too am floating, searching the seamless horizon for seals sighted in this spot. What can she be talking about, I wonder.

Her husband Chris, also in the water, advances the conversation:

"We've been watching *L'avventura*—"

"The movie?" I interrupt.

"Yes, the movie, but it's slow, two hours and twenty minutes—we broke it up over two nights. Last night was the finish."

Again Barbara: "Do they find her? Did she jump off a cliff, or drown, or just disappear deeper into Sicily?"

Hmm. I am a hair-trigger away from my old behavior, habits acquired during the theatre days when customers did not understand movies in accordance with my expectations.

But that's no way to have a conversation, I think, especially about a favorite film like *L'avventura*.

"What if the plot wasn't the point of the film?" I ventured. "Anna—she matters only in so much as she brings Monica Vitti and Gabriele Ferzetti together. In looking for her they find each other but are then not able to connect. That's a bigger concern than what happened to Anna."

The name on my passport is Anna, not Ann. I was born Anna Marie Porotti.

I take a breath and look for Bruno the Boxer, swimming in the deep water.

"This way, over here," I shout at my dog, mindful that summer's warm temperatures have brought in seals and where seals come, sharks will follow.

Chris nods. Barbara—she's still puzzled—she's looking for clarity, a definitive end.

"Just look at it!" I say. "Beautiful pictures of unravaged Baroque Noto, or Vitti's polka dot dress."

"Yes," Chris says, "her clothes were beautiful."

Yes indeed.

I am colonizing.

We have all been in the water a while, my fingers are feeling prune-y. I stand up and begin speaking:

Ann and Dave in the dining room, L'avventura

"In 1960, when *L'avventura* came out, two other equally great movies were released: *La Dolce Vita* and *Rocco and His Brothers*. Fellini and Visconti. Along with the Antonioni they gave a political and emotional history of what had become of post-war Italy. *Rocco* follows a Sicilian mother and her three adult sons who move to Milan to find work. There are nearly three hours of domestic drama about an underclass looking to exit their poverty and violence. The people in the movie could have been our grandparents, people facing dead-end lives. Except that Cavi and Ardelia had the wit and the courage to get out decades earlier. *La Dolce Vita* is about another Italian world altogether—about the poverty of privilege. It's Rome as a spiritual wasteland populated by the high and low, but far too many of the idle rich. *L'avventura* is after something different. A culture besieged by modernity, with characters who don't know what they feel. Some idea of Italy has been

Split sign

lost and we are waking up in The Day After. But the tragedy generates this astonishing beauty. As my friend Toni likes to say, "the beautiful lies close to the terrible."

That's what I said, as I worried about my sea-going dog. I can be a little pedant, and I had just given one of my mini-lectures.

The word "L'avventura" means adventure or, depending on your audience, a mid-life affair. So it was entirely appropriate that in 1996, when Dave and I were kicking around names for our new restaurant, we agreed to call it *L'avventura*. Of course I did love the film, although I came to be less enamored of the Italian word once I learned that one simple little apostrophe somehow made it impossible for the phone company to retrieve our number when it was requested.

"I can even remember what Ellen and Ted ate that night," Dave went on to say. "When their apps came there was lots of grinning over the food. They had ordered shrimp and arugula, the dish we discovered at that cafeteria in Padua. Remember—we were having our own meal and I looked over and saw somebody eating something pink and green, so I got up and walked by his table as quietly as I could. I counted the number of shrimp—five—and asked a waiter about the greens. We went for the Giottos and left with a recipe."

Like the shrimp and arugula, we stole almost everything we made. The cookbook I may someday write will be called *Stolen Dishes*.

AT THE END of the evening when Ellen and Ted came in, I looked over at her and thought about how, for so many years, she had been my *confidante*. The wise woman. We had talked mostly about men, about who to love and about how to work within the boy's club. I was happy to see her again, after her long sojourn in the West, but I was post-*confidante*.

When you are cooking and managing a restaurant in your late fifties, you simply put one foot in front of the other. For those years, it now seems, all I did was work. The work was physical, boring, and important. I often became overtired, as on the New Year's Eve when I was manning the grill and also making risotto to order and my eye filled up with blood. I kept stirring the rice and banking the fire. And, in time, I came to feel what I had always wanted to feel: competent and integrated.

When it came time for her to leave, Ellen walked over to the bar, looked through the glass blocks at the people in the lobby moving toward the auditorium, and said something prophetic. "So the theatre and the restaurant are now like Siamese twins."

Ellen didn't know how right she was. Back in 1997, when we decided to run both spaces off of one electrical service, my builder said to me, "What are you going to do when you don't want to do this anymore? Now they're joined together and you'll never get 'em apart."

IN 2017 I returned to Casa del Grivò. Along for the ride were Meleesa, Dave's sister, and her daughter Kate; I was showing them my Italy. On our last day in Friuli, Toni drove Kate and me into Udine so she could shop for presents. Then he came back for us with Meleesa—she had hiked up to the local castle and back—and all of us went to San Daniele for lunch. Toni ordered the most giant plate of pale pink prosciutto, two cheeses—a latteria and a chèvre—pickled wild mushrooms like Cavi used to send with me to college, artichokes in a light pesto, much bread. We drank a great bottle of Friulian Sauvignon, the perfect wine to pair with the queen of cured meats. It was eaten quickly. Then Toni ordered another bottle and more prosciutto. We ate it all. Espressos lifted our bodies out of the chairs. 76 euro.

We drove back from San Daniele the scenic way, past abandoned castles, churches still showing damage from the 1976 earthquake, little villages for sale, streams with cute ducks, fields of mustard. More gelato for Meleesa and Kate, more driving for Toni.

In the car, Toni got talking about how he has so many plans and ideas for things he wants to do, but he says Paola is tired, and very involved with teaching school. She is not interested in more house renovation or business projects. He says that menopause has recently hit her very hard; they are both fifty-two. Toni's belief is that women reach menopause and their bodies say, "OK, you can quit now."

Toni caught me off guard in that moment. Oh my God, I thought, what had I done without even thinking it through? When Dave and I first started talking about building the restaurant I had also been fifty-two. During the construction phase it had often seemed to me that I had attached myself to my rocket of a husband, but, truth be told, I was the one who was blasting ahead, sensing it was my last chance for a career challenge. Some part of me knew I was running out of time. Now, as I inspect my yearly diaries from the restaurant years, tucked in among my prep-cooking schedules, tax deadlines, wine orders, and endless appointments, there is a calendar of my irregular periods. They were a complete havoc. When we closed L'avventura, on the Wednesday before Thanksgiving in 2005, I was sixty-one and fully out of menopause; it had been a long and bumpy ride.

Ann and Bruno at Cape Cod, 2013

23
I GIVE IT AWAY

Once, in 2004, when I was looking to sell only the restaurant, I described the theatre to my lawyer as a "good small business that behaves itself."

Stable audience, occasional hits, no bill-paying drama, minor capital improvements, experienced employees: I could check those boxes, but one thing I had failed to notice as the decades passed was my own growing lack of interest in running it all. The early days of L'avventura consumed me: I had stopped working box office at the theatre, or making the deposits, or doing the payroll. What I did was pay the film rentals, speak to my booker Jeffrey Jacobs every Monday about the film grosses, and travel as much as I could. After closing the restaurant in 2005, and finding tenants to rent the space, I was happiest with an airline ticket in my pocket, to places like New York, Cape Cod, Madrid, Morocco.

And that's where I was—Morocco—on January 18, 2008, when Vinegar Hill opened the highest grossing film in its thirty-two-years of exhibition. *There Will Be Blood,* starring Daniel Day-Lewis, Paul Dano, and Ciarán

Hinds, clocked in at 158 minutes. The sheer length of the film allowed for only two shows on weekdays and three on the weekends. Director Paul Thomas Anderson's epic of the rivalry between oilmen and the church for control of the West unfolded with gushers of violence and not a whisper of romance. It played forty-nine days, grossing $39,682 in ticket sales while making another $9920 from concessions. In film rental VHT paid Paramount Pictures a total $20,170—a little over 50% for weeks one through six, and 35% for the last week.

For much of the rest of 2008, the theatre limped along. Julian Schnabel's poetic story of a man with locked-in syndrome, *The Diving Bell and the Butterfly*, made a scant $9000 over three weeks; others, like my unloved baby *The Band's Visit*—later an Emmy-winning musical on Broadway; or the animated *Persepolis*, about an outspoken teen in Tehran; or the most orphaned of all, Oscar-nominated from Romania, *4 Months, 3 Weeks, 2 Days*, about abortion during Ceausescu's brutal communism, did not break $2000 for their individual weeks. I relinquished all film selection over to Jeffrey, and his pragmatism guided VHT through the summer.

By July, Dave and I, along with our young boxer Bruno, had moved to the Cape for several months. This was the first year our renovation of the old cottage was truly finished and we invited everyone to drop in. The cavalcade of visitors reveals an undeniable fact: we were re-centering our lives at Cape Cod. As much as I loved running a hotel for my friends and children, I was equally happy to share the beach simply with my dog; and I had the spare time to write a poem about it.

> *Might have been the end of summer. September 13.*
> *Long walk with Bruno in the morning, more wading*
> *but could not get wet above the waist. Shoveled sand from the side of*
> *the house until*
> *It seemed unhealthy. But then I was very warm.*
> *So into the high tide I went. A solitary field,*
> *no one on the beach or in the water.*
> *I swam jetty to the far jetty, and looked up to see*
> *a man staring at me. Maybe the water was cold*
> *and I just hadn't noticed. As I came out*
> *there was Claudia walking on the beach*

with her little dog. She wore long jeans, thermal top
& hoodie. My bathing suit dripping, we greeted &
decided both outfits were possible depending
on what you wanted from the day.
Later, Lu ran up
yelling that there was something I had to see.
A single white Mute Swan swimming
in the ebbing tide. Big, amazing curvy neck, and so WHITE.
Wow, wow, wow. And then the swan opened its wings
to move further up the shore and Sir Bruno made his
unavoidable presence known. We stayed on the sand
until the swan flew away—heavy take-off,
and it began to get sun-setting cooler.

AS WONDERFUL AS such days may have been, it was becoming impossible however to manage a movie theater from six hundred miles away, a fact a conversation with my projectionist-manager soon revealed.

On the day I walked into the lobby after a three-month absence he came up to me with a sad face.

"I've been taking money," he said. "I needed cash to help out my father."

After I caught my breath, I managed to ask, "Why didn't your siblings help out?"

The answer was quick, and devastating. "Oh, they weren't interested."

And I guess I wasn't interested either, not anymore.

A business can die in your heart, long before it really dies.

It turned out that some $5,000 had been quietly siphoned off during the time I had been away. It was done by forging the numbers on the daily sheets, something not difficult to do when a business runs on all cash. I had not known how right I was when, some years earlier, I had begun saying things like "I'm just staying open to employ my employees."

The way things ended at the restaurant was disturbingly similar. In the fall of 2005, about a month after an earlier return from the Cape, our head chef announced that he had scheduled an operation. He gave us only a week's notice, and it wasn't clear when he might be able to cook again. It felt like the last straw. My daily calendars tell the story: in the first five years with L'avventura, the entries are hopeful and forward-looking. Then they begin to record mere routine, and the dulling of the senses from the daily chores. Refrigerator Patrol, aka *garde-manger*, an early morning attentive sorting of produce and proteins for the day's service, lost its Zen pleasure for me; passion declined into diagnosis.

Dave and I decided it was time to close, and I, briskly, left town for the occasion. On the Wednesday night before Thanksgiving, after working the front of the house, Dave gathered the wait-staff—Barbara Tinsley, Courtney Hall, and Scott Robinson—by the bar and said, "Well, tonight is our last night. We're closing." Then he handed each of them a check for five hundred dollars.

The announcement didn't come as a complete surprise. We had put the restaurant/theater complex up for sale about a year earlier. As a *Daily Progress* article noted, "Husband-and-wife entrepreneurs David Wyatt and Ann Porotti are selling two-business properties priced at $1.5 million." In the intervening months a few people had come around to kick the tires but there had been no real takers. It turned out that selling a business is about as hard as starting one.

I don't remember how I found BK; I suspect I asked a friend in the realtor world, and the answer was, "BK is the guy who sells commercial buildings." We had a lay of the land meeting at 220 West Market, and then the waiting began.

The initial meeting with BK took place in late winter and the contract I soon received is dated March 16, 2007. The typed asking price of One Million Two Hundred Thousand Dollars has been crossed out and my handwriting has replaced the word "Two" with the word "Five." Next to the change a date has been written in—4/2/07—along with two sets of initials, AP and BK.

A few weeks later we got a call to meet in his office.

The meeting took place at the top of a big bank building downtown. Once we got into the office there was lots of glass rather than the usual Virginia paneling and a spectacular view over Charlottesville's Downtown Mall. BK's wife was in and out with a lot of chitchat about travel to Israel. The place felt prosperous, and very confident: these people know how to sell things. I felt I had come to the right place.

"So what's up," I said. "Why are we here?"

"Well, I have an offer for you."

"Really—so soon?" The few offers that had already come our way had taken months to unfold, before they fell through.

"So who is it—who is the buyer?"

"Someone who is willing to offer $1.4 million."

"That sounds pretty good—I mean, we expect to bargain, right?"

"That's how it's usually done. And it's not far off of your asking price."

"OK—so who is it?"

"Me."

Some things don't quite affect you at the moment they happen. I felt surprised, a little shocked. But something seemed off, as I listened to BK continue to talk. Then I began to feel desperate, forced into a corner. I didn't think; there was a visceral nausea as if a part of my body had been violated.

I had only one question: "Does this mean that you will get both commissions? One as the broker for the seller, and one as the broker for the buyer?"

"Sure—that's how it would work."

Dave wasn't saying anything, but he was looking at me.

At this point I was not thinking about money at all. The offered price was better than fine. But I did feel that I was being taken, taken by someone who was smarter than I was. I don't want to be here; I don't want to be with this man.

I jumped up out of my chair. "Let's get out of here," I said to Dave, as I headed for the door.

At the time, I might have said that I was acting on principle. But the fact is I was being impulsive, responding to the feeling of being pushed. So I ran away.

It turns out that the practice I deplored is fairly standard. And, in the end, I sold the building under very similar circumstances—and eight years later—for a little more than half the amount BK was offering.

Sometimes I don't do things because, as Dave's son Luke likes to say, "It doesn't smell right."

And, if I had agreed to BK's terms, I would have missed out on all the drama of those final years.

After Dave and I returned to Charlottesville in the fall of 2008, and my manager came to me with his story about taking money, I really did feel that it was time for me to go. My little endgame was also playing out against the nationwide financial meltdown and a presidential campaign. On one of the daily sheets from that October, the ticket taker has written, as if in explanation for that night's paltry box office, "Debate tonight." It was probably the last time Obama went up against McCain.

Meanwhile, I had located a man who agreed to lease the theatre from me and to keep it running. We agreed on a turnover date in early November, 2008. He kept the doors open for five more years.

At the end of a run of thirty-two years, the last movie shown under my management was Bill Maher's *Religulous*. It's not a film anyone would ever wish to watch again. We nevertheless showed it for twenty-eight days and made over $16,000 in ticket sales. Its fleeting popularity had everything to do with the emotions stirred up by the politics of that fall; people wanted to have their superstitions confirmed. On my last night in business, October 30, 2008, five days before Obama was elected, we brought in $182.50. We had sold tickets to ten adults and fifteen seniors.

It would be seven more years before I finally found someone to take 220 West Market Street off of my hands. These were the years in which I cashed my tenants rent checks, paid off my construction loan on L'avventura, and tried to find peace with the end of my working life. By the spring of 2013 I found a realtor I could trust, but it took him nearly two years to find a buyer who would follow through to closing. The behavior of several developer suitors was comical when it wasn't pathetic, and, finally, it just wore us down. Most memorable was Mr. JaMatiCar who, with a low-ball offer, insisted on a six-month Inspection Period where he put $10,000 in escrow with his broker, then missed his deadline to cancel, but took his $10K back anyway. My task would have been to sue him for the deposit.

Frustrated, I wrote to my broker, "I'm just trying to learn this as I go. But I see that being a realtor means not getting between the shark and the seal." Mostly, I was the seal.

I came to realize that there was no curb appeal attached to the Vinegar Hill Theatre/L'avventura complex, even though Dave and I thought Russell Skinner and Edith MacArthur's design was one of the best small, new spaces in Charlottesville. When it was built, we affectionately called it Charlottesville Bauhaus. But unlike the wave of sentimentality that followed the Paramount Theatre's closing in the early '70s, there was no movement to rescue. Vinegar Hill Theatre was much more about ideas and an aesthetic than historic preservation. Still, whoever bought the building had the possibility to design a major portal into downtown and that opportunity would shape Charlottesville's urban footprint as much as restoring a 1930s movie palace. Our corner piece of land with its perch and striking visibility advertised prime real estate for a developer with imagination.

IT ALL STARTS in West Texas in the winter of 2015. Dave and I have taken a winter vacation, down at Big Bend National Park. After hiking the strenuous Lost Mine Trail, I notice pale-pink spotting in my underpants. I know that this is not normal for a woman at seventy years. I go to see Margo Gill, my PCP doctor. She does a PAP test and says, "The cells are irregular, but let's do an endometrial biopsy at my office and bring your husband because it can be painful."

The biopsy, even though it hurts like hell, doesn't yield enough tissue to explain my symptoms. Dr. Gill orders a transvaginal ultra-sound which, even though the technician assures me of no pain, also hurts like hell. Turns out, I have grown a clementine-sized tumor on my left ovary and there is also an odd mass in my uterus. Dr. Gill refers me to Dr. Linda Duska at UVA's Cancer Center.

Two weeks go by, waiting to get that UVA doctor's appointment, which lulls Dave and me into thinking nothing is going on. Then on March 16—it's a Monday—we see Dr. Duska and there is urgency in the air. The upshot is surgery on Friday, March 20, where they take out my left ovary and fallopian tube. The robotics drive around my abdomen laparoscopically. While I am in recovery, Dr. Duska calls Dave, who is waiting downstairs. "Did she have some sort of infection?"

Home with chicken soup from friends, and the Elena Ferrante *My Brilliant Friend* novels, I accent the positive to well-wishers.

But, alas, I speak too soon.

A week later at nine at night, the phone rings. It is Dr. Duska. "You have Stage 1 cancer—in your left fallopian tube." I am alone. I hug the dog, and think, What does this mean? The word cancer makes life go silent, like a bout of deafness from water in your ears.

I am terrified but, frankly, I'm thinking more about the two airline tickets in my pocket. Up first is an April girly rendezvous in New Orleans, followed in mid-May by a month-long Bosnia-Croatia-Italy-Berlin journey.

Dr. Duska opens our next meeting with, "We've come at this sideways." What that meant is this: here comes Operation Number Two, which will remove all suspicious players, including the right ovary and fallopian tube, the uterus, the cervix, the omentum, and a sampling of groin lymph nodes. I have quietly been mounting a campaign to Save the Uterus—a personal favorite for heart health, orgasmic power, and as my children's first home. The doctors, and the family members, are not listening, perhaps because the protocol for fallopian or ovarian cancer comes with a juggernaut that steamrollers alternatives. Radical Hysterectomy, followed by six cycles of chemotherapy.

I came to believe that if I had to endure this bodily invasion, I would bracket the unpleasantness with vacations. Thus, Meleesa—herself a cancer widow—and Margaret, a breast cancer survivor, and I spend four April days at the Green House Inn, on leafy Magazine Street enjoying French Quarter Fest. We eat like champs at Pêche, Coquette, and The Butcher, and inhale the urban mischief of New Orleans dancing to Cory Ledet's zydeco. During a rainstorm, we slow things down, and tuck into the elegant Jazz Playhouse for vocalist Sasha Masakowski and her NoLa family band. Everything goes better with champagne.

The day before the second operation, I call Dave at his office in Maryland. "I'm going to leave town, they can't stop drilling." I have just endured a painful and ineffective guided biopsy of my liver. He tries arguing me down, and finally yells into the phone, "If you fucking die because of not having this operation I'll never forgive you!"

Then he cancels his Thursday classes and rushes home to Charlottesville. He finds me distractedly weeding the day lilies. "It's OK," I say, "this is my problem and I'll deal with it." But I was really scared and glad to have him nearby, not in Maryland, in case the robotics cut the wrong line.

Unlike operation number one, recovery after the second surgery lingers. The worst feeling comes from the gas that they blow into your abdomen to separate the organs so the robots can scoot around without accident. But the tiny incisions look lovely; my total now is up to six.

Next, I repair the European vacation. Touring of the former Yugoslavia will be replaced by a modest trip to Venice, to Friuli to see Toni and Paola, and to see Luke, now living in Berlin. I have only thirty days to recover, and truth be told, when I fly on June 1, my body is not prepared for the confinement of airline seats. Travel proves uncomfortable and debilitating, and by the time we return on June 17, five days before I am to start chemo, I feel exhausted.

June 22, 2015

Meleesa and I spend the weekend pulling weeds. She and her daughter Kate have flown in from Seattle to be with me for my first chemo cycle at UVA. Luke, pursuing his musical career in Berlin, sends encouraging words about our recent visit with him there. "It was great to see you, looking as vital as ever, and Dad, cuter than ever with his pasta belly."

Dave remembers being told that chemotherapy is measured in proportion not to a patient's weight but to her surface area. However they calculate the dose, a woman standing five feet high and weighing one hundred and twenty-five pounds may not require a large amount of what the nurses call the "mixture" but is nevertheless subjected to a drip set to fall so slowly that any one session is likely to consume the better part of a day.

I had been warned that I might have a reaction to my initial dose of Taxol. Dave remembers that when the drip started I rose up in the hospital bed, turned red, and said, "I have a fire in my chest." The pain inside deepened long before my audible protest; what I came to realize was that the preinfusion cocktail of Benadryl, steroids, and anti-nausea meds produced a syndrome where I can hear what is going on but I cannot speak or open my eyes to register pain.

I don't remember saying anything; I thought I might be burning from within.

Dave must have called the nurse. They pumped more steroids and resumed the chemo in thirty minutes. I remember being in a knocked-out sleep for a while but then in a kind of uncomfortable twilight that lasted until we left the hospital at six pm. We had been there since seven. The next morning, I said to Dave, "My leg and foot are made out of crumbling stone. I'm afraid to walk."

Later that week we made arrangements to decamp for Boston, live at the Cape, and continue treatment at Massachusetts General Hospital.

July 7, 2015

We arrive at MGH for a one o'clock consult with our new oncologist and find our way to the ninth floor of the Yawkey Center.

"It was awful, I don't know if I can continue." My voice trails off as I describe the first chemotherapy session at Virginia to hematology fellow Dr. Rebecca Porter.

"Benadryl put me out, out! And when the Taxol went in I couldn't sit up and say 'Help.'"

"Maybe the premedications can be done differently," Dr. Porter answers. "How are you feeling now?"

"Tired. When I go to bed, I can't find any quiet inside."

"So, you went to Italy after the second operation?"

"Yes—for the white wine treatment."

"And you had your children when, exactly? With ovarian cancer the risk is decreased by having children early."

"Pretty early—Ian at twenty-three and Courtenay at twenty-five."

As Dr. Porter and I talk there is a knock at the door, and Dr. Don Dizon, my new oncologist, comes in. He is short, smiling, and a beautiful shade of brown.

"I think you're gonna be fine," he says, above his bow tie.

"It was like a hammer—the chemo," I answer.

"Your response was fairly typical," he responds calmly. "Actually it was the solvent in the Taxol—not the drug itself—that caused the reaction. Here we find we're very successful at getting it in. And I agree with UVA on six cycles. My thinking is based primarily on your histology. You may have Stage One cancer, but it's Serous cancer—actually Grade Three cells."

"Serous—I hadn't heard that."

"It's a high grade; the cells may not have spread but they are quite virulent. That's why we're recommending chemotherapy at all."

OK, I think, the new news is a shock.

Climbing out of my reverie of alarm I hear Dr. Dizon in conversation with Dave about alternatives to the dose-dense chemo I was served at Virginia.

"Rebecca—Dr. Porter—came up with an idea and it's what I am leaning toward. We can do weekly treatments," Dizon says.

I struggle for a response. "Weekly? Seems like too much to someone who is negative about the whole thing."

"The drug goes in easier and it's a shorter treatment day, two and a half hours rather than six. Less toxicity, it's quickly becoming my preferred approach."

I nod. Something is being agreed to without much being said.

"It will mean more driving in and out. Where will you be coming from?"

"The Cape. We have a cottage in Dennis."

"That's not bad, about an hour and twenty minutes. Actually, I was just up at Truro for the Fourth. About to go on vacation for two weeks, at 3:30 this afternoon."

"Where to?" I ask.

"Guam. That's where I'm from. My mother is turning seventy."

"My age. So, you could be one of my children."

He smiles and says, "I was going to say nephew."

MY TIME AT Mass General in cancer treatment for the five remaining cycles of chemo is to be broken down into thirds and spread across fifteen weeks. I expect to cross the finish line on October 20 and then to drive back to Virginia.

Actual daily life becomes more muted, less a sports contest, although cancer care is often marketed as a battle. I never felt sick from the cancer but I am plenty sick from the chemo. But at the MGH Infusion Center I see patients fighting to stay in this life. I am looking at them, rarely at myself, hoping to see lessons in courage and poise.

I live to walk out to the low tide and swim. My cousin Barbara and Bruno the Boxer keep me to that schedule, and on Tuesdays, when Dave and I drive to Boston for my infusion, Barb will send me an email:

Hi.
Bruno and I had a swim from 3–5. Shower at 5, he had dinner at 5:11.
I am leaving eggplant parm for you as well as cake!
I will check him at 7.
Xox Barb

"IT'S NOT HELPFUL to be urged to cheer up," I say to Dave. "The most helpful people this summer have come with no advice. Barb's been great—she just swims with me, makes me food, and asks no questions. But then she's had cancer too."

"Well, you've known each other all of your lives. She's more like a sister than a cousin. And maybe her work with children has taught her that not everything can be fixed."

"I used to believe that—that things can be fixed. Now ... kindness and quiet, that's my wish. It's going to be a long time before I'm myself again."

My hair falls out, so I shave my head. Then my nails crack and lift. I procrastinate in writing or calling friends, but they find me. I can't focus on much in the way of reading except cancer self-help, but then I fall into William Finnegan's surfing memoir *Barbarian Days* and begin to imagine Life after Chemo. Brainiac activities like knitting or listening to music hurt my ears and eyes. But I do get the MGH team to drop the Benadryl from the original 50 mg liquid to a 12.5mg tab—do they think I am a hippopotamus! And in my desire to be a living person with a life, not just a patient, I learn how to be my own nutritionist. What I do not get to do that summer is to be a mourner at my friend Ruth Drexler's funeral. She dies on August 19, 2015, in Crozet, Virginia with her son Josh at her side. She was the great moviegoer, and she is ninety-four.

October 13, 2015

Dave is sitting in the lobby of the infusion center reading *Under Western Eyes* when I walk out and say, "Let's get out of here." Even though it is five o'clock and we arrived at 1:30, it is too early for the infusion to be finished. I sprint toward the elevators.

"What's up—what happened?"

"I've been waiting for three hours and the session hasn't even started yet. My nurse is in bad shape—she tried to do a stick and each time she blew a vein. 'Oh, this is feeling like a challenge today,' she said. 'Let me find another nurse.' That was it—at that point I got up and left."

As usual, each of us being exhausted in our own way, we drive back to the Cape in silence. I have completed only four cycles—twelve weeks—at MGH, plus the initial heavyweight single dose at UVA. But I am facing three more sessions, and my body and spirit are broken. My platelet count has repeatedly fallen below the legal number for chemo treatment. To spur the plow and get this thing done, I have been given a drug, Neulasta, to inject in my belly to stimulate platelet growth but it isn't working. I am frustrated, and exhausted, and done.

Next morning the phone rings and it's Dr. Dizon's office. A nurse says, "He is wondering if she wants to come back today or tomorrow."

"No," Dave answers. "Yesterday was just too much for her: the wait, the blown veins. We'll come back next week for the final session; we'll see the doctor then."

Over coffee I tell Dave about a dream I had last night—I think it's the first dream I have had all summer. "I dreamed my mother came for me. She was wearing one of those colorful pantsuits she sewed for herself and driving her big Chevy. Oh, it felt so good; it felt so real. You know, when you wake up and the dream feels real?"

Dave looks puzzled. "Yes—actually I dreamed that you called me and said, 'I just bought another dog.' And that felt real too."

My phone begins buzzing. It's Barbara, asking if I want to walk out to the low tide.

"The dream of my mother was about love and protection—that she came for me," I say, "that she wanted to protect me."

"Well, she wasn't very good at it while you were alive."

"But this time it felt so real; I really liked that feeling."

"But dreams *are* real—they're all about what we want, or didn't get, or something like that. And so you have made the mother you didn't quite ever have, or maybe you have just plain forgiven her. It's a good dream, and it worked if it made you feel good."

"So your dog dream—what's that about? We already have Bruno. You mean one dog is not enough to rescue me?"

"Maybe so. I mean this whole thing has been for you like another experience of abuse, awakening all those old feelings. So, rescue, sure—why not?"

"You know, I've been feeling a lot more tender toward my mother lately. Maybe she didn't protect me from the abuse, but she herself was treated so badly—really like Cinderella. And my father didn't see her for all that she could be."

"And she left you this place. This foothold in the sand is her; this is what she gave you."

"Yes, and I really don't hate it, despite it being associated with this terrible summer. In that infusion room yesterday, it felt like purgatory. All the docility. There was an old lady, and they couldn't find her veins either, and she kept saying, 'I'm sorry,' as if it were her fault. And then there were all the conversations I couldn't help overhearing—people speak so loudly there. Then, there was this old guy just staring at me who wouldn't let me out of his sight. Pure purgatory. I know you don't believe this stuff, but for a lapsed Catholic it never quite goes away."

"I do believe in it—I just believe it happens *here*. That's what I've been saying all summer: that we've entered a kind of limbo or purgatory or whatever and we cannot ask too much of ourselves. We just have to put our heads down and get through it. And, of course, you only get out of purgatory with the help of someone else's prayers."

"Maybe that's why my mother came to me, maybe she was praying for me. I really do feel that I crossed a line yesterday; I don't think I can go back. I'm so tired of not feeling alive, of not being in my life. And I look totally gray."

"Honey, I've always thought that you are one of those people who look the way they feel inside. The worst actress in the world. If you feel good, you look good."

I hold out my arms and inspect my veins, especially the left ones. "Well, today I'm getting my head shaved. The hair is supposed to begin coming back three weeks after the end of treatment."

Dave is wrong about going back to Mass General for one final session; I am done with chemotherapy. Five cycles will have to be six; I will live with whatever risks have been incurred. For us, the ordeal of treatment is over and, two weeks later, we drive back to Virginia.

BUT WAIT, WAIT, I forgot the closing. Or the Casual Closing, as my lawyer came to call it. On May 8, 2015, one week after operation number two, I sat down at the Nest Realty offices with Deanna Gould and sold the property at 220 West Market Street to Light House Studio. Light House is an outfit that trains Charlottesville-area kids to work with video and film. They will call their new operation Light House Studio at Vinegar Hill Theatre.

It had been a long time—our mutual contract was signed November 8, 2014, with a 120 days Study Period—since I had agreed to sell my life's work to the Charlottesville non-profit. And one reason I went with Light House, and at a price so much less than I had once been offered, was because I believed they were not going to tear the building down.

But I missed the moment, the dramatic instant when the property that was mine for forty-two years passed to new owners. The sale got buried in a fog that held my cancer. For eight calendar months I thought of nothing except getting well. At the actual closing I was barely upright, still feeling the anesthesia from my second operation. I have no memories to share.

Thankfully, sometime after the sale, the *Daily Progress* asked me for a comment. I tried to convey my enthusiasm for the new owners, for their respectful incorporation of the Vinegar Hill Theatre name, and for their desire to renovate the property without erasing the original building. Here's what I wrote:

Vinegar Hill Theatre and its younger sibling, L'avventura Restaurant, were for me like a great pair of boots. You want them. You buy them. You love them.

They carry you into a life you could not have dreamed.

Over the years, they see the world with you, ignite a local film community, and reveal the mysteries of simple Italian food. But a thousand movies, and many bowls of bucatini all'Amatriciana *later, these boots—that stood the rigors of running two small businesses in corporate America—are frayed and tired. My guess is that Light House Studio has strong boots that will carry it into realms of artistic excitement, at this slightly goofy building on the edge of Charlottesville's Downtown.*

VINEGAR HILL THEATRE

FINAL WEEKEND
"MUCH ADO ABOUT NOTHING"
2:00 & 4:30 - SAT, SUN
7:00 - FRI, SAT, SUN
"FRANCES HA"
9:20 - FRI, SAT, SUN
WE CLOSE MON, AUG 5TH

24
FORTITUDE AND FATE

I started writing this book in the fall after walking out of chemo, and it has taken me a little over five years to finish it. In that time, I was to experience many recognitions, and not a few reconciliations too.

"ARE YOU THE Vinegar Hill lady?"

I am walking across the downtown mall toward the Violet Crown when a voice comes toward me out of the darkness. The Violet Crown is the movie theatre that replaced Vinegar Hill Theatre—by beginning to show art house films—in the fall of 2015.

I whip my head around and see a young man seated at the Mudhouse Café. He seems to be talking to me. I rarely know anyone on the Mall, let alone get hailed.

But I stop and say, "Yes, I am." There is a woman and a child of stroller age with him.

"I found one of your old schedules in a drawer," he continues.

"Which one?"

"It was white—"

"—With a big red Japanese-y design," I interrupt. "That was our first. Do you have the purple and yellow one, the second schedule? From April 1976? That's even more rare. We spent a fortune on printing those. You should frame it."

"OK," he says. "My Dad took me to Vinegar Hill all the time. We saw everything."

"Great. Any favorites or memories?"

"The black and whites—they were the best. So my wife and I—" The woman next to him nods, and we speak our hi-hi's.

"I bought a screen and a projector and now we show movies to our son. We want him to see movies the way they were meant to be seen."

"Who was your Dad?"

"Walter Ross."

"The music professor? He was a devoted customer. You learned at the knee of a master."

I do remember him. Standing there, I realize that Walter was even younger than the son I am now talking to when he came, that first year with a handful of people, to see *The Red Shoes*. I wonder if Walter memorized the dialogue between ballet impresario Boris Lermontov—"Why do you want to dance?"—and dancer Victoria Page. "Why do you want to live?" she answers. That exchange was a kind of secret handshake among dedicated filmgoers.

"I wish I had your business sense," the son says.

"Really? Did you lose money?"

"Oh, I'm a terrible businessman."

"Well, then you *do* have my business sense."

Then I say, "I've got to run—I'm meeting my husband to see *Twentieth Century Women*."

"That's great," he says. "So, you still see movies."

ANOTHER BIG MOMENT occurred at the Cape. I was on the beach with my granddaughter Zoe when an old friend walked up.

"Zoe," I said, "this lady was the flower girl at my first wedding. To grandpa Chief."

Even though Janice and her family spend a week every year at the Silver Sands, a condominium just down the beach, it had been a long time since we had actually talked. Janice grew up in the house next to mine on Mellen Street and her mother Emily and Anita were best friends. She played my Hamilton piano after I left for college, and her father Dominic once refinished all the maple kitchen furniture in the Cape cottage. Janice was part of my deep past, although we had never been adult girlfriends and especially not after I asked her kids to leave my beach when they were daytime drinking.

But, after her husband came down with kidney cancer in 2015, we have come to treat each other with more tenderness. During my early days of chemo she sent me a bottle of red wine with a card offering prayers for my recovery. Recently I had learned that her husband's tumor had come back but I did not know this directly from her so we had to talk around the fact.

"How are you?" she asked.

"Good—all my numbers are right where they need to be. And your husband?"

"He's OK. I try to keep it quiet—don't want too many folks asking about it." Since her teens, Janice has been a tall stunning brunette, with an ageless curvy body. She had married her high school sweetheart, an older guy, and had three kids very quickly. Her long chestnut hair now has streaks of grey, but her face still read as young and sexy. What she held in her brow was worry.

"I know—who wants to be a patient?" I offered. "Some friends shy away from you when they find out you have cancer. I have lost a few. Maybe they thought I was contagious."

Janice was quiet for a long minute, and then she said, "I had a friend when I was young. She was thirty and I was twenty. We worked together, and she was kind of like an older sister to me. Well, she got breast cancer. For a while she was in remission, and then it came back. Even so she wanted to connect and so one day she brought over a lasagna. But you know, I did a terrible thing. She gave it to me and I freaked out—I threw it away. I was afraid for myself, for my children. Just to have it in the house.

"That was a mortal sin. I am so ashamed of myself for doing that. But I was young. Wouldn't it be great if we knew how to behave at the beginning?"

I looked up at the sky. "But then," I said, "we wouldn't have to live our lives, and besides, nobody would want to hang out with us."

I was happy when she let me hug her. Then off she hurried, her gauzy beach dress blowing, to sun bathe on the low tide flats.

Zoe smiled. "Janice is pretty," she said.

I WENT BACK to the theatre one more time. It was a year and a half to the day after we had signed the sales contract with Light House Studio. Despite their savage renovation of the restaurant space, where they had torn out all of our beautiful cherry booths, they had decided to preserve the auditorium more or less as is. The event being held there was part of the Virginia Film Festival and offered an afternoon showing of the documentary, *Liv & Ingmar*. But the real draw was that Ullmann herself was going to speak after the screening.

Dave and I drove across town to the theatre's no-man's land parking lot, now even more than ever a mixture of big potholes and urban weeds. We walked past the tower where yellow cannas and pale pink abelia had once edged the building. Strolling toward the back garden under the cedar lodgepoles, I tried to remember our pergola filled with Dublin Bay roses, fighting for height against the orange honeysuckle, and Eddie's Rose, a wild climber from Heronswood nursery that flung a thorny roof over the low perennials. Back in the day, the plants ruled the garden, but for many months no one had pulled a weed, or watered a bush. Malt liquor bottles and fast food styrofoam littered both the plants and the walkway.

It was totally ruined.

Once in our seats, I looked around at the auditorium. It felt strangely familiar there. Then I said to Dave, "This is a pretty nice little space."

The Virginia Film Festival MC got up. As part of his opening remarks, he said, "Isn't it nice that they've fixed it up."

The comment caught me off balance—it felt like a rebuke. And even though I had just been admiring the place where I had once tucked everybody in, I also realized that when I became a landlord, and began renting out the theatre, I *had* stopped caring about the inside, and had let much of it go. The chairs needed to be replaced, and had not been; the paint on the floor was scuffed away.

But until my last moment of ownership and even beyond it I had not stopped caring about the outside. David and I kept working the garden and then invited a friend to keep it up for us when we spent the summer away. She had put in a *parterre* of bricks and lots of special plantings—irises, hydrangeas pruned to Standards, eye-catching annuals. People walking by the hillside continued to admire it. After the sale, my friend volunteered to maintain the outside and asked Light House what she might plant. "Oh, whatever," was the reply. She came over and began removing much of her hard work.

Liv & Ingmar unfolded with a sense of constant sorrow, threading the phases of their May-December relationship: love, loneliness, pain, friendship. When they met, he was forty-six and she was twenty-five. Theirs was a *coup de foudre*.

Bergman, commenting on their explosiveness, was sure they would set themselves on fire. The documentary combined footage from films they made together—*Persona, Hour of the Wolf, Scenes from a Marriage, Shame, Saraband, The Serpent's Egg,* and *Face to Face*—with outtakes from director Dheeraj Akolkar's recent interview with Ullmann.

"Painfully connected" is the phrase that gets repeated in Ullmann's narration. She offers it as the reason why she and Bergman could not remain together as a couple even as they maintained a forty-two-year friendship. Bergman was not just older, he was furiously jealous and sometimes violent about Liv's attention to others, including their daughter. The beginning of their love, however, took their breath away.

Once, in a schedule from 1978, I described Bergman as "the world's greatest filmmaker."

After the film, Ullmann walked into the auditorium and the audience came to its feet, clapping. She had been on screen many times in this space—*my* space. Her face was fuller, her cheeks just as rosy, and those beautiful full lips still drew you in. She laughed and smiled when she talked even if the message was serious. At one point she said, "You have to listen to your life."

In the end, the audience didn't want to let her go, and when the questions were finished, she was surrounded by fans. Clearly the screening was over.

We were sitting on the front right, just a few seats into the third row. Dave leaned toward me and said, "Let's go out the side door." So we slipped away.

Outside the wooden handicapped ramp the city had required us to build was beginning to disintegrate. You slipped when you walked on it; it was covered with mold. The hillside garden I had so loved caring for was overgrown now. Where the big bed of peonies had once been, there were three cedars, planted by the restaurant tenant. They looked to be twelve feet tall and had begun casting their black shadows on the bricks of the patio. Wiregrass was everywhere; summer had come and gone. Dave placed his hand in mine, and, as we walked out of the ruined place, I saw that his two Dublin Bays, cut to the ground during the Light House renovation, had insisted on growing back and were now sending up one last blood red rose.

Back to 1957

In the crane shot that won't leave me alone I am swooping over the Cape of my childhood, dropping down on a desolate beach framed by dunes like mountains and a pale green tide. I glide in on my cameraman's chair. Small children cuddle on a blanket—is one of them Barbara? I am with them now, we are so young. A child's stillness, not lonely but precious, relaxes into the tender breezes. It's August, the end of summer when all the other children have left to get ready for school.

"Who are you? Where are the others?" *I ask my younger self.*

How far we all come.

The scene shifts to the pause after our mid-day meal. Having stuffed us with antipasto and risotto, my mother and aunt force us to wait two hours before we can swim again. Once the wait is over my father Gene will take us back down to the beach, where he pulls us through the water like an overprotective tugboat.

My brother Rudy sits struggling through The Mill on the Floss, *a book he will never finish. Cousins Billy and Barbara have to kill time too, but they are younger, not as impatient as I am. Nodding over some historical romance, I have only one thought: when will my life begin?*

Then I hear the wooden screen door close, and the reverie is over.

I know where this goes. It goes to Dave and me. I remember all the good days, days in the eighties and nineties, and even in the fall I had cancer. It is our beach now, our time.

We lie out at the low tide in the sun, get wet and then walk away from the umbrellas and beer coolers toward the cut between our beach flats and Sandy Neck. After a good half-hour we come to the channel where there is a strong current even at the lowest low tide. The channel never goes away, and is always ready to take you some place. Over the years, on its northern edge, it has carved a fine white sandbar.

We sun ourselves as Bruno, who has followed us, remains on the lookout, keeping stray walkers away from our high ground. We nap until the incoming tide wakes us.

"Time to go," Dave says.

"No. One last swim," I counter. "Never know when we'll pass this way again."

I search the horizon for visitors, and seeing none, peel off my bathing suit. Dave does too. We dive into the cold, clear water and, in a blink of an eye, the current carries us a hundred feet. When I resurface, I float on my back and look toward our lookout, who has suddenly been joined by a processional of our former dogs—Sylvania, Norma, and Voisine. Bruno is the old dog now, with white on his muzzle and rashes on his legs. He no longer runs down the beach at a mile a minute. We have to urge him on, and he often looks back to see where home is. I hope he will last a little longer, but I know that the end is near.

This is exactly where I want to be.

THE CREDITS

CREDITS ARE ALMOST my favorite part of a movie, although I once saw a film directed by Andrea Arnold—*American Honey*—where the credits rolled alphabetically, first names only. It was a completely deglamorizing experience.

I needed a lot of help on this book. From the first written page, in 2015, when I thought my title could be *Boyfriend Bonanza*, Howard Norman firmly said, "No, not that." Afterwards he set up shop as a faithful *consigliere* to my fledging attempts at memoir.

Leslie Gossage, another first to read, also read last—noting a final round of typos and exclaiming "fabulous" as she red-penciled. My daughter, Courtenay Leahman, wrote up her vivid under-age working memories in *Popcorn*, *Women in Love*, and *The Year of Living Dangerously*. David and Ellen McWhirter drove Route 20, north and south, to get VHT started, as David kindly remembered.

During four years of dedicated reading, Meleesa Wyatt encouraged me how to eliminate the "chunky parts"; Peter Sils, often on site after hours at Fellini's, reflects on meeting his wife Jean Dunbar there; cousin Barbara DiVitto kept me straight on who hit who with the bread board; candy dude Jody DeRitter fondly remembers the era of "surly, rude, and inert"; executive cheerleader and repeat reader, Marie Hawthorne, advocated "pussy power," sending flowers with a card that read, 'Author, Author'.

Bob Schultz, writing to advise, told me the book was better than I knew; Bob Kolker, as he took in the final version, shared thoughts of his own "silent father;" Phil Halapin taught me to think so I could write with my heart; Joe Quinn, source of early photos of Ian and Courtie, became a late reader with the best shoulder notes; architect Edith MacArthur Forde remembers driving to cozy L'avventura in a snow storm; Suzanne del Gizzo loved "the sense of women's adventures and pure joy of being alive." And like all great teachers, Caroline Rody insisted on deepening the book's opening.

Luke Wyatt insisted that the VHT logo and typeface be the "look of the book," and then found the most egregious typo; Pam Friedman got me thinking about the issue of audience; and Reid Oechslin came over the mountain to talk with me about the changeover dance—one of his many talents.

Photo/Graphic Credits: Edith MacArthur Forde sketches the new VHT lobby and her Dream; law school days friend Edie King shoots early Chief and me, and him with the kids; Peter Bacque visits Cape Cod; Reid Oechslin takes the cover photo, *Dial M* installation, designs VHT schedules, and the Italian Film Festival poster; Tim Coffin snaps Dave and me in Yosemite; Joanie Bullard begins with film cans and takes VHT lobby and renovation shots as well as wedding photos; Moss Dix imagines Mighty Joe Corn.

Billy DiVitto shingles my Dennis cottage in 1993 and makes a Polaroid; Doug Magee photographs Barb and me at her 1979 wedding; Cape Cod neighbor Elaine Cifiuni frames a tableau of Barb, Rudy, Billy, and Ann in 1959; Berlin visitor Gesine Zeller-Martin caught Bruno and me on the beach; James Wyatt found two restaurant owners in a moment of rest; chef Jonathan Hayward set his self-timer and shot the L'avventura staff before Saturday service. I took the family photos.

Laura Roseberry designed the book, thereby providing a parallel narrative with photos and graphics that were soft and beautiful, girly and serious. Her illustration of The Dress worn at the Townwatch/City Council stand-off brought back bittersweet memories of the last years of Vinegar Hill Theatre.

And lastly, Toni Costalunga taught me what it feels like to love a beautiful place.